Praise for *The Mindful Millionaire*

"Peterson opens your mind to the story you've been telling yourself about money, then shows you how to craft a new one that better fits who you are and what you're here to do."

—Jonathan Fields, author of *How to Live a Good Life* and founder of Good Life Project

"If you want to win the mental game of money AND the real game of money, THIS is a playbook with the science and tools to make it happen. Pages 30-35 alone are worth the tiny investment."

—Todd Herman, author of *The Alter Ego Effect* and Inc 500 Fastest Growing Company Recipient

"The world is full of gurus advising you on how to make more money, make the most of your money, or at the least stop losing your money. Very few actually get inside the real reason that money becomes such an issue for so many people. Leisa Peterson finds the internal obstacles that are the key to financial abundance like no other. I really recommend this book." —David Ralph, host of Join Up Dots Podcast

"Leisa Peterson outlines a fresh, provocative, holistic path for moving from scarcity to prosperity. She artfully weaves together her own journey to wealth with stories of millionaires and illuminating statistics that show the simple, effective, and mindful steps millionaires take. Leisa will help you clear the clutter from your mind, heart, and behavior to make conscious financial choices that bring peace and happiness to your bank account—and to all areas of your life."

—Alexia Vernon, author of *Step into Your Moxie: Amplify Your Voice, Visibility, and Influence in the World*

"A powerful book that should've b̲ this climate where so many peopl

T0003331

nourishing their minds, it's no wonder why countless people are unhappy. Leisa does a great job of teaching you how to get rich both financially and emotionally."

—Justin Stenstrom, editor
in chief of EliteManMagazine.com

"An excellent book from a real financial pro. Sharing many of her personal experiences with money, Peterson offers a realistic look at your money issues. More importantly, she offers feasible solutions for those seeking true prosperity in their lives."

—Elizabeth Sinclair, business strategist

"This is a non-fiction masterpiece with guts! Leisa shares her journey to wealth with such clarity and honesty that there's no possibility of failure for the reader. You can't help but be inspired to clear the obstacles blocking dreams as her words touch you and remind you how incredibly powerful you are!"

—Holly Riley, author of *Allowing:*
A Portrait of Forgiving and Letting Life Love You

"Leisa is a master teacher who has the ability to explain the inner truth of finance at a very simple level so that everyone understands. When Leisa appears on our program, it's an event. She always offers incredible insight and practical advice. Leisa teaches and empowers others to manifest their dreams. She's heart-centered and her passion resonates deeply with our audience. Leisa is one of our most requested guests. Highly recommend The Mindful Millionaire!"

—Ryan McCormick, host and executive
produce of *The Outer Limits of Inner Truth*

"Because she deeply understands the value of this inner journey, Leisa is able to unlock people's potential in a way that very few people can.

This skill shines throughout *The Mindful Millionaire* and you will gain SO much from devouring the words therein."

—Ed Lester, coach and creator of The Abundance Index

"*The Mindful Millionaire* gives the gift of practical wealth-building strategies while simultaneously helping readers overcome something often overlooked—the scarcity mindset. This is a must-read for anyone who wants to define and experience what true prosperity means to them and create the life of their dreams."

—Ande Anderson, MS, RD, co-owner of AVAiYA University

"Wow, Lisa's vulnerability around your experiences and the stories are really powerful. As someone who works with trauma, I know how important it is to have our stories shared. Thank you for offering a vehicle to both have stories witnessed and healed."

—Julie Smith, MHS, LMFT, CSPAT, licensed psychotherapist and trauma-responsive advocate

THE
MINDFUL
MILLIONAIRE

Overcome Scarcity,
Experience True Prosperity, and
Create the Life You Really Want

LEISA PETERSON, CFP®

ST. MARTIN'S
ESSENTIALS
NEW YORK

This book is intended solely as a source of inspiration and information for readers who wish to take charge of creating a healthier financial future for themselves. Examples are provided for illustrative purposes only. With the exception of references to the author and her immediate family members, I have changed the names and identifying characteristics of people mentioned in the book to protect their privacy.

If the reader needs advice concerning the evaluation and management of specific legal or financial matters, he or she should seek the help of a licensed, knowledgeable professional. Additionally, if you are working with mental health professionals, please obtain their permission prior to beginning the processes highlighted in this book. Nothing in this book is meant to serve as medical nor financial advice in any way.

First published in the United States by St. Martin's Essentials, an imprint of St. Martin's Publishing Group

THE MINDFUL MILLIONAIRE. Copyright © 2020 by Leisa Peterson. All rights reserved. Printed in the United States of America. For information, address St. Martin's Publishing Group, 120 Broadway, New York, NY 10271.

www.stmartins.com

The Library of Congress Cataloging-in-Publication Data is available upon request

ISBN 978-1-250-26191-5 (trade paperback)
ISBN 978-1-250-26192-2 (ebook)

Our books may be purchased in bulk for promotional, educational, or business use. Please contact your local bookseller or the Macmillan Corporate and Premium Sales Department at 1-800-221-7945, extension 5442, or by email at MacmillanSpecialMarkets@macmillan.com.

First Edition: 2020

D 10 9 8 7 6 5 4 3

To Aidan, Zoe, and Tim—
I love you (and our adventures)
to the moon and back.

CONTENTS

PART III: A GUIDE FOR THE MINDFUL MILLIONAIRE

FOREWORD

I could tell you that this book will change your life, but your life is already changing in every moment.

No matter where you come from, what you look like, how much money you have, or how much money you make, you're reading or listening to this book because you know there's something more. I'm excited because what you seek is within these pages.

The Mindful Millionaire is a truly special book. The first time I read it, it brought me to tears. The second time I read it, I realized how much I'd missed the first time. The third time I read it, I realized that I've only read a handful of books three times in my whole life. Every time I read it I uncover something new. It's helped me immensely in my own life. I'm not just saying that.

You deserve a life you love. You're likely closer than you think. In fact, you're probably only a few steps away, but when you're stuck it's so hard to see. This book isn't about how to best invest in your 401(k) or minimize your taxes. There are plenty of books that can help you do that. It's a book to build your life on. It's a road map to a richer life. A life where you feel fully alive. A life where you're happy and at peace.

This book is about so much more than money. It's about life and everything that is. It's deeply spiritual, but it's not new-agey or cheesy or wishy-washy or full of fluff. When I was working seventy hours a week chasing the next client, the old me would have been skeptical of a book like this. Who is this Leisa from Sedona talking about energy and chakras and purpose and mindfulness? I would have written it off, likely never picked it up. But this is one of the best books about money I've ever read.

When you're working for money or want to buy something, being mindful is about deciding whether it's worth the hours of your life you're trading for it. Remembering that you can always go out and make more money, but can never get back your time.

This is why it's so important to build your financial life so your money is making money for you and you don't have to trade your time for it—investing in the stock market, building passive income through real estate, and building businesses all become ways to make more money in less time. You'll learn about all of it in this book.

We live in a world where we're always running after something—whether it's the next raise, promotion, a million dollars, or some retirement in the distant future. Or we're running away from something, like the credit card bills we're never opened, a hurtful memory from childhood, or a stirring inside that's wondering if we're making the most of our life. We jam-pack our lives and then wonder why we feel stuck.

I encourage you to stop chasing and stop running, just for a moment. This is an opportunity to do the work you've been putting off. Freedom is freedom of mind.

You might be tempted to read this book as quickly as you can to pull out the key points and rapidly integrate them into your life. But I encourage you to slow down and take your time. Create some space in your life. For this book and for the you you've yet to become.

The first time I read *The Mindful Millionaire* it was over three weeks, reading a few pages every morning, feeling everything that came through me.

Pay attention—to the wisdom Leisa so generously and lovingly shares and how it makes you feel. Take the time to listen to what's inside you. Don't rush it. Leisa wrote this book for you, not herself. She didn't need to write it, but she couldn't not. I watched her pour everything into this book.

Leisa has a truly unique gift and has designed a path that will transform your relationship with money. After spending many years as a financial advisor for the wealthy, she realized the reason most people feel stuck wasn't about the money at all. It's about what's at the soul level. What's hidden inside. We can all learn how to save and make more money, but it doesn't matter if it doesn't help you live a richer, fuller life.

Let go of everything you think you know about money, because it's probably what's holding you back. Bring everything that stresses you out about money with you. Let Leisa be your guide and be open. This is your path. You're in the right place. This isn't going to be easy, but it's worth it.

Listen to what this stirs inside of you. Take a deep breath. Look around. The more you look the more you'll see. Wonder. Feel without judgement. Know without knowing. You are already everything that is and will be. There is no more important work than this.

This is your life.

—Grant Sabatier, author of
Financial Freedom and creator of Millennial Money,
Brooklyn, New York,
October 2019

AUTHOR'S NOTE

WELCOME!

Whether you've arrived here because of deep struggles with money or the realization that no matter how much money you have, it's still not enough, there's something here for you. You may have tried a myriad of ways to feel better about money, but sooner or later all roads eventually bring you back to feeling a sense of lack.

The difference between how you feel now compared to in the past is that something has shifted inside. You're ready for a solution, maybe even desperate for the opportunity to take your life to that elusive next level—to where your finances are flourishing and, far more important, where you're feeling a sense of peace, ease, and joy about your money and your life.

While it has probably felt like your financial challenges and frustrations are about money, what you'll be learning inside these pages is how money is rarely the real issue. Instead, the problem is your thoughts, feelings, and beliefs about money. The common thread running through them all requires you to look inside yourself to understand them, so you can identify the inner conflicts that are causing the outer frustrations. For many, this may feel like you're taking a giant leap into the unknown, because it's the opposite of how you've been trained to think. Normally we're told that if you fix your finances and create wealth for yourself, then everything will work out fine.

As a certified financial planner (CFP) who has worked in the money business for over twenty-five years, I saw how traditional money management solutions work for some but not for everyone. During my career I've witnessed countless people, myself included, struggle with the emotional aspects of money far more than the financial part. My suspicion is that many people know it has something to do with their past, and yet, without a guide or process to go through, it is just too intimidating to dive into. Then there's the fact that, for many of us, we've got a ton of pain wrapped up in our money stories, which means we'd prefer to never have to revisit it.

Unfortunately, avoiding pain is often the exact challenge that prevents us from improving our lives. And, if you're like me and my clients, we were experts at avoiding unwelcome feelings that the past could bring about, especially regarding money. We'd rather have stood on our heads, chanted a gazillion mantras, and run a marathon than explore what was happening under the surface.

Yet living without uncovering the story beneath it all causes us to live with a lot more fear than when we understand and release it. The more fear we have, the more likely we are to live in one of two ways with money: either apprehensively or aggressively. When we're apprehensive about it, money remains elusive and hard to come by, and when we're aggressively pursuing it, even though we may earn a lot of money, it can be riddled with problems. In either case, our fears cause us to play life in such a way that prevents us from losing rather than truly thriving. This is why you can have all the money in the world and still be operating from a lack-oriented mindset.

Perhaps you've asked yourself the following questions and at the same time were afraid of their answers:

"What's wrong with me that I can't make my money work?"
"Why does it always seem so easy for others and so difficult for me?"
"Why can't I stop worrying about money?"
"Why does it never seem like enough?"

The good news is that I've written this book for those of you who can relate to what I'm sharing. If you're currently living paycheck to paycheck, feeling the pressures of having debt, and not sure how to turn your finances around, you'll be learning new ways to shift how you think and act so you can earn more money, get out of debt, and better manage your finances while feeling greater ease.

Or, if you're doing okay with money but have found that no matter how much you have, your feelings of disappointment and lack of fulfillment won't go away, you'll be learning new ways to transform how you think about yourself so that you're able to live with greater peace of mind and contentment.

While you may or may not want to become a millionaire, it's true that when you have a net worth of over $1 million, you are a millionaire, but let's be clear: that's all it means. To become a Mindful Millionaire does not require you to have $1 million but to *feel like a million.*

How you get there is up to you. It may be that you *do* want to have $1 million in the bank; it may be that, instead, you treasure social connections and set your sights on having a million followers; and then again, it may be that you feel like a million bucks and that *is* enough. The freedom that comes by knowing yourself and treasuring how you feel is better than having all the money in the world. Becoming a Mindful Millionaire is about having confidence in your ability not just to cope with the basic challenges of life but to thrive in any and all situations that come your way—with your money, your health, and even within your relationships.

This book is not a magic pill, nor is it a get-rich-quick scheme that is going to tell you how to become wealthy in no time at all, or how to solve all your problems by the time you finish the book. Instead, it's a proven process you can carry out from the convenience of your home in about thirty minutes a day over the course of a few months' time. While it is not easy, as long as you show up and do the work, you'll be learning how to reinvent your financial future along with transforming how you feel about yourself.

The reason this work can be life altering is because it helps you clear out the guilt, shame, and regrets of the past, so you change the running commentary in your head and feel greater confidence in yourself and your potential to create the life you really want to be living.

If you're looking for a book that tells you to think positively and to visualize and affirm all the things you want in life, this isn't that book. Research tells us that positive thinking alone is actually detrimental in most cases because it decreases your motivation to change your behavior.[1] Instead, this book is about digging into self-understanding—the "why" behind what you do with money—so you can consciously and proactively shift your behavior going forward.

How you feel about money is often a reflection of how you feel about yourself. If you feel really good about money—similar to how you feel about someone you love and care deeply about—your experiences with money will reflect those good feelings. However, when you dislike, distrust, or disengage from money, the opposite occurs and money becomes a source of great anxiety and stress. Shifting how you feel about yourself shifts how you see the world and your money.

This is what happened for my client Debra, a self-described personal-growth junkie who had spent many years growing her coaching business. But no matter how hard she tried, she could not get ahead financially. Unable to get out of debt and earn more than just under $100,000 a year, even though she had a doctorate and many years of experience, meant she was at her wits' end by the time she began the work highlighted in this book. She knew her working-class background and family stories of there never being enough were limiting her potential. Going through the eight-step process you'll be learning in part 2 helped Debra break through her scarcity patterns while bringing her attention to the importance of being grounded and connected into her body as well as her actions.

After that, Debra found resources that amplified her awareness of being fully responsible for her own success. Within one year she was earning well over $100,000, including having weeks where she earned $20,000 and months where she earned $40,000. Becoming responsible for her results and her life also led to getting back together with her estranged husband. After that, not only did she pay off all of her debt with her husband's assistance, she created a detailed plan of how she can become a millionaire within the next seven years. The transformational process Debra experienced was life changing and the perfect example of what can happen as a result of diving into this work headfirst.

Although the word "prosperity" typically means a state of being that comes as a result of having a large supply or abundance of things, I've changed how I define it. Instead, prosperity is the belief in one's own potential to fulfill your needs and wants without limitation. When we are living in fear, lack, and stress, our decisions can't help but be impaired, which can result in feelings of limitation. Only when we understand the "why" behind our decisions can we take back the reins of life.

I've written this with the understanding that what we most want is always within reach. This is true prosperity. It doesn't necessarily mean that everything is running easily and smoothly or that upsets don't occur; they most certainly do. What it does mean is that within each of us is a limitless source of power that is waiting to be tapped. And because of that, if you don't like the way something is going, you have the power to change it—even if all you're doing is changing your perspective toward it. When you feel truly prosperous and empowered to create the life you really want to be living, you're going to do it. This book will show you how to create this as your reality.

HOW DOES THIS BOOK DIFFER FROM MOST FINANCIAL BOOKS?

I discovered the principles you'll be learning about after facing way too many tragedies that brought me to my knees. These "wake-up" calls, which started in 1999, forced me to pay attention to the fact that, regardless of how successful I was in the external world, even in becoming a millionaire by my midthirties, I was spiritually bankrupt.

It would take years to discover why that had occurred and what I could do differently going forward. Everything I share is what I learned and lived in my own life. Starting with the process of gaining control of my mind and continuing through many tiny shifts that added up to dramatically transforming my life and my relationship with money. I've drawn upon many fields of study—biology, neuroscience, philosophy, spiritual teachings, and psychology to create a synthesis of some of the best and brightest teachings ever given. My contribution has been to use these awe-inspiring teachings to develop an intuitive process that anyone can follow.

GETTING THE MOST FROM THIS EXPERIENCE

I'll caution you that this process isn't for the faint of heart. You have to want a better life so badly that you are willing to "lean in" even when it gets uncomfortable. When I first started doing this work with my clients, I noticed that it took a while to take hold. It's like they couldn't totally "hear" what I was sharing, and I later realized it was because they were so trapped inside of fear that they had trouble believing in their own potential to change. This is why the first part of this book helps you notice where your limiting beliefs are coming from and helps you open your "ears" of awareness to new possibilities.

As you read through this book, spend the time you need to gain a solid understanding of the depth of the concepts and ideas you encounter along the way. Test their framework in your own life. Always seek clarity. Take time to slow down and relax if things get too intellectual or heady. This is a journey and not a sprint.

As you move through the eight-step process featured in part 2 of this book, you'll be surprised and delighted to see a new side of yourself emerging. In due time you'll feel prosperous on the inside while creating more material wealth on the outside. But first you'll be learning how to uncover and let go of that which stands between you and prosperity. How far you go is up to you, and what you take away can be customized for your own needs and wishes.

YOU ARE PART OF A WORLDWIDE COMMUNITY

One of the most powerful parts of the journey you are about to embark on is knowing that you are not alone. I help you remember this in three ways:

1. Throughout the book you'll be hearing about my own money experiences and the experiences of several of my clients who've taken this same journey. You'll see how we overcame and broke free of our past and created new money stories for ourselves that aligned with our deepest wishes and dreams.

2. By purchasing this book you also have access to additional tools, money stories, resources, worksheets, questions to ask advisors, and meditations. Simply go to www .mindfulmillionairebook.com to register and obtain free access.

3. By joining our worldwide community of readers you'll be connected with others who are learning the power of the Mindful Millionaire right alongside of you. All you have to do is go to the Mindful Millionaire Community Facebook group and request access by clicking on "Join Group." Share your stories and your wins.

PROLOGUE

Now that I've shared the premises of this book, let's discuss where we're going and how the process is going to work. The book is divided into three main parts:

Part I: A New Language for Personal Finance. In the first part, you'll learn the keys to the Mindful Millionaire way of being. You'll begin by understanding your current relationship with money so you can uncover the patterns of fear and scarcity that are holding you back. You'll learn how to shift out of resistance and step into willingness. You'll discover what prosperity means to you and the steps you want to take to bring more of it into your life. Through this process, the new language for personal finance will prepare you psychologically, emotionally, and spiritually to create financial wellness for yourself and your loved ones.

Part II: The IPROSPER® Process. The next part includes nine chapters that guide you through an eight-step process, starting with a navigational guide to walk you through what to expect. In each of the following eight chapters, I share one of the core principles that will help you transform your relationship with money. Each chapter includes an introduction, stories, and commentary to the stage of the process, along with exercise sections that include "Mindful Moments of Reflection" and "Mindful Moments of Action." The principles in these exercises enable readers from all backgrounds, cultures, socioeconomic classes, religions, and so forth to learn how to transform their mindsets as well as their practical experiences with money. Think of this part as the main course for your personal development and self-mastery.

Part III: A Guide for the Mindful Millionaire. This part reviews what prosperity in real-life action looks like, providing you with guidance and suggestions for putting the tools and practices you've learned into daily application. Think of this part as the grand finale before you start your new life as a Mindful Millionaire.

PART I

A NEW LANGUAGE FOR PERSONAL FINANCE

1

A TALE OF TWO (MONEY) PATHS

M any children have big dreams of one day making the world a better place. I wasn't one of them. Not that I didn't want to help people. I did. But more important to me were all the ways I was going to be rich. I would think about it incessantly—the clothes I'd buy, the homes I'd own, the places I'd travel, the shoes I'd wear.

My dreams were filled with the life my parents could not provide but I badly wanted. The more struggles my family had with money and the more they fought about it, the bigger the void inside me grew and the more determined I became to earn money—lots of it. Putting money as my North Star made life simple: if I couldn't have what I wanted when I was young, all I had to do was figure out how to get it later in life. It would fill me up and give me the satisfaction I didn't think I could get any other way.

By the age of thirty-five, I had achieved many of the dreams I'd set out for myself, and by many people's standards I was wealthy. But the process of getting there—all the rationalizations for doing what I did to get the money—meant I had become really good at convincing myself that the end justifies the means, that as long as I got what I wanted, nothing else mattered.

THE PURSUIT OF MONEY

Chasing money, success, and fame is the epitome of the American dream. Reading books like *Rich Dad, Poor Dad; The Richest Man in Babylon;* and *Think and Grow Rich* filled my mind with the idea that anyone could do it. You just had to learn the game. The deeper I went, the more I could feel myself compromising.

Like a drug addict who needed another and yet another fix, I believed that money was the thing that satiated me better than anything else. Getting rich was my siren song pulling me toward the rocks of Homer's *Odyssey*. God help anything or anyone that got in the way of what I wanted. I was a woman on a mission. Rather than being pulled toward my death, I was being drawn toward my own emotional bankruptcy.

Earning money became all-consuming, requiring a lot of work, planning, and strategizing. I learned quickly that there were no short-cuts. The more I wanted, the harder I had to work to get it. Working for someone else left me putting in longer hours, taking on bigger projects, and assuming greater responsibility. My evenings became shorter and my weekends revolved around chores.

Perhaps you can relate?

If you're like I was, you find that chasing money leaves you over-looking the true meaning of life. Depending on what you do for a living, this could mean feeling forced to compete and connive to get ahead, or fear of being passed over for a promotion or pay raise. If you're self-employed, you may find yourself tempted to deceive to get the sale, out of fear of not earning enough to stay afloat. Other than those proverbial few who make success look easy, many find themselves feeling like they need to do whatever it takes to make money, no matter its toll.

At some point, you may ask yourself, "Is any of it worth it?" For some, the answer will be no, and they'll make changes. But what if you can't say no? What if you can't back away? Perhaps your finances don't allow it, others depend on you for their livelihoods, or you're already so addicted to the money game, you can't break free.

MONEY AND FEELINGS

Money is so powerful that it can blind you to the realization that you have a choice about how you live your life. On one hand, it makes sense you want to have more money, because it can be incredibly satisfying and brings feelings of euphoria and enjoyment. On the other hand, life can become so complicated and expensive that no matter how hard you work, you never feel like you're getting ahead, nor do you ever feel like you've "arrived."

Before the age of thirty-three, my main interest was climbing to the top of the corporate ladder. With this goal in mind, I became a business development executive at a large bank, where I managed relationships with a handful of the largest companies in the world. I was driven, logical, strategic, and not the least bit interested in my own emotional health.

My goals for success overshadowed everything, including my relationships, even with my three-year-old daughter and my husband. Nothing was allowed to get in the way of my ambition, and every decision revolved around getting ahead. I felt pride in my ability to stay focused and achieve my goals. It never occurred to me that what I was doing was anything but ideal.

Until one day turned everything upside down.

I was in the middle of negotiating one of the biggest deals of my career. Arriving home after a particularly long day, I found my mother and grandmother waiting for me. They asked me to sit down on the couch and proceeded to tell me that my estranged father had been brutally murdered. The shock of hearing how he'd been killed sent me into an emotional tailspin. Although my father had tried to be a good one, his many years of drug abuse combined with an inability to control his anger had caused my family to push him away. Now I was hearing how he'd been killed in a horrific manner, and all of a sudden my life no longer seemed to make sense.

After my father's death, all I could think about was how sorry I felt for him. His entire family, including his mother, had disowned him, and then he was killed in a terrifying way. Strangely enough, I couldn't stop thinking I was in some way responsible. The guilt and sadness consumed me.

As I fell deeper into my sorrow and grief, I began to untangle my life and question everything. Who was I? Why I was here? Why was I so tormented by negative self-talk? And what could I do to help myself feel better?

The more questions I asked, the more I realized I had absolutely nothing to offer myself, nor did I know anyone who could help me. I felt so alone I even weighed the point of my life and wondered if it was worth continuing. Feeling helpless was something I had resisted my entire life, and yet now it was staring down at me and I had no choice but to surrender into the abyss of unknowing. It was absolutely dreadful.

THE HEALING PATH

Up to this point, I was what you would call a "do-it-yourselfer" with just about everything. I'd never seen a therapist. Instead, I relied on talk therapy with friends. I'd mostly avoided religion and questioned anything that had to do with the idea of a father figure in the sky that deemed you a sinner. I figured that I already did a great job at talking down to myself and had plenty of naysayers who challenged me on a regular basis, so there was no need to invite someone else in, including the idea of a God who might judge me and see how messed up I was. This left me in a pickle when it came to figuring out how I was going to answer all these questions that were bubbling up inside.

Shortly after my father died I was on lunch break in downtown San Francisco when I walked into Stacey's Bookstore on Market Street hell-bent on finding something to help me understand my father's death. I left the store that day with not one, but eleven books on death, dying, and meditation, thus ushering in a new phase of my life that continues to this day. Here, I began a healing process that brought me into the depths of my soul, eventually leading me back to the connection between my life and my money story.

IS MONEY YOUR TOOL OR YOUR MASTER?

After my father's death, I became more and more disenchanted with my corporate career and kept changing jobs in search of a place that fed my soul and my wallet. I transitioned from business development to marketing and then to mortgage banking and underwriting, eventually settling into the role of financial advisor.

As I moved through the different jobs, I noticed a stark divide among people and the various ways they reacted to money. Some of my clients and friends treated money as a tool; they didn't seem to have strong feelings about it one way or the other, and no matter what happened with money, they seemed to take everything in stride. Often, they were multimillionaires who not only understood how money works but had mastered their relationship with it.

The majority of people, however, were those who either grasped at their money tightly or avoided it altogether. They handled it as if it were their master and used it as a barometer to decide if life was working out or not. If their financial affairs didn't go as planned, they were angry, frustrated, and focused on finding who was at fault. If things were going well, they took it for granted. Although I hated to admit it, this group of people behaved just like me.

After watching how people's attitudes affected their experiences with money, a few questions began to stick out in my mind: "Why do so many of us feel like money is in greater control of our lives than we are?" and "Why do we feel the need to sacrifice, badger, and compromise ourselves in order to get money?"

Conversations with my clients confirmed that people who treated money like it was a tool often felt a sense of peace, regardless of how much they had. Working with these people as their mortgage banker and, later, as their financial advisor, I saw how common it was for things to go their way. And even if problems arose, their calm attitudes led them to quickly find resolutions. They had restraint when it came to facing challenges and didn't let their lives get turned upside down when things didn't work out as planned.

In stark contrast were those who felt controlled by their money. In this case their attitudes about and experiences with money were entirely different. Whatever *could* go wrong *would* go wrong. Many times these were the hardest clients to work with because, when challenges arose, I'd find myself on the receiving end of their anger. It was like their feelings created a ripple of energy that magnetically attracted further chaos and pandemonium, and I couldn't help but get caught in the fray.

It was only when I asked my clients how they felt about money that I began to unearth the vast world that was playing out under the surface. Within minutes of sharing, my clients would reveal intense stories of the past that elicited fear, sorrow, resentment, regret, shame, and guilt. The more they revealed, the more clear it became how repressed their memories were and how much emotion was hidden inside. Never before had someone asked them such personal questions about their relationship with money. The emotional floodgates opened beyond our wildest imaginations.

My clients, almost in unison, would share comments like, "I've never thought about this before," "I've never told anyone about this," or "I can't believe that I wasn't more aware of myself and my money." Many times, my clients got so emotional that they'd become too self-conscious to want to talk again. I would later learn that just by talking with me about money, they each experienced a personal awakening. From there, nearly everyone started making changes: one left her husband, another quit his job, another bought a house, and yet another started a side business. The awareness of how they felt about money caused them to take stock of their lives and make life altering changes accordingly.

Listening to my clients' stories brought me full circle to my own money story and the many ways I continually made choices from a place of scarcity. I noticed how deeply I believed that only by achieving wealth would I ever feel safe, and that gave me license to repeatedly sacrifice myself in pursuit of it.

Research conducted by Sendhil Mullainathan and behavioral scientist Eldar Shafir, authors of the book *Scarcity: The New Science of Having Less and How It Defines Our Lives*, found that, "Scarcity captures the mind. . . . Scarcity is more than just the displeasure of having very little. It changes how we think."[1] They also found that scarcity causes people to become myopic and single-mindedly focused on the problems at hand rather than seeking to find helpful solutions. Once your focus becomes "tunneled," you become less likely to consider all of your options, including those that would provide you with a solid resolution. This causes us to become blind to our own potential as human beings. Research into such ideas, combined with my own experiences, proves that whenever scarcity is present, whatever we believe to be true for ourselves cannot help but become our reality.

This is what happened for me. Watching my parents fight about money constantly served as a reminder that surely there was never enough to go around. Looking back, I can see how my childhood was defined by a scarcity mindset, even though I was great at earning, saving, and even investing it from a young age.

I'll never know if it was this mindset that caused me to beg my mom to take me to the bank and get a checking account by the time I was ten, or the fact that I lied about my age on a credit card application at JCPenney when I was twelve. What I do know is that my parents watched me with curiosity as I gradually began to have bigger savings accounts than they did.

Strangely enough, no matter how much money I saved, I thought about it all the time. This sense of perpetual fear and worry was my mainstay. It didn't help that I was also struggling with undiagnosed depression and suicidal thoughts starting at about the time of puberty. All of this combined together caused me to decide early on that if only I could become a millionaire, everything in my life would be better.

Even after becoming a millionaire many years later, I was still consumed by wanting to feel financially safe. My fears were so strong that I did not believe it was possible for me to leave my lucrative financial advising practice to follow my passion of helping people deal with their money fears. It didn't matter that my husband and I had saved up enough money to retire early; I couldn't get up the nerve to quit my job. But then something happened that changed everything.

THE PATH FINDS ME

In December of 2013 I was sitting in my doctor's office among several other patients. Not accustomed to waiting, a flash of irritation crossed my mind as I checked the time on my phone once more. How much longer would I have to wait?

I glanced up to see a dark-haired man in his midfifties walking briskly into the waiting room. Addressing everyone in the room in a soft and compassionate tone, he said, "You might want to leave now." His warning sounded definite and firm, yet mild-mannered enough that hardly anyone paid attention to him.

Before I could register what he was doing, he pulled a large gun out from under his vest and started to move quickly toward the offices beyond the waiting room.

The receptionist shouted at him: "Sir! Sir, where are you going? Sir, you can't go back there. Sir!" She stood up to get his attention, but he ignored her. Then she saw his gun. "Everyone out!" she shouted, with no thought for her own safety, only ours. "He has a gun! He has a gun! Get out of here!"

At that, everyone in the waiting room jumped to their feet and rushed to the elevators. My heart was racing and a burst of wild energy coursed through me; a jumble of thoughts swirled through my head. One part of me was thinking, "He's serious! He's going to kill someone!" while another part thought, "He isn't going to do anything bad."

When I reached the elevator, I stopped to take a breath. The alarm had spread, and people were running in all directions. Time slowed down, the way it so often does during calamities, and I took a second to consider where to go.

Just then, the elevator door opened in front of me. I hastened inside with a few other people. Someone punched the button for the ground floor, and we all took a deep breath. Just as the elevator doors were closing, a hand stopped them from shutting. Everyone froze. If the hand belonged to someone like us, we could be saving that person's life. If it belonged to the shooter, we were not coming out of the elevator alive. A woman next to me started praying out loud, and then another person joined her. I was surrounded by a melody of prayers as a few more nurses scurried in and the doors finally shut.

I've read that upon facing extreme terror or imminent death, human beings can go through an out-of-body experience.[2] I think this is what happened, because one moment, my eyes were glued to the elevator doors, and in the next, my life flashed before me. I thought about my family, realizing that I might not see them again.

Yet I also realized that if I were to make it through this alive, things were going to change. In that moment, I felt just how much I wasn't living; I felt how much my fears had been holding me back.

Experiencing such intense emotions in that elevator stripped me of all feeling for just long enough to notice that I was not my fear. I was much more than my fear, and all my internal stories of not being good enough, not being safe enough, not being enough were glaring back at me in that moment. I could sense the ridiculousness of how I'd been living. I closed my eyes and thought, "It can't be over yet! I'm not done yet! I'm here to live fully; I get it! God, please give me another chance. Please . . ."

AFTERMATH

My incredible, loving, and supportive doctor lost his life that day. His kids lost their father, and his wife lost her amazing husband. Two other people were shot, and the gunman took his own life at the scene. I grieved for everyone who was affected by this and other violent deaths that have become far too common in our world.

The shooting made me see more than anything just how precious life is and how fortunate we are to be alive. Interestingly enough, research shows that when people experience high levels of trauma, the reticular activation system, which is responsible for wakefulness and sleep-wake transitions in the brain, releases noradrenaline.[3] This stress hormone is part of the so-called fight-or-flight response that promotes alertness and vigilance. It also enhances the formation and retrieval of memory, which could explain the feelings I had of watching my life flash before me in the elevator. That reaction alone brought hyperawareness to the fact that I could no longer allow money to dictate my life. It also made it clear that I could no longer afford to hide behind my fears.

Within a few months of the shooting I left my financial advisor job to start my company, WealthClinic. If you've ever seen the movie *The Matrix*, you'll understand that it was as if I'd taken the red pill. The red pill and its opposite, the blue pill, are metaphors for the choices between the path toward knowledge, freedom, and the brutal truths of reality (red pill); or the path to security, happiness, and blissful ignorance of illusion (blue pill). In choosing the red pill, we've awakened to see the world as it really is and are no longer willing to believe in our own lack as human beings. Becoming our fullest expression of ourselves while acknowledging and learning to love our fears and failures means we get to enjoy life on our terms.

From this vantage point, nothing compares to the joy you feel when you spring out of bed every morning excited to see what is going to unfold. The joy is limitless. From this place of understanding, it becomes easier to see just how terrible money can be when you've made it your "why," and how awesome it is when money becomes one of your many "hows."

True, lasting prosperity is an unknown frontier in our compulsive society, as much as it's a wide-open doorway into personal liberation. The Mindful Millionaire methodology can become a trusted guide for entry and continual exploration into these uncharted territories. Thank you for giving yourself this gift.

2

THE POWER OF YOUR MONEY STORY

Always borrow money from a pessimist;
he doesn't expect to be paid back.
—AUTHOR UNKNOWN

Not many things in life possess the kind of power that money wields. At its core, it's a form of expression, and its main functions are a medium of exchange, a unit of account, and a means of storing value. In addition to expressing value in the form of currency, it expresses personal, familial, and collective values (what is held as important), as well as beliefs (what is believed to be true). Money can also express that which is hidden from conscious thought, including limiting and fear-based beliefs, mental blocks, and "shadows," which refers to the unknown dark side of the personality and was a term coined by Carl Jung.[1]

On its own, money is neither good nor bad. Yet the more your values are in alignment with the ways you engage with it, the better you feel about money. This is because money serves as the currency of your relationship to the world. You are paid for your work, and you pay for services and products created by others. You may also receive money through inheritance, gift, or lottery. You pay the government taxes to take care of the basic needs of the community to which you belong. Not much happens in the world without some measure of money.

THE POWER OF MONEY

Money has been given so much power that even if we try to ignore it, we can't for long. It affects our relationships, our lifestyle, our health, our environment, and even how we think about ourselves. Many of us have placed it high on a pedestal, hoping that it will do us right. The problem is that money was never supposed to be given this type of power.

Money is a tool that was created to help us live in the world more easily. Rather than exchanging a cow for a horse for transportation, now we have money that gets us access to a car, as well as to food. Something that was meant to be simple and straightforward has strayed far from its roots and has attached itself to our ideas of value, self-worth, and beyond. This has played with our heads quite a bit, including the fact that many of us believe that money is bad in some way. However, this simply isn't true. Yes, it can serve as a reflection of the people and societies who are using the money—for better or for worse—but the "badness" of money is not inherent. In fact, it is quite the opposite.

Money, at its core, is about trust, the trust between human beings that says money is worth what we think it is worth based on the stability of the systems we created so we can cohabitate. To me this means money is the ultimate form of connection, love, and cooperation.

While the external value of money is what we pay lots of attention to, and what we can often idolize, it is the internal value and how we feel about it that carries even greater significance. Here again, the perception of money changes depending upon who has it. When money is used to support values and beliefs that are oriented toward service, cooperation, and growth, it reinforces a healthy and positive feeling about money. Conversely, when money is used to perpetuate fear-based beliefs or to manipulate or harm others, it results in negative feelings toward money. Not that this covers all the possible scenarios, but hopefully this gives you an idea of how money merely reflects the intentions of its users.

The process of understanding money and your relationship to it is far more complicated than most people realize. For that reason I am here to help you unpack what's going on under the surface so you can get to the root of where your money challenges are coming from.

It's not all that different from the process an arborist would use to understand what's wrong with a tree. She knows that to understand why the leaves are turning brown she must explore what's happening at the root level—especially because roots are vital to the health and longevity of the tree. In the same way, in order to diagnose what's happening for us, we must dig deep into the roots of our money story to be able to transform it, reviewing and resolving whatever issues we find along the way that are diminishing our own vitality and longevity. We begin this process by understanding how our beliefs affect our roots, and vice versa.

MONEY BELIEFS

Money beliefs are assumptions held to be true. They may be true or they may not be true, but you assume they are true until you change your mind. Your thoughts arise from your beliefs; they serve as a filter from which you perceive reality. Your beliefs are the lenses through which you create, interpret, and interact with the world. The problem with beliefs, which most people don't realize, is that they create a sense of separation between yourself and everything else.

Money values and beliefs can be conscious, those that are apparent and obvious to you, as well as unconscious, those that are hidden from your awareness. Beliefs that are consciously known and understood are typically not much of a challenge. However, unconscious beliefs are the ones we have to be more mindful about. That's because they can often play off your worst fears. An example of an unconscious belief is when you do not know that you do not trust yourself with money and so you find yourself unconsciously self-sabotaging your finances whenever you have extra money available. All you consciously know is that your spending behavior frequently gets you into trouble.

When you find yourself in conflicting money situations, the tendency is to think about giving up, wondering how you could be so irresponsible to have let this happen yet again. However, when you discover more about your unconscious beliefs and how they are creating your conflicts, things can get far easier. Now, instead of blindly walking into situations where conflicts are likely, your self-awareness helps you develop contingencies and alternatives for ensuring success. This is why learning about your money beliefs can lead to greater alignment with your money. The more conscious you are of your beliefs and the areas where conflicts exist, the easier it becomes to make better decisions with money.

TWO TYPES OF BELIEFS

There are two types of beliefs: direct beliefs that arise from your own experiences and knowledge, and indirect beliefs that arise from others' beliefs, knowledge, and experiences. Beliefs affect your judgment and determine whether something should be desired, resisted, or ignored. Direct beliefs come mainly as a result of the physical, emotional, and mental events that have occurred in the past. Indirect beliefs come from other people's experiences that we are conditioned to, that are imprinted on and taught to us.

When your beliefs and values are integrated and in alignment with each other, you feel a sense of flow about how you fit into the big picture of life. The opposite occurs when your unconscious beliefs are running the show. For example, let's say you've been hemorrhaging money, spending carelessly on things you don't need and cannot afford. You tell yourself you're going to start living within your means, and at first you're good at following through. After a while, however, you slip back into patterns of spending too much. Although you logically knew what you wanted to do, your behavior reflects the exact opposite, and now you're left confused.

As you can see from the next two charts, your beliefs come from a vast array of inputs and include many things you have little control over, including your biology, your ancestors, the economy, and the education system. As much as we think we are in control of our lives, when you see these charts, you start to realize just how much conditioning we've actually received.

Beliefs allow you to live on autopilot because these "shortcuts" save you time from having to think deeply about situations as you navigate through life. This may be okay for mundane activities, but when it comes to important decisions around money, career, relationships, and your health, your unconscious beliefs can lead you astray. An example of this would be if you find yourself struggling with money as an adult and notice how similar your situation is to what your parents went through when you were growing up. Your familial beliefs led you to make decisions that led you right back to where you first started.

CONSCIOUS AND SUBCONSCIOUS BELIEFS

The conscious mind is what allows us to access cognitive and rational thinking so that we have the ability to accomplish tasks, including researching, organizing, categorizing, and planning. This reliance

DIRECT MONEY BELIEF INPUTS

Money Belief Inputs

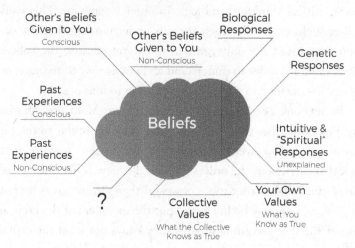

© 2018 WealthClinic

INDIRECT MONEY BELIEF INPUTS

Money Belief Inputs

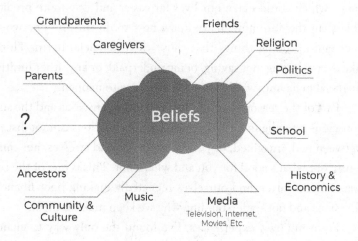

© 2018 WealthClinic

on the conscious mind is what led our ancestors to create the critical systems we needed to live together, including our financial, legal, scientific, medical, and business systems. All of these rely upon willpower, critical thinking, and logic in order to operate. This works well enough, especially when there is understanding that the conscious mind isn't the only game in town. Yet because the subconscious mind is harder to understand and not as easy to manage, our society has decided to pay as little attention to it as possible.

In his book *The Power of Your Subconscious Mind*, Joseph Murphy, PhD, describes the conscious mind as being similar to the captain of a ship who gives out the orders. Yet it's the crew under the deck that carries out the orders. Hence, the crew is like the subconscious mind that is a lot more powerful than anyone gives it credit for. The captain may be in charge, but the members of the crew are guiding the ship according to what they know, not what the captain knows.[2]

While we instinctively and without much understanding allow the subconscious to affect the conscious aspects of our mind, the opposite isn't quite so clear. Unfortunately, we're still learning how to get our conscious thoughts to better guide our subconscious actions, which could make our lives far easier and way more predictable than they are now. If we knew how to do this, no one would ever end up doing things that cause them financial harm. Things like overspending, not saving, being underpaid, or any other limiting financial behaviors would simply never have to happen.

Part of the reason that we must bring the conscious and the subconscious into alignment is because the subconscious cannot discern between real, imagined, or perceived threats and stresses, nor can it figure out what's good for you and what's not. This is one of the reasons why we often find ourselves repeatedly making poor financial decisions and not understanding why we keep making them.

From my own experiences, I've found the only way to change our unconscious thoughts is to bring them out into the open so they can be witnessed. This is why practices like meditation, hypnosis, mental training, physical training, journaling, and habit-creation exercises are so important—because they are all oriented to helping us change our behaviors by tapping into the subconscious.

YOUR BELIEFS FORM YOUR MONEY STORY

As I mentioned earlier, when you bring together all the aspects of your life's journey—your belief systems, all your familial and personal experiences with money, your core values, your education, your past challenges, as well as your understanding of money—you end up with your own personalized money story. This story tells you where you and your family have been with money, the experiences and teachings that came from it, and what you can do differently going forward.

Most of us don't want to look into our money story for fear of what we might learn about ourselves. It takes a great deal of courage to be willing to look within to examine what's happened in the past—especially when it requires you to look into the memories and emotional experiences that up to this point felt better left dormant and unexplored.

A study published in 2013 by Cambridge University[3] suggested that most children under the age of seven have grasped all the main aspects of how money works and formed "core behaviors which they will take into adulthood and which will affect financial decisions they make during the rest of their lives." This study demonstrates the power of parental influence and how much is learned and absorbed about money when we are young. It also helps explain more about how traumatic events that occur when we are young can continue to affect our money, our relationships, and so much more. At least until that trauma can be consciously released through various practices, some of which are featured in part 2 of this book.

Understanding that your money story starts early and realizing that it was your three-to-seven-year-old brain who was trying to put the pieces together, brings forth a new perspective. At that age, how you felt mattered far more than what you were thinking. If you experienced emotional upsets or traumatic events during these years, especially around survival and money, it is likely that you are still living with imprints of those experiences in your life today. We are born as emotive beings who feel our way through life, especially when we are young; it is how we make our decisions as children. It is these types of patterns that you will be learning how to shift going forward, as you move through this book.

To be clear, no two people are alike. Each person sees and experiences events in their past differently. This is because we are the ones giving meaning to everything happening to us. Which explains why your siblings may have very different money stories even though they grew up in the same home. Events in and of themselves have no power to affect how we feel one way or another. It's what our position about them was that affects how we live our lives.

The following statements from my clients illustrate the emotion, behavior, and circumstances surrounding one's money story:

"I grew up in a home where it was always stressful. My parents fought about it a lot, and they were often found shouting at each other about not having enough of it."

"We grew up poor, and there was a time when we lived on food stamps."

"My grandmother had money and she used it as a weapon to hurt my family."

"My father used money to control my mother and sisters."

"My mom always wanted us to feel very loved and accepted because she hadn't felt that way growing up. She used money to buy us things, even when she couldn't afford them, and would say it was her way of showing her love."

"My father wasn't a good employee, and so he got fired from his job a lot. That didn't stop him from buying things with credit cards. Of course, the bill collectors were always calling and harassing us."

"My mother loved shopping; it was her passion to get the best deals, and she would always be clipping coupons for sales. We didn't have the money to pay for her shopping, so my dad would scream when the bills would come. He was so mad at her."

"We grew up comfortably, but money was treated as something that was not to be discussed. I didn't learn anything from my parents about money, and that really hurt me when I was just starting out and discovered credit cards."

"My mother made all the money, and my dad was beholden to her for how much power she had as a result. He had a hard time finding a way to support her, and what mattered more than anything is how much we depended on her for everything."

Reading these, you can see why it isn't always easy to break free of the past and hit the restart button. We believe our stories far more than we believe in our own potential as human beings. Not only do beliefs determine behavior, feelings, and attitudes, they also determine perceptions. The good news is that once you really see something, from a fresh perspective rather than through the "eyes" of past conditioning, it doesn't take long before that's all you can see.

By questioning your interpretations of what's happened in the past, you gain new perspectives to help you see how your experiences led you to believe certain things that ultimately caused you to doubt yourself. When you eliminate the beliefs that constrict, diminish, and negate yourself (also known as "limiting beliefs"), you create new possibilities for how you see yourself and how you engage with money.

HOW BELIEFS LIMIT REALITY

It is important to know that much of a person's financial situation can easily be improved once the limiting beliefs that are causing the trouble are identified. For now, I want to explore a few contributing, and often unconscious, factors that fuel the creation of our limiting beliefs.

We're Not Talking Enough About Money and Our Feelings About It

During the sexual liberation in the sixties and seventies, a lot of energy was spent exploring how we could feel more comfortable with our physical bodies and desires. In the late eighties and nineties we looked more deeply into death and dying, partly because of the AIDS epidemic and also as a result of Elisabeth Kübler-Ross's groundbreaking work on grief in her book *On Death and Dying*.[4] Thanks to Kübler-Ross's efforts, people were able to finally talk about death in ways that allowed them to stop fearing it, and this diminished its stigma. By opening a discussion, her work changed death and grieving from a living hell to a beautiful part of life.

Then in the 2000s we moved into exploring shame, courage, and empathy, thanks to Dr. Brené Brown, a research professor at the University of Houston. In her TED Talk about shame,[5] Dr. Brown liberated viewers from the idea that they were alone in their shame and instead revealed it to be a very normal aspect of life. However, even after all of these conversations about tough topics over the past fifty years, money and our fears about it have yet to be brought fully out of the closet.

Part of the reason discussions about money have remained hidden from view has to do with the fact that exposing where you are with money can usher in a flood of emotions, including shame, greed, guilt, and regret—not that it is always bad, just that we have a lot of feelings about it and don't yet feel comfortable talking about those feelings. Plus, there is the reality that when a person's financial problems get really serious, it becomes all the more difficult for that person to reach out and ask for assistance in a culture where money talk isn't totally accepted.

This is one of the reasons money can cause people to consider suicide. Shame and feelings of isolation become greater than the afflicted person feels able to handle. This causes him or her to lose hope that something can be done to make it better. Researchers believe that it's one of the top causes of our growing suicide problem in the United States.[6] While no situation with money should ever be so bad as to cause someone to take his or her own life, money shame can and does cause some to feel like they have no other choice.

Hiding old wounds can lead to an altered state of reality, where we live our lives acting as if the pain weren't there. This is a chronic condition that is rampant throughout our society. I truly believe it is one of the main reasons we are dealing with so many problems with our mental health, the health of our bodies, in personal relationships, and also with our money.

Plus, whenever we've gone through severe emotional hardships, it matters a great deal whether the emotional pain was dealt with at the time or whether it was suppressed. If suppressed, avoided, or ignored, then no matter how much time has passed, it is still affecting us in ways we probably don't fully understand. Knowing the truth behind our struggles is incredibly important if we ever want to eliminate the stuck feelings, especially those that involve shame, guilt, and despair. Holding on to them leaves us incredibly vulnerable to their showing up in counterproductive and unexpected ways.

Realizing that money conversations are among the last taboos left in our culture helps us understand what is happening at a deeper level. We are often so afraid of saying something wrong or divulging too much information that we completely avoid talking about money. No one wants to be the person who reveals what a mess his or her finances are, or about how much (or how little) that person earns, or the fact that a recent Hawaii vacation was fully paid for by credit cards that can't be repaid. It feels way too vulnerable, exposing, and shameful, which makes us want to hide it, sometimes even from our closest family members.

I had the good fortune of spending several hours on a flight with a doctor in his eighties who had been a general practitioner for his entire career. When he heard about what I do, he said he believed that many of the ailments and diseases in his patients were a result of their problems with money. He was so relieved about this work that he started crying, explaining that he felt like talking about money in an open way would help people avoid disease if they could catch it early enough.

We Aren't Educating Ourselves nor Our Youth About Money and Financial Management

A huge contributor to our challenges with money has to do with how little priority is given to financial education in our culture and public education system. Even though personal financial management education has been proven to be highly effective in helping students prepare for their futures, in the United States, we still are not universally teaching our children about money in the K–12 system. Sadly, only seventeen states in the country require high school students to take at least one personal finance course.

Financial literacy has been proven to be tightly linked to financial wellness, according to a study by the 2019 TIAA Institute—GFLEC Personal Finance Index (P-Fin Index).[7] The study confirmed that people with high financial literacy scores (67–100 percent on the P-Fin Index) also scored higher on measures of financial wellness. This was measured by likelihood to save money both for retirement and for other investments, to track spending, and to be able to come up with $2,000 cash within thirty days.

My experiences with trying to bring financial education into public schools revealed just how deep the shame and resistance goes. One of the reasons teachers aren't talking about personal finance is that they themselves often don't have enough knowledge to be able to teach it. They also are products of an education system that left out the topic unless they happened to study it in college. Even then, what you learn by getting a finance degree is limited in scope when it comes to practical personal finance. Additionally, the school system is jam-packed with requirements for how the school day is controlled. Without a heightened focus by our government and administrators, change is unlikely to happen anytime soon.

Another aspect to this lack of financial education is how it penalizes the economically disadvantaged even more than those children who come from middle- and upper-class homes. Economic equality only becomes possible when a society believes in the importance of financial education for all people. Students could better understand each other and how they fit into the world through the simple action of having an opportunity to talk about their money stories in their classrooms among their peers. From what I've seen inside the schools, there are limitless possibilities that can be created when we're ready to pay greater attention to the value of personal finance in our education system.

When money is not taught in schools, we leave it up to parents to teach their children how to handle it. If parents are good with money, those skills are more likely to be passed on; and if parents are not good with money, their kids are likely to follow in their footsteps, too. Some students, like me, may make the effort to learn how to manage money regardless of their parents' problems with it, but that is not the norm.

More than anything, I want you to leave this part of the discussion knowing that if you've had a tough time learning how to manage your money, it is not your fault. It is all too common, and our educational system hasn't supported your success.

As you learn more about the importance of taking charge of your financial situation, my sense is that you will find it a lot easier to understand money than ever before. Having the courage to question your beliefs is what gives you the power to control your financial destiny. When you are no longer living in the fog of what you have adopted or been taught to believe, you return to your rightful place as the driver of your own life. It is here that you can choose to create what you most want for yourself financially and beyond.

We've Wrapped Up Our Feelings of Self-Worth into Our Money

By far the most transformative work I've done to change my own and my clients' relationships with money comes down to looking inside of our experiences with past emotional trauma. I learned foundational aspects of this work under the guidance of one of my dearest friends and my spiritual teacher, Holly Riley,[8] and have also been inspired by the work of Byron Katie.[9]

By applying Holly's methods to my work, I started to notice that when people are dealing with repetitive negative behaviors with money, there is always a belief buried deep inside of their subconscious minds that is oriented to proving their own lack and limitation. Most of the beliefs that are causing the problems were created as a result of emotionally challenging situations as a child. From there, we find ourselves in a position of unconsciously wanting to prove that something isn't right within us. While the situations differ from person to person, it's like our problems in life, and with money, become a cry for help from the child within.

By using a combination of deep inquiry and intuitive guidance, we're able to uncover the belief systems that were created in the past. It starts by setting an intention for what you are ready to learn about yourself and continues through the process of asking yourself detailed questions (which you have access to in part 2). These questions help you tune in to yourself and awaken the ability to feel your past. The process of learning to feel again will likely involve going through stages of anger, grief, guilt, and shame. Similar to the process of giving birth, there are expansions and contractions, highs and lows, and even a time where you might ask yourself if you will be able to survive. At each step along the way, parts of your past are sloughing off, like a snake sheds its skin, so you can eventually feel a new sense of self emerging.

The reason this is so important is that early experiences with parents and caregivers can become the lenses through which we view our self-worth. As children, our parents and caregivers are at the center of our universe. If they think badly of us or if we were treated poorly or abused in any way, we end up internalizing their negative opinions, criticisms, and judgments. From there we end up incorporating them into a damaged sense of self-worth. Because of our naïvete, there is no perspective from which to cast doubt on this understanding.

Harmful childhood experiences, even when we do not remember them, can force us to close our hearts in an attempt to protect ourselves from further pain. Of course, there is no such thing as a perfect parent. No one is immune to the challenges and pitfalls that come with the role. Plus whatever is learned as a child can be passed down to our children unless it gets released, thereby breaking the cycle of trauma.

In the end, everyone has some degree of baggage left over from our childhood, and to deal with it, we construct layers of emotional scar tissue to cover up our unhealed wounds. This protective barrier can inhibit a person's ability to live fully and freely. Additionally, depending upon the severity and number of "adverse experiences," a child encounters, research has shown these to cause a long list of health and wellness-related challenges, including financial problems later in life.[10] All said, when traumatic events occur both in youth and later in life, they can leave us struggling to find our footing financially.

At some point we realize it's time to overcome and rise above these past circumstances. Learning how to do this requires the ability to change your mind, your beliefs, and your heart in such a way that you can recognize the full scope of what happened and see it as part of your own personal evolution. You cannot change the past, but you can choose what you do with it going forward.

We're Not Taking Responsibility for Ourselves

It's tempting to get wrapped up in the belief that your financial challenges are caused by one of two reasons: (1) your own misgivings and strings of bad luck, or (2) something outside of yourself, including the fault of other people, unfair and discriminatory treatment, the government, or other people's errors. Either way, blaming yourself or others makes you go through life trying to protect yourself and rearranging your circumstances in hopes that it will fix it. Unfortunately this approach only works for so long, because in both situations, you aren't taking responsibility for what's happening. Even in cases where you blame yourself, there is still a lack of accountability at the deepest level. This may be hard to understand, but it's critical if you really want to change things for the better.

Much of the time, responsibility is about being in charge and being held accountable. Then there is blame, which is not only about being responsible but also finding fault in someone or something. Blame is about finding a wrongdoer, even if that wrongdoer is you. Once someone is guilty then all the attention can be directed toward that person and away from the actual problem at hand. Blame occurs as a result of a belief in the value of diverting responsibility to avoid having to accept it.

The reason we're tempted to blame is because we're not confident enough in our ability to take responsibility. I know firsthand how this works, having grown up in a home where life was a continual battle and there never seemed to be enough. Put frankly, where there is no confidence in the ability to solve the challenges at hand, blame feels like the most viable option for survival. The challenge that we must face at the end of the day, regardless of our past, is the fact that in order to create financial wellness for ourselves, we must take full responsibility for our lives and our success.

When it comes to the beliefs we have about money, our first responsibility is to identify the limiting beliefs we're holding on to. Our second task is to question these beliefs and assumptions vigorously and repeatedly until we get to the bottom of why we think and act the way we do. Our third task is to stop engaging in the process of making ourselves, or anyone else for that matter, wrong. As long as we're doing that, there is always going to be some form of judgmentalism taking place behind the scenes, which prevents us from becoming aware of the beliefs we're holding on to. When we drop the judging, we also drop the tendency to self-recriminate, which gives us the space to fully examine our lives and the beliefs we've been living within. Without that added pressure, we're finally free to create new beliefs oriented to prosperity rather than fear and lack.

3

STOPPING THE WAR WITHIN

For me, the opposite of scarcity is not abundance.
It's enough. I'm enough. My kids are enough.
—BRENÉ BROWN

As you are probably becoming aware, getting crystal clear about what's underneath your money challenges is not an easy process. Getting to the bottom of your money fears, worries, and problems involves getting to the bottom of your scarcity mindset. Although it is a well-researched topic in behavioral economics, and widely discussed in popular culture, my experience is that we, as a society, do not fully understand the ways a sense of scarcity is affecting us, nor do we understand how to go about eliminating scarcity ways of thinking. In fact, my impression is that once this belief system takes hold in a person's life, it is rare to ever be free of it. Which is why I became so adamant about finding a solution.

The reason a scarcity mindset is so hard to change comes down to the fact that we've connected money to our value as human beings. Which means that without some serious emotional and spiritual epiphanies, no matter how much money we end up earning, saving, or investing, deep inside we still hold on to a sense of lack and deficiency about who we think we are.

IN SEARCH OF YOUR WORTH

I had a dream while writing this book that illustrates how some of this works. In the dream, I was at a party surrounded by incredibly fascinating people who were funny, charming, well-educated, friendly, and wealthy; everyone really seemed to have "it" together. They said the "right" things, acted the "right" part, had the "right" jobs, went to the "right" places for vacation. I knew these people were the kinds of people I revered and looked up to. It felt exciting to be in their presence.

Suddenly, from out of nowhere, a gorgeous, well-dressed, and perfectly manicured man and woman appeared and hustled everyone out of the room so that we were the only three people left. I stood there looking at them wondering what was going to happen next. They asked me to take a seat at a table.

I felt very uncomfortable with the way they were looking at me as I sat down. The man proceeded to ask me what I thought about the group, and I told him how attractive everyone was and how much fun they were to be around. He asked me if I wanted to be like them, and I said "Of course!"

Without pause, he then launched into telling me everything that was wrong with me in comparison to those in the group. He talked about my biggest fears, the things that people have made fun of me for, my struggles with money, my challenges in my business, and my difficulties with fitting in. He said things that caused me to feel terrible about myself, and it hurt so badly that I was unable to speak in my own defense.

The woman then pulled out a piece of paper and explained that they had the ability to make all my deficiencies go away so that I could become just like the people at the party. They knew how to give me another chance, and it would only cost $1 million to go through the process. When I gasped at the number they whispered to each other for a few minutes and pulled out another piece of paper, saying that because they liked me they would do it for $200,000. When I still looked at them in dismay, they came back with yet another piece of paper that said it would only cost $100,000 to get started.

Having a sense that they were now in the ballpark of what I would spend to get their help, they painted a picture of how it would feel if I were to become smarter, richer, more attractive, more social, and a better communicator than I currently was. They talked about how much money I would earn and how many people would revere me. They talked about how much better my life would be now that everything I wanted was finally mine.

I could feel the yearning for a better life grow with each of the things they said, and it made me very sad. I could feel how much I had wanted these things and yet still hadn't gotten there on my own. I could feel how good they were at playing up all of my insecurities so that I would want to pay them what they were asking.

With all of those emotions stirred up inside, all I could do was take a long deep breath and exhale.

Within seconds of exhaling I felt a wave of loving understanding sweep over me. It brought tears to my eyes because I knew it was the truth. This supportive presence wanted to show me what was happening from a higher level of consciousness.

It began to tell me how everything being offered by the couple were things that people most revered in our society—money, success, beauty, control, and attention—and that the reason we want these things is because we are trying desperately to fill up the hole we feel inside. Further explaining how this hole is a result of believing that we are our experiences rather than something far greater than all of our experiences combined.

The loving presence then detailed how even if we were to change our external circumstances, sooner or later the dissatisfaction would resurface. This is because we wouldn't be getting to the root of why we are experiencing life the way we are and changing it from that level. Only by approaching it this way could we ever hope to change how we feel about ourselves and have it "stick."

The presence then revealed that the pathway to fully accepting and loving ourselves comes from feeling self-compassion and self-forgiveness and, most importantly, from no longer telling ourselves we are wrong, bad, or lacking in any way. It could never come from what these people were offering me, because all that would do would be to encourage greater self-doubt. Love is the only way to move through our feelings of scarcity, and as the love grows, it eventually becomes the foundation of our being—like water mixing with water. We are and always have been love and so by releasing scarcity we return back home to our loving self.

When I woke up I knew this was meant to be shared here with you, to bring to light how often we scurry around trying to decide which consequences with money and success are going to bring us the happiness we seek. This happens because we think things like prosperity are "out there" waiting for us to find them. In reality, it can only be found within.

Sadly, we've been hoodwinked into believing in our own lack as human beings far more than we've been taught about our own brilliance. The norms of our society combined with what's offered up by the media have lulled us into docile acquiescence. They sell fear and discontent at every turn to motivate us to buy and consume things, while in the same moment, causing us to become disconnected from the loving sense within, leaving us without a strong internal compass with which to navigate life.

Stuart Wilde, an inspired author and teacher, stated, "If you want to disempower people, offer them a perpetual diet of scary problems that they have no power to fix." Further explaining, he said that the best way to cause people to feel insecure is to create a world where "only the important men at the top have the power to protect them, heal them, provide for them, inform them, and so on."[1]

Thankfully times are changing and people are becoming fed up with this approach. Although it cannot happen fast enough, we do not have to look far to see evidence of these outdated ways crumbling before our very eyes. We welcome in a new era of activists who are no longer willing to freeze inside of the "scary problems" and instead are willing to devote their lives to the spirit of change.

THE ENEMY WITHIN

When I first started exploring the topic of prosperity and abundance, I'll admit I approached it with a healthy degree of skepticism. Coming from the world of economics and finance, abundance meant exploitation. Capitalism, at its worst, proposes that anything of value that is in plentiful supply should be used to make lots of money, regardless of how sacred and precious it is. When money can be made, it's considered an "opportunity" to exploit, regardless of the toll it takes on our bodies and our environment. From rain forests to fish to the labor of human beings, the way the majority treats abundance on this planet is atrocious. This left me doubting whether or not abundance was something I would ever want to openly discuss with others.

A few months after starting my company, I was teaching one of my first money courses, and in between classes, a student sent me an article about what it meant to be living in abundance. In it, the author spoke about living with the idea that everything we want and need is readily available to us.

Something about this message being delivered while I was teaching about money caused me to realize that I was unwilling to believe in the potential of abundance. This made me so emotional that I found myself curled up on the floor in a ball sobbing without the ability to catch my breath. As I lay heaving with emotion, it hit me just how much I'd been living in fear and scarcity my whole life, never allowing myself to feel supported and embraced by all the

beauty, magic, and vastness that always surrounded me, never allowing myself to enjoy just how good my life really was.

From that vantage point, I could see how much time I had wasted
in a prison of my own construction: all the times I had passed by
opportunities to enjoy life because of how much things cost and
the many destructive ways I had treated my family when I put the
acquisition of money before them.

This vision reminded me of a recurring nightmare I'd had many
times over the years. In the dream, I'm waiting in a long line for food
and feeling very hungry. By the time I get to where the food should
be, it's gone and there's nothing left for me to eat. This dream was
a metaphor for my fears that there would never, ever be enough for
me. In that moment, I knew this wasn't just about the belief of there
never being enough food, but also about a belief in the limitation of
my own self.

Within minutes of having this realization, I could feel years of
negative self-talk and judgment being shed from my psyche and creating an energetic shift inside of my body. Feeling, for the first time,
free of the burden of thinking I wasn't enough, or at least free from
the belief that filling the hole with money, success, or other status
symbols would ever tame my fears. Instead, I saw what mattered
was believing in myself as an abundant being.

When you achieve a moment of realization, like you will be
reading about many times throughout this book, it means that all
of a sudden you understand something you haven't before. Realizations increase your ability to apply what you know to your life and
your money. It's like that moment when everything seems clear,
concise, and simplified. Plus, realizations can compound on one another so that you feel like the puzzle pieces are all coming together
at once.

OVERCOMING LACK MENTALITY

After my breakthrough, I resolved not to repeat the stressful patterns of the past and began noticing and questioning self-doubt whenever it appeared. Watching my thoughts closely helped me notice how often our fears are exploited in order to get us to buy things we don't really need.

In his popular book *Influence*, Robert Cialdini describes scarcity as being incredibly powerful at generating demand in a vast number of applications.[2] Like Pavlov's dogs, we cannot help ourselves from taking action to obtain things as soon as we find out that they are less than readily available. Issues of self-worth cause us to be drawn to things in limited supply, hoping that by consuming and possessing them, we will become more valuable ourselves. When we are living in scarcity, we cannot help but be a cog in the wheel of an economic machine that rewards the few at the expense of the many.

When we believe in our own value outside of success and possession of things, we're free to create our best life on our terms. This is the ultimate freedom. Believing in yourself means you can see money as a wonderful thing but not something that will be the ringmaster of happiness. This allows you to stop elaborating on money as a cure-all and admit to yourself that money isn't why you enjoy life, it merely increases enjoyment, especially when you know you actually don't need a lot of it to be happy.

I saw how fast a person's attitude can change about money when my mom found out at age fifty-seven that she had stage 4 ovarian cancer. Up until that moment, as long as I had known her, she'd suffered from bipolar disorder as well as ongoing bouts of depression and severe anxiety about not having enough money. While she was often seen as a jubilant person, behind closed doors she was plagued by some pretty severe internal demons.

After she received her diagnosis however, the strangest thing happened. Instead of feeling depressed and melancholy, my mom became radiantly committed to living her best and fullest life possible. In knowing her time was limited, she started taking better care of herself, making better choices with money, living in the moment, and being incredibly deliberate in her actions. Gone were her mood swings, and in their place was a woman living in absolute joy as much as humanly possible. No longer was she focused on how bad she felt about herself; all she saw was her own greatness.

This was not what I was expecting from someone who had just been given a death sentence. Yet my mom's mindset had completely transformed before my eyes. Instead of being stuck inside of scarcity, she faced her fears and made a choice to live happily with whatever time she had left.

THE SEVEN SCARCITY PATTERNS

Going back to what I was referring to in the previous chapter about unconscious beliefs being buried inside of us, which cause us to prove our own lack and limitation, I've developed a model that helps you more closely examine your own scarcity patterns surrounding money. The idea here is to provide you with an easy way to identify your limiting beliefs, depending upon which challenges you are encountering with money.

As you read through each of the following patterns, pay special attention to those that resonate most with you.

1. I Do Not Feel Safe or Supported

The first scarcity has to do with your fears of not being able to create a sufficient and sustainable income. This belief stems from feelings of not being safe or supported by life, perhaps showing up as a fear that you are just a few bad moves away from destitute poverty.

In 2012 Allianz Life Insurance Company conducted a study[3] with 2,213 women ages twenty-five to seventy-five with household incomes of $30,000 or higher. The study found that the belief about being close to financial ruin, otherwise known as "bag lady syndrome" persisted among even the most successful women. Nearly 50 percent of the women interviewed said they "often" or "sometimes" fear losing all their money and becoming homeless, with 27 percent of the higher-income earners ($200,000+) sharing that they too worry about becoming destitute. And after the fear of losing a spouse, the thought of running out of money in retirement is what 57 percent of the women said keeps them up at night.

This is the belief that plagued my mother for much of her life, and as a result it was passed down to me through conditioning. The fear of having the ground fall out from beneath me is something that kept me from investing in the stock market as much as I knew I should. Even though, as a financial advisor, I am aware the data supports a gazillion reasons why the stock market isn't all that risky as long as you have a ten-to-twenty-year time horizon. Yet no matter how hard I've tried to put my fears to rest, if I were to invest all of my investable assets in the stock market, I would not be able to sleep calmly at night.

Here are a few examples of how this belief can be affecting your life and your money:

- fearing taking risks and losing your money
- fearing having money (that you could lose)
- feeling like you have to work hard to barely get by
- thinking that earning money is more important than anything else

Questions that help you understand if this is a scarcity pattern affecting your life are: Am I living in continuous fear of the pressure that comes with getting by and surviving? Do I struggle with taking risks out of fear of what I could lose?

2. I Do Not Feel Worthy of Having Money

The second scarcity relates to not feeling worthy of the desire to have money. It stems from a deep-seated fear that your feelings do not matter, which is often connected to your relationships growing up. When it comes to money, this scarcity affects your own feelings about spending and debt: you find yourself regularly facing situations for which there isn't enough money to cover your spending. The more you experience this scarcity, the more numb you may become when dealing with your financial challenges.

Research conducted by Steven Hayes and Elizabeth Gifford[4] found that one of the main causes of psychological problems is the habit of emotional avoidance. Their research supported the fact that avoiding one's feelings is the attempt to escape or avoid certain private experiences and is both pervasive and harmful to human functioning. Also noting that because of its pervasiveness in our communication norms and how it is built into human language, this avoidance can be extremely difficult to detect and change.

Not being in touch with your feelings, you may find yourself becoming desensitized to the pain that arises as a result of having high amounts of debt. This means that you do not worry about accumulating more nor do you worry about paying it off. You may also become hypervigilant about avoiding any discussion or consideration of doing anything different from what you are doing now. This condition, over time, causes debt to appear like a prison that cannot ever be escaped. Further, according to meta-analyses of several research studies, it is likely that more severe debt is related to worse mental and physical health.[5]

Here are a few examples of how this belief can be affecting your life and your money:

- an accumulation of high amounts of debt without a strategy for paying it off

- a strong need to hide feelings that gets channeled into spending money
- a lack of ability to save money
- a refusal to pay attention to spending behaviors

Questions that help you understand if this is a scarcity pattern affecting your life are: Do I feel worthy of having money? Am I avoiding my emotions when it comes to money?

3. I Do Not Feel Powerful

The third scarcity has to do with feelings of not being in control of your money. It stems from a sense that no matter what, you will not be powerful enough to control your conditions in life.

According to several research studies,[6] how people feel about their own sense of power or lack thereof, can lead to self-objectification, which is a phenomenon that makes them see themselves as tools for the satisfaction of the urges and needs of others. Denied their own autonomy, self-objectified individuals do not see themselves through their own eyes but rather through the viewpoint of others. This leads them to deprive themselves of the inner essence that defines what it means to be an autonomous human being.

Without a sense of being powerful in the world, especially as it pertains to money, you may find yourself struggling with confidence and consistency in managing your money. The less empowered you feel about yourself and your own capabilities, the less likely you are to accomplish your financial goals.

Here are a few examples of how this belief can be affecting your life and your money:

- feeling powerlessness with earning, saving, spending, and investing

- having an ability to create a budget but struggling to stick with your plan
- striving to be in control of your finances, but never feeling like you are

Questions that help you understand if this is a scarcity pattern affecting your life are: Am I procrastinating when it comes to taking better care of my financial situation? Do I avoid confrontation with myself and others when it comes to money?

4. I Do Not Feel Appreciated for My Contributions

The fourth scarcity relates to the fear of not being loved and appreciated. Whenever you are holding this fear, there is strong discomfort in asking for and receiving what you most want. You may also struggle with gaining a sense of what it means to be your own sovereign being. When you feel unlovable, you have to work hard to give the appearance that everything is fine. You may end up trying so hard to avoid wallowing in your feelings that you cut yourself off from getting what you really need in order to feel better.

With money, this pattern can result in not being paid according to the value you provide. And rather than asking for what you need to be paid, you end up settling for what you are given. This pattern leads to giving way too much of ourselves without receiving enough back in return, so that we end up being underpaid for our efforts.

Contrary to what some spiritual views would lead you to believe, it may not be true that it is better to give than to receive. While it is wonderful to give and share with others, it is also important to receive back in return, especially when your livelihood is at stake. If a person is always giving more than they receive back, it can easily turn into a depleting situation that builds financial distress, resentment, and frustration. Instead, it is important to engage in reciprocity and ask for fair compensation for the value you provide to others.

A few examples of how this belief can be affecting your life and your money follow:

- underearning chronically
- feeling like you have to sacrifice in order to get what you want
- not being able to get ahead financially or to grow wealth
- struggling to ask for help from others

Questions that help you understand if this is a scarcity pattern affecting your life are: Do I feel like I have something to prove to the world about my own value? Do I resent others when it comes to how much they are paying me? Do I feel well paid for my efforts?

5. I Do Not Trust Myself or Others When It Comes to My Money

The fifth scarcity relates to the fear that you will never feel fully empowered to act in your own best interests when it comes to money. This stems from a lack of confidence in your ability to speak your truth and to trust yourself and others to take a stand for what you most want.

People who do not trust their own knowledge, beliefs, and feelings cannot help but suffer from a lack of self-trust which leads to self-sabotaging behaviors like deferring to others, flip-flopping with decisions, and second-guessing. When you are living in one extreme or the other (either gullibility or lack of trust) you likely feel a sense of limitation and frustration rather than confidence when it comes to money. However, as you come into balance between being too trusting and not accepting anything anyone tells you, you'll find yourself becoming a more trustworthy person. What this means is that you will be more reliable, consistent, and truthful in your own behaviors which in turn causes you to be naturally drawn toward others who are living in the same way. It can also lead you to establish goals around the management and investment of your money so that it aligns more closely with your moral, social, and ethical desires. Plus, one of the biggest benefits of self-trust is the confidence that comes by knowing you will never give up on yourself.

A few examples of how this belief can be affecting your life and your money follow:

- not feeling like you can speak up when you disagree with others, particularly those who are managing your money
- frequently changing your mind about how you want to manage and invest your money
- feeling the need to compromise your values in order to get money
- selecting financial advisors for the wrong reasons—(for their confidence and bravado, rather than for knowledge, compassion, and experience)
- trusting advisors too much without establishing checks and balances

Questions that help you understand if this is a scarcity pattern affecting your life are: What lies am I telling myself when it comes to my money? Am I being honest and truthful with others about my money?

6. I Do Not Feel Like I Am "Enough"

The sixth scarcity has to do with feeling that you are not "enough"; it can also show up in feelings of not being smart enough or not having enough (no matter how much you have). This stems from a lack of confidence in who you think you are. Just about everyone deals with this scarcity belief at one point or another. We live in a society that reinforces the idea that one's "enoughness" only comes as a result of what we do and accomplish in our lives—that we must earn our "enoughness." The problem with this belief is that it leads us to constantly strive for more, never knowing when we have earned the right to tell ourselves, "Yes, you are enough."

Here are a few examples of how this belief can be affecting your life:

- an inner struggle between listening to your mind (reason) and your intuition when it comes to making money decisions
- difficulty in setting a clear vision for what you most want with your money

Questions that help you understand if this is a scarcity pattern affecting your life are: What gifts of understanding and awareness am I hiding from myself and others? What is my intuition telling me that I am not listening to?

7. I Do Not Feel Whole, Complete, and Prosperous

The seventh scarcity has to do with feeling incomplete in your own self. Without a sense of our own wholeness, we seek to find that which will fill us up, and, depending upon our tendencies, it may involve other people and material "stuff" to help us feel complete, or it can involve letting go of all worldly attachments and relying on the Divine to complete you. In either case, the underlying issue is that you do not feel whole without some sort of dependency outside of yourself.

Instead of trying to accumulate relationships and money or trying to be extremely pious, the challenge you face with this scarcity pattern is how to merge the reality of your true nature with divine consciousness. As you do this, you discover that there is an illusion, brought about by scarcity, that indicates you cannot be wealthy and spiritual at the same time.

A few examples of how this scarcity belief can be affecting your life follow:

- struggling inside between knowing when to surrender and "let things happen" versus "making things happen" with your money
- questioning if it is possible to be a spiritual being and at the same time have great wealth

Questions that help you understand if this is a scarcity pattern affecting your life are: Am I renouncing wealth in order to be spiritual? Or am I renouncing spirituality in order to be wealthy?

JUSTINE'S STORY

When Justine first came to me for coaching, she was struggling financially, and the more we spoke, the more I knew she was dealing with issues around feeling unworthy. With a long career as a very successful nurse, she explained how she often found herself buried under piles of debt and had reached the end of her rope. Although she worked long hours and made good money, there were always situations that left her struggling financially—car breakdowns, manipulative boyfriends who stole from her, expensive coaching programs that exploited her desire to get her side business going, as well as the need to help her retired parents whenever possible.

As we got into exploring Justine's past, I discovered that when she was young, her greatest passion was dancing and moving her body. However, her parents wanted her to play the piano, as it was something that her mother had always wanted to do herself but never got the chance. Her mother could afford lessons, so there was no question that Justine would become a pianist who could perform recitals for her friends and family. As much as she tried to tell her mother how little she wanted to play the piano and how badly she wanted to dance, her mother would not listen. Even when she asked to simply be allowed to also take dance classes, her mother refused, saying there was not enough money to pay for both dance and piano.

When Justine's memories came forth, we started to identify the many beliefs she had created as a result of these struggles with her mother. They included the following:

- Her feelings and desires did not matter to those whom she was closest to. (As in 2: I do not feel worthy.)
- There was not enough money to pay for the things she wanted to do, only the things she had to do. (As in 3: I do not feel powerful.)
- It was more important to do what her parents wanted her to do so that she felt loved. (As in 4: I do not feel appreciated.)

In adulthood these beliefs became severe hindrances to Justine's life. This is what often happens when the wounded child within us was not able to get what was most wanted. Just like many children who are resentful of how they've been treated, this inner child has a tendency to wreak havoc in our lives when left ignored.

As a result of how she felt, Justine often found herself buying things in order to make her feel better about life, which resulted in spending more than she earned each month.

Yearning to fill the void from her unmet childhood needs resulted in Justine feeling like she deserved to buy the things she wanted and needed without restriction. In the end, by spending and using debt to fill the gap, she got what she wanted, and at the very same time she proved she wasn't worthy of those things by going into debt to pay for them.

As we reviewed the issues of worthiness and frustration Justine felt a sense of love and forgiveness rise to the surface of her awareness.

By noticing her own feelings of unworthiness, Justine could see how much animosity she was holding on to toward her mother. In forgiving her mother she was able to release her own sadness and frustrations while realizing how her mother had always done the best she could.

As she continued through the forgiveness process, Justine was able to let go of the guilt and shame she'd been holding on to for much of her life. From there it was like her emotional logjam had been loosened. In that moment, Justine took a long deep breath with tears in her eyes and shared, "I can see how much I've sabotaged my own finances as a result of what happened when I was young. I was trying to feel better about myself, but I see now that I am whole and complete as I am. I do not need to spend money in the same way going forward. I want to change my finances and take charge of my life. I am finally ready to do this."

Breakthroughs like this can make all the difference with our relationship with money. In owning her truth, Justine was able to start facing her fears, addressing her blocks, and claiming her dreams, including the idea where she could someday be free from living in debt. She started by listing all her income and expenses so she could come up with a plan for reducing expenses gradually.

All of this happened because Justine was able to resolve the conflict between her inner beliefs, her own truths, and the fears that were motivating her spending behaviors. Justine was officially on the right track to breaking free of her scarcity patterns, and even though there were plenty of times when it didn't feel like much progress was happening, she knew the potential was there to turn things around for the better.

By understanding the seven scarcity patterns and noticing which of these patterns have affected your relationship with money, you begin the process of unraveling your limiting beliefs. In part 2, you'll have the opportunity to go even deeper into these patterns to increase your awareness of the balance between scarcity and prosperity within your energy system. Through this process of self-evaluation, you will develop the skill of reading scarcity energy and sensing intuitively the best way to respond to any given financial situation. Developing this skill requires practice and conscious commitment to learn from your experiences, which leads to a decrease in your fears and a strengthening of your spirit.

4

OVERCOMING RESISTANCE TO CHANGE

Most of us live two lives. The life we live, and the unlived life
within us. Between the two stands Resistance.
—STEVEN PRESSFIELD

When people learn what I do, they often want to share their money
stories with me. No matter what kind of story it might be—
tragic or triumphant, sordid or uplifting—I appreciate hearing the
many ways money has played out in people's lives: the highs and the
lows, the success stories, the choices, the squandered inheritances,
the missed opportunities, the roles of black sheep in the family, and
the relationship challenges, to name a few. In those moments, I'm
reminded just how much we have in common with each other.

IT'S A CHOICE

Throughout history, people have found themselves living two financial lives: the first serving as a direct reflection of one's relationship
with money, and the second remains unlived in great part due to
resistance. Whether we like to admit it or not, we're all procrastinating about something we'd like to do differently when it comes to

money. If we can move past this resistance, we get to see what's on the other side waiting to be discovered and enjoyed.

Nowhere else have I seen as much resistance in life as with money. It's almost a national pastime, and yet those who overcome their resistance are the ones who are most likely to achieve what they want. Or, rather, only those who *do* overcome it can ever hope to see the other side of life, which is where the most satisfying parts are waiting to be both revealed and enjoyed.

This is why it is so important to bring our money problems, worries, and fears out into the open: so we can understand what's tripping us up and preventing us from creating our most masterful forms of prosperity; so we can be sure to not allow the "resistance to defeat us," as Steven Pressfield warns against in his book *The War of Art*.[1] The best way to notice where and when resistance is appearing is to ask yourself the following questions:

> Are you limiting your potential when it comes to money?
> Are you settling for less than you're capable of?
> Are you easily sidetracked or derailed when trying to improve
>   your money situation?

If the answer is yes to any of these questions, then ask yourself:

> Where is the resistance coming from?
> What are you most afraid of?

There are no right answers to these questions. Simply notice how you feel and pay close attention to what you think about as you tune in to your thoughts and feelings. This awareness can help you make three bold moves toward your resistance. The first is to become aware of where you are right now. This takes being honest with yourself and trusting that whatever you are feeling is valued and appreciated without judgment. Notice the intensity of resistance, especially if you are feeling shame, guilt, and fear of the unknown.

Next, you can think about where you want to go with your money. What goals, dreams, and aspirations do you have for your future? What do you most want to create for yourself going forward?

And finally, you can think about the gap between where you are, where you want to go, and how resistance is affecting your ability to move from one place to the next.

NAVIGATING MONEY CHALLENGES

By understanding the gap that is constructed as a result of your most pressing fears, you become more mindful of exactly what is causing you to settle for less than you want. From here it helps to look more closely at what is happening under the surface of your financial challenges.

I was first inspired to explore the difference between money problems and money worries by author John Armstrong[2] and further developed these ideas into my own theories in highlighting the difference between money problems and money fears.

Money problems are those that need to be taken care of right away. They result from not having enough cash on hand to pay for something important, like when your car breaks down, you need to pay your taxes, or you're facing a family health crisis. When money problems occur, you can do one of three things: get more money, lower your expenses or, in some cases, go without. You don't need lots of experience and knowledge to solve these challenges; instead, it's about deciding what to do, moving past any resistance, and then taking action. To get the money you may have to work additional hours to make up the shortfall, or you may choose to borrow to pay for it.

In general, this is what most financial books are designed to help you with. What matters most is that you take charge of the situation at hand and deal with it as quickly and efficiently as possible. If you're only dealing with occasional money problems and you're able to resolve them on your own, then you're doing great. No need to dive in any deeper.

On the other hand, if you've got money challenges that keep repeating themselves and aren't easily resolved, this is when you want to ask yourself if you're dealing with money fears.

Money fears stem from your unconscious beliefs, feelings, and emotions. Often they are taking place in your head and have been playing in the background of your thoughts and actions for many years. You don't have to have money problems to have money fears, but money fears have an uncanny way of causing money problems. Money fears are complicated because they come from so many different places that it can be difficult to pinpoint why they are happening and how best to handle them.

The primary difference between treating money problems and money fears has to do with getting down to the root causes so that the basis of the condition can be removed. It is similar to when doctors prescribe medicine to lessen the symptoms of a condition versus when they're able to help a patient get to the point where they no longer have the condition. I think we'd all agree that while it may be easier to deal with symptoms, until we heal the root cause, we aren't really done with the problem.

When left unchecked, money fears perpetuate unworthiness and lack. Just like when you water a tree, the water extends to every aspect of the tree—the roots, leaves, branches, and flowers. In the same way, money fears, which directly connect to the scarcity patterns highlighted in the previous chapter, cannot help but extend to every aspect of your life.

When you are making decisions about money while at the same time worrying about the outcome of your decision, you are far more likely to do what you have been conditioned to do, which may not lead to the best decision. This happens because fear leads us to lean on indoctrinated belief systems rather than our own knowingness. In contrast, when you are making decisions from joy and abundance, your decisions are far more likely to bring about prosperity.

I've found that the better you understand, acknowledge, and work with your money fears, the more easily you navigate life. Thich Nhat Hanh said it all too well: "The only way to ease our fear and be truly happy is to acknowledge our fear and look deeply at its source."[3] While there is no quick fix or easy solution, the process you will be guided through in part 2 will help you circle through your issues again and again, each time through a different stage of awareness. The goal is to blaze a trail that allows many discoveries to reveal themselves.

UNRAVELING YOUR MONEY FEARS

Let's now explore a few of the most common deep-seated money fears and some ways to move forward without them holding you hostage.

Fear of Power and Authority

In the breakthrough work that I do, I have seen situations in which people have adopted a skewed understanding of power as adults. Instead of seeing a person's power and authority as something that comes as a natural part of being alive, it is thought to be coercive and forceful in nature and therefore something to be avoided. We are likely to think this way because of having witnessed plenty of situations in which power and authority were abused and exploited. When this occurs there can be a tendency to avoid being in positions of power out of fear of how you'll be seen by others.

Growing up in a home where my father was in charge of spankings and discipline caused me to have a fear of authority figures early in life. I can see how these fears that started young continued to play out in many ways over the years and led me to think that power was more about forceful domination than anything else.

My father, similar to many others, parented in the same way his parents had, which was to reward him when he was good and to punish him when he wasn't. The premise was that you did whatever was needed to control your children, which often involved fear and intimidation. Under this model, to be powerful meant that one person decided what others could and could not do, which essentially means that the person with the power had control over those who didn't.

Both parenting and the work environment all too often make use of the carrot-and-stick mentality, in which, if a child (worker) does what the parent (employer) wants him or her to do, then the person is rewarded. If not, the person is penalized. When this happens repeatedly over many years, we learn that we need to do what the people in power want us to do in order to get the things we most want. Left unchecked and unquestioned, this sort of reward system may lead to feeling overpowered by others. When you include money in the equation as one of the most common forms of reward, both in work and in relationships, it makes sense that we can end up feeling disempowered and resentful about money. It's no wonder money has turned into a representation of oppression and control for many of us.

As we become accustomed to this conditioning, we cannot help but perceive a strong difference between right and wrong, win and lose, black and white. When we then find ourselves in situations that demand some sort of response, we may react in one of two extremes: either trying to act like we are powerful and in control, or its opposite, which is submitting to those who seem to have power over us. Neither reaction is optimal, as both are based on an underlying belief that having dominance over others is a sign of strength and being sensitive and accommodating to others' conditions is a sign of weakness. We can see the effects of this belief system playing out through society, in politics, in finance, in education, in business, and in the home.

When money gets misidentified as being something that determines how powerful a person you are, it's easy to see how things take a turn for the worse. When this belief gets perpetuated, you end up having a society in which it is believed that those with money have power over others, and those who don't are powerless. From there you can see how beliefs like "money is the root of all evil," "rich people are bad," and "it's selfish to want a lot of money" get formed.

True power, however, is not about force nor dominance over others; it resides in the human experience of inclusiveness and respect. Inspired by the significance of life itself, true power uplifts the human spirit to a place of meaning, substance, and understanding. It is focused on motives and intentions, rather than a preconceived outcome. A perfect example of power rather than force is what happened when Mahatma Gandhi led India to gain independence from British rule. Employing the essence of *satyagraha*, a Sanskrit word that means "insistence on truth," Gandhi refused to use physical force against the British. Instead, he sought to eliminate antagonisms through moral power. This was not about inaction but determined passive resistance and noncooperation. This use of "soul power," rather than antagonistic pressure, is similar to the path Martin Luther King Jr.'s famous speech, "I Have a Dream," entreats us to follow.

As we've discussed, the outer world has an uncanny ability to mirror our inner world. In the spirit of trying to improve ourselves, we notice the good and the bad and the light and the dark, and we find ourselves thinking about how to overcome the negative. We believe that if we can force these parts of ourselves to go away, then we will feel whole and complete. In fact, the exact opposite occurs, and by resisting these aspects of ourselves, we end up feeling fragmented and cut off from who we really are. However, by learning how to embrace, allow, and accept all parts of ourselves, free from judgment, we learn how to restructure the way we consider power and authority, choosing to see this as a way through fear rather than perpetuating it.

Fear of the Past

While challenges in our youth have a lot to do with our money worries, so too do events that occur in adulthood, those that cause us to feel emotional, physical, or mental stress. In their book *Mind over Money*, Brad Klontz, PsyD, and Ted Klontz, PhD, explain how money disorders are "persistent patterns of self-destructive and self-limiting financial behaviors."[4] They explain that these behaviors result from "distorted beliefs" that are developed as a result of "flashpoint experiences." Financial flashpoints are painful, distressing, and/or dramatic life events that are so emotionally powerful, they leave an imprint that lasts throughout adulthood and can become the foundation of our financial life.

In my coaching practice, I've often seen people who have undergone emotional hardships in adulthood that end up affecting their views on money. From serving in active combat in the military to going through a painful divorce, we continue to carry the trauma of these events in our minds and bodies way beyond the occurrence.

Trauma is an overwhelming and seemingly unbearable life experience that undermines how we feel about ourselves. Absent of releasing it, many find these disorders obstructing and interfering with one's natural evolutionary process of growth while limiting the ability to achieve financial goals.

My own experiences with post-traumatic stress disorder (PTSD),[5] which I experienced for several months after the shooting, have shown me just how much of an impact the continuation of disturbing thoughts, emotions, and feelings can have on one's well-being. It can be so destructive that you have little to no interest in taking care of your responsibilities, including your finances. Or even if you do, the emotional instability you feel results in financial mishaps, like increased spending and credit card usage, missed payments, poor job performance that affects your income, and otherwise poor financial decision-making.

Later in this book you'll be exploring the benefits of mindfulness practice and how to apply it to your money transformation, which essentially means changing how you perceive money. You'll also be learning how to practice moment-by-moment awareness in a systematic way that teaches your nervous system to become more calm, steady, and peaceful. The more you do this, the more you realize that you are not your fear and, as such, fear no longer has to rule your life.

Fear of Being Responsible

One of the most common responses to difficulties and emotionally charged financial situations, especially when we are living in scarcity, is to react with blame. We blame ourselves, blame others, or even a higher power, like God, the stars, or Mother Nature. The reason we are drawn to blaming something or someone for our pain, or to make excuses for why something happened, has to do with our immediate desire to avoid pain. We think that as long as we don't have to feel it, everything is going to be okay. The problem is that when we create excuses to explain something, we're also diminishing the opportunity to learn from our pain.

Excuses are sneaky. Their job is to convince you that whatever happened in the past is the reason for why you cannot have, do, or be what you most want. They are so obscure that you don't even realize they're there, nor do you think they can ever be questioned. They are attractive because they allow you to assign responsibility outside of yourself, and the ego loves this arrangement.

I spent much of my first thirty years learning how to blame everyone but myself for just about everything. It was an effective way to not have to accept responsibility for all the shitty things happening in my life. I figured that as long as I could find fault in others, then I didn't have to look inside of why I kept attracting these painful situations into my life.

I lived in this state of denial until the day I received the news about my dad's death. Something about the horrific nature of his death caused me to snap out of the pattern of blaming others and finally point the finger toward myself. I think this is why I fell apart so fast after his death. I couldn't blame him and I couldn't even blame those who had killed him, because I knew how effective my dad was in harassing and provoking others. Instead, I decided to take responsibility for myself and see what I would find under the covers of my psyche.

It would take years to figure out *I* was the one causing all of my problems. Not because I was a bad person doing bad things (which was my fear all along), but because I was not capable of seeing my own part in how my life was playing out. To be clear, this realization was not about creating more self-criticism; instead, it was about learning how to control my mind and my reactions. Only from that state of awareness could I ever hope to notice what was happening in my life and how not only did I play a part in it, I was the only one who could change it for the better.

Taking full responsibility for one's life does not happen overnight. It requires learning how to live above and beyond excuses especially when things don't turn out as planned. Being courageous in the face of uncertainty. Knowing that while we cannot control outcomes, we can control our intentions. Accepting this allows us to focus on living intentionally while managing mishaps along the way. If you can be patient with yourself and apply this approach to money, without forcing or expecting too much too soon, you'll be amazed at the beneficial events that can occur in your life.

Fear of Failure

Have you ever been so afraid of failing at something that you were powerless to take action? How many times have you stopped working on a money project out of fear of not having it turn out the way

you want? For many people fear of failure is one of the biggest obstacles to turning around their finances. We get so afraid of having
something not work out that we can't even find the energy to try new
things.

First of all, I want you to know that no matter what your experiences with money have been, you are not a failure. Not in the past,
not in the present, and not in the future. It's impossible, so I want
you to let that go right now. Whether you have money or not, you
are not and cannot be a failure. The whole point of this book is to
help you learn tools that break through any sorts of self-imposed
beliefs and barriers that are blocking you from what you most want.
There is a very good chance that much of what you will be learning
is new to you and will help you do things differently in the future.
Allowing yourself the benefit of knowing you are, and have always
been, doing the best you can will help to remind you of the fact that
you are not a failure.

No matter how hard we try to avoid it, most of us will stumble
and fall in life. Doors will get slammed in our faces, we'll make decisions we later regret, and we're going to lose money one way or another. Imagine what the world would look like if Oprah Winfrey had
given up on her dream to build a media conglomerate when her first
boss told her she was too emotional for television. Imagine if Warren Buffett had given up when he was rejected to attend Harvard
Business School, or if Steve Jobs had given up when he was fired by
Apple Computer in the mid-1980s. Imagine for a moment what you
could do when you no longer have a fear of failure.

Sara Blakely, the founder of Spanx, tells a story about her father
and how he taught her to approach failure growing up.[6] As you
may know, Sara is a self-made billionaire, having started a company
to solve one problem for women, namely how to make our curvy
bodies look better in form-fitting clothing. Growing up, Sarah was
asked at the dinner table every night by her father, "Tell me about
what you failed at today." Sarah then explained that by talking about

what she had failed at and knowing her dad would be looking for her stories, she learned that failure was in fact *not a bad thing*! Instead, it was considered a perfect way to learn in her home. By the time she started her company, she was conditioned to believe that failure was a precursor to success. In Sarah's case, this belief helped her become one of the most successful women business owners on the planet. Imagine what effect this belief could have in your life.

By letting go of your fear of failure and any silly thoughts that you are already a failure allows you to become willing to try new things. Willingness is a game changer because it means that instead of thinking to yourself, "I can't," you are now thinking, "I could," "I may," and even "I can." While I am not a big affirmation person, I do know that telling yourself "I can do it" is incredibly uplifting and soul redeeming. Which reminds me why one of my favorite childhood books was *The Little Engine That Could*.[7] That book made it clear early in life that our thoughts mattered.

Working within the eight-step process featured in part 2, you will be going inside of your money story so that you can unearth the root causes of your money fears, worries, and resistance. This will feel like a peak-and-valley phase of growth and, for that reason, you won't always want to continue moving forward. This is because you've likely become attached to life as you know it and disassembling your fear-based belief structures can feel like a death-and-rebirthing process.

Giving up the old ways of being often requires us to mourn and grieve before we can create the space needed to grow into and realize the new. As you learn how to nurture and appreciate all the stages of your past that have brought you to this point in time, you'll be able to move beyond your pain and constriction that have been holding you hostage. You'll learn new ways to resolve fearful patterns as they arise, drop away emotional scars, and develop grounded strength, paving the way to a newfound confidence that allows you to navigate life with greater agility and ease.

5

THE TAO OF MONEY

Money is only a tool. It will take you wherever you wish,
but it will not replace you as the driver.
—AYN RAND

The challenge now becomes how do you go from where you are
today to where you want to be in the future? Or rather, how do
you change your money story so it stops reflecting scarcity and starts
reflecting prosperity?

MINING FOR GOLD

For a moment, imagine you are holding in your hand a large clump
of dirt. From the outside, it looks like any other ball of dirt, with
pieces breaking off into tiny specks. Your hand is getting dirtier the
longer you hold on to it. The ball is heavy, and yet if you were to
break it open you'd see that inside is a one-inch solid ball of gold.

By its nature, the gold is a brilliant yellowish color and is dense
and malleable. Regardless of how dirty it looked on the outside, it
retains its "goldness." Neither economic collapse nor a currency crisis

can strip away the value of gold. No matter what you do with it and how long you keep it, it remains pure. Its goldness is unchanging.

This ball of gold is a lot like us. Over time we've experienced many trials and tribulations, which can lead us to build up psychological layers around us. Years go by and layers get added without realizing that the many treasures we bring into the world are becoming hidden from sight. The walls come in the form of beliefs and stories about who we think we are and who we're afraid we are—all of which are locked up tight inside of us, just like the gold being covered up with dirt. After a while, because we can see the only layers of dirt, we forget what it is like to be the gold inside. And even though we have a sense of being destined to achieve great things, mostly we're left questioning ourselves and what we're lacking.

Gold is a symbol for what is purest, most excellent, most enduring, and most valued in terms of human aspirations, behaviors, and relationships. When you realize you are the gold and it is your essence that is wanting to radiate out, you no longer have to question your own potential. Instead, you see yourself as a seed of potentiality and see your struggles with money as merely teachings on the road of life. When this happens, you can feel how life is inviting you to love and appreciate every step of the journey for all the beauty it represents.

The more you feel this, the more "goldness" you end up creating in the world. Now, rather than trying to prove anything, you are focused on living your truth for its own sake. From here, money becomes a reflection of the love you feel for yourself appearing in the form of currency. When you love and accept yourself, you can't help but love and accept the world around you. When you love who you are, fear no longer controls you and you become the unwithholding lover of life.

WHAT'S LOVE GOT TO DO WITH IT?

For many of us, our understanding of love hasn't always been clear. I used to have a very skewed idea that love was about being good. As long as I was a good person, a good partner, a good friend, a good manager, a good daughter, then I was worthy to be loved by others. I believed love was conditional and determined by others. If they deemed me acceptable, then I would be loved. If not, then I was an outcast.

What the world and our various forms of media generally refer to as love is intense emotion, usually romantic, that combines possessiveness, control, and physical attraction. When this kind of love doesn't work out as planned, anger and dependency arise out of attachment. This causes emotions to bounce back and forth from one extreme to the other and feels very unpredictable. How you feel about someone depends upon how they are treating you in the moment. Clearly these aren't descriptions of true love, and, sadly, believing these explanations of love impacts how we approach loving ourselves.

How you feel about yourself shows up in everything you do. No love, no money. Lots of love, lots of money. This isn't to say that just because you love yourself money will come falling from the sky, but it is to say that whatever you're thinking gets reflected in your relationships, including the one you have with money. It's no different from how we think about our bodies. Health and wealth can both serve as expressions of how we feel about ourselves.

The most beneficial state of love a human being can ever feel is unconditional love. This is a sense of devoted affection that does not have any expectation, limitation, or condition applied to it. It is an indication of our intention to be a kind and loving person, and it doesn't matter what's going on outside of our own self.

When you decide to love yourself or others unconditionally, it means that you refuse to exclude yourself and others from your affection no matter what. By making a decision to love in this way, you are creating a stable energy field of unconditionality that prevents you from being a victim to what goes on in the world. What this means is that even if someone's behavior harms you or you don't like it, it doesn't change your lovingness.

True love is unconditional, unchanging, and permanent. It does not end because of how you feel one day or because of something that was done or not done. It is a state of being that is forgiving, nurturing, and supportive. It comes from the heart and not the mind. Love isn't judgmental; it is deeply intuitive and focuses on the good of all. Unconditional love is limitless and boundless. Put simply, it's about feeling a warm embrace with all of life, including yourself.

Before we can love others, we must fall in love with ourselves. When we do this, it becomes the pathway that guides us through life. Unconditional love begins by learning to treat ourselves with mercy and kindness and continues by lifting others up through our presence. Love comes in many unexpected ways and expands the more you surrender to how it makes you feel.

Learning to love myself took many years. It wasn't until I saw the conditionality I was applying toward myself that things started to shift. The only way I could get around it was the opposite of what you might expect. I started by finding the things about myself that I did not like, the things I wanted to change and eliminate.

Looking for what I didn't like about myself required unbridled self-honesty. That's because, far too often, the tendency is to numb out the aspects of ourselves that we would like to change but don't feel capable of changing. Which occurs when we're not in regular dialogue with the symbols of our inner selves. So to start becoming more aware of what's happening within our psyches we need to explore all the ways we're making ourselves wrong, inadequate, and insignificant, paying close attention to the inner narrative of criticism, doubt, and lack of self-compassion. As your awareness moves you up and out of your numbness, you begin to notice the perceived gap between how you're talking to yourself and what lies beyond this limited sense of self. This opening gives you a chance to feel the beauty of your natural state of being.

Meditation practice plays an important role because at first you need to have enough control over your mind that you can catch how you are talking to yourself and pause when you notice the tone has taken a turn for the worse. Stopping or at least curbing the negative voice inside is critical and makes all the difference in the quality of one's life.

Instead of making yourself feel bad, you can began speaking kindly and appreciatively toward these parts of yourself, even those you tried to avoid in the past. Eventually you'll be able to do the same toward how you think about others. Criticism, judgment, and condemnation cannot be incessantly playing out in the background of your mind if you're wanting to engage in the practice of unconditionally loving yourself. It simply doesn't work.

In time this practice will help you feel love and acceptance of yourself. Your compassion may even extend to loving the parts of yourself that remain in denial and wish to dwell in the mistakes of the past. Don't worry if it takes days of repeatedly reminding yourself about how you are always doing the best you can in any given moment, especially on those days when you make mistakes. Slowly but surely, the love you feel inside grows. Instead of making yourself wrong, now you are making yourself right, which increases your sensitivity toward balance and imbalance. Noticing when you are balanced in your self-talk and when you are not gives you the confidence to keep practicing self-love.

As you move into greater states of unconditional love, what matters more than anything is who you are and who you have become. What you have become is an unconditionally loving person who has deep value and appreciation for herself.

THE YIN AND YANG OF MONEY

Part of the reason many of us struggle with loving ourselves unconditionally has to do with the fact that we are constantly pushing away the pain, fear, and discomfort that comes with life. At the same time, we're striving for anything that makes for a cushy life, including status, significance, and glamour. This causes us to feel like we are being pulled in vastly different directions, rather than living in balance as explained within the teachings of the Tao.

The Tao is a Chinese philosophy that highlights the natural order of the universe, and it is activated by one's own individual wisdom through daily living experiences. The Tao is trying to capture the elusive balance between the extremes that come with being human.

The Tao more than anything is about understanding and accepting yourself on your own terms. Since the nature of who you are is ever changing, the less time you spend trying to resolve the various contradictions and struggles that life brings, the better. Instead, you want to find your own personal adjustments to the rhythm of the natural world and to follow the way of the universe. This is done by stressing the importance of harmonizing with nature by balancing the yin and yang and developing chi (energy, often in the form of breath) through meditation and detachment.

One of the most polarizing topics of our times, especially with money, is in the area of masculine (yang) and feminine (yin) qualities of what it means to be human. Masculine and feminine energies are not solely based on gender. Any person can embody either energy or both. Masculine energy is typically more externally focused and driven by having direction in life with a mission or a goal to accomplish, to "make things happen." Feminine energy is inward and spiritually focused while being oriented to opening to love, mothering, compassion, kindness, caring, and supportiveness, to "allow things to happen."

The challenge we find with money is that the polarity of the masculine and feminine within us are most commonly found at their extremes. When this happens we struggle to find a middle ground or at least the pathway to living a life of harmony and acceptance of all parts of ourselves—both the masculine and the feminine.

I have wrestled with this conflict for many years, feeling like I needed to be someone other than who I was, especially when I was so interested in mastering the art of money. As a woman working in finance, I could not help but lose myself inside of the masculine/yang energy of pushing toward achievement, engaging in competition, wielding my high-powered jobs to evidence strength, and doing whatever I could to control my external conditions. This is what I thought I was supposed to do if I wanted to have money and be seen as a leader in the world. This unbalanced and one-sided "yang-ness," where I was lacking yin energy, caused me to lose my way many times. I thought if I got off the hamster wheel, even for a short while, I would lose momentum in my career.

During those times, I was especially repelled by the soft, opaque world of the shifting energies that come with the yin. I thought my money would be lost by succumbing to the subtle energies of letting things happen on their own. My mind was stifled by the idea that materialism brought happiness and security. I could not see how it was my pushing forward and obsession with materialism that was causing me greater pain and far less life balance.

The trick was to realize that life is about becoming more accepting of all parts of ourselves—the yin and the yang, the masculine and the feminine, the fear and the love, the attachment and detachment. To close the gap between all of it so that ultimately you feel like you are a powerful being who can navigate your way through the challenges of life and come out feeling like you are enough.

Take a moment right now to think about where you fall within the spectrum of the yin and yang. Notice how you may feel more comfortable with one than the other.

- **More Yin-Focused:** This includes those who have avoided money due to fear of harm, greed, competition, and selfishness—so much so that you end up feeling like you have to expend a lot of energy to stay out of trouble with money. This struggle leads to self-doubt and loss of confidence surrounding your own potential. These struggles consistently make you feel like you are not enough.
- **More Yang-Focused:** This includes those who have thoroughly embraced the cultural practices when it comes to capitalism and making money. You're focusing so much time and attention on earning money that you've found yourself making too many compromises and sacrifices in order to keep the money rolling in. This ongoing battle results in becoming tired and "yanged" out after years of overdosing on activity in the external world. This tugs at your heart because you feel like you have to compromise your deepest desires to have money.

As we resolve any internal conflicts between the yin and the yang, we learn that life isn't so much about being one way or the other as it is about finding balance between the extremes. Balance means you're able to be both yin and yang, depending upon what you're working on in any given moment.

Being prosperous means paying less attention to money and more attention to your beingness. Being yin and yang without making yourself wrong heightens the enjoyment of life itself. From here, money becomes the tool for how you go about creating harmony and balance in life. Earning money and taking care of your finances is done out of the joyfulness that comes by experiencing life. Your money activities arise out of the expression of your inner aliveness. It becomes an effect of your mental attitude, and when you think, "I love you, money; I appreciate you; I value you," you know it is coming from sheer joy and gratitude for all that you are.

6

CLAIMING YOUR PROSPERITY

Abundance is not something we acquire.
It's something we tune in to.
—WAYNE DYER

One of my past clients told me a story that really changed how I thought about money and the magical things that happen when we're ready to manifest prosperity for ourselves. Many years ago when Teresa was going through a period of deep introspection in her late twenties and early thirties, she quit her job, got into meditation and spiritual thinking, and couch-surfed for several years. She spent much of her time sitting in introspective thought and creating vision boards about what she wanted her life to look like in the future.

Part of this process included deciding she wanted to have $3 million in the bank by the time she was forty. She got to thinking that this was how much money she needed to make the most beneficial impact in the world, and, accordingly, she went about visualizing and meditating on it for days at a time. Several months after she began this practice, she bought a lottery ticket, which was outside of something she normally did. A few days later, she remembered to go online to check the status of the ticket.

After entering the numbers into the website's search engine, she was shocked to receive a confirmation that she held the winning ticket: she had won $3 million! She couldn't believe it. She kept checking her numbers over and over, each time confirming that in fact she had definitely won the lottery. Realizing that it was Friday night and the lottery office was closed until Monday, she decided to put the ticket in a safe-deposit box and wait it out until she could call the lottery office when they opened Monday morning.

Teresa was beside herself with anticipation. She then spent the next sixty hours thinking about the fact that her life was about to drastically change. She thought about what she would do with the money, where she would go, and the ways she would live her new life. She thought about the fact that she had set this goal only six months previously and now it had already come into reality. She did her best to remain calm, but her mind was racing with excitement and anticipation, so much so that she could barely even sleep.

On Monday morning, Teresa called the lottery office to find out what the next steps were now that she had won. The person who answered the phone told her that it was impossible that she'd won because someone else had won that lottery drawing. Teresa must have checked the wrong drawing, the lottery rep explained. She had not won the money. The realization that she wasn't going to get the money sent Teresa into a deep funk that lasted several weeks.

After overcoming the severe disappointment, Teresa could see that while her affirmations had caused her to readily believe that the lottery winnings were hers, there was no reason why she had to give up her dream just because of what had happened. Instead, the false win with the lottery made it all the more clear that her goals were within reach if she could just hold on to this deeply envisioned dream until it became her reality.

Interestingly enough, within a few months of this happening, a business opportunity landed on her doorstep beginning a series of real estate deals that brought her closer to the realization of her goal. After a few years of rapidly growing her real estate company, she found herself sitting on a bank balance of more than $1 million, and, sure enough, by the time she was thirty-nine, she had accumulated more than $3 million, just as she had envisioned.

She later told me that she felt certain that the weekend she spent believing she'd won the lottery led her to create the wealth that had continued to grow since that time. For those two days, Teresa had thought beyond a shadow of a doubt that she had won $3 million and from that time forward it was a part of her consciousness. She simply knew it was going to happen.

Teresa's story showed me the power of what can happen when we become absolutely positive about what our future is going to look like. I feel like my own journey to becoming a millionaire wasn't all that different. I made a conscious decision early in life that there was no reason why I could not reach that goal one day.

By becoming so deliberate with my thoughts, I was refusing to allow any and all limiting beliefs to determine the outcome. I simply knew I would figure out a way to do it and never allowed myself to question the potential. In interviewing many millionaires over the years, I have discovered that they too were operating from a very similar mindset—not that they all knew they'd be millionaires but that they were very determined to create freedom for themselves. Looking back, I think Teresa and I had each discovered our own way to access the limitless power we have as human beings.

GREATER AWARENESS MEANS EVERYTHING

What happened for Teresa and myself helped me understand just how much the beliefs a person carries can affect his or her wallet. People who are wealthy are neither smarter, faster, nor more resilient by nature than anyone else. One thing they do have in common are their beliefs about what is possible. By the time someone earns money consistently for many years, they gain a belief system that favorably supports their ongoing success. Their beliefs confirm that not only is it likely their income will continue, they no longer recognize obstacles as standing in the way of their success.

Rarely have we witnessed times of such huge prosperity for so many people, and as a result, there are more millionaires than ever before in the United States. According to data from the Credit Suisse Research Institute, completed in 2019, there were more than 18.6 million millionaires nationwide,[1] which marked an increase of 1.26 million from the previous year.[2] Overall that represents millionaires as being about 7.6% of the U.S. adult population.

Sadly, even with that many millionaires in the United States, when people are asked if they think they can become millionaires in their lifetimes, only 29 percent believe it is possible.[3] Yet with estimates that people are becoming millionaires at the average rate of 3,452 every day, it is expected that there will be more than 20 million people reaching this level by the end of 2020. The question to ask yourself is "Do you see yourself as someone who can achieve this goal?" And, for that matter, "Do you even want it?" To be clear, whether or not you become a millionaire isn't as important as what happens to you in the process of becoming one or even in allowing yourself to move in that direction. Which is why I think the following quote by motivational speaker and author Jim Rohn hits the mark perfectly:

> The real value in setting goals is not in their achievement. The acquisition of the things you want is strictly secondary. The major reason for setting goals is to compel you to become the person it takes to achieve them. The greatest value is in the skills, knowledge, discipline and leadership qualities you'll develop in reaching that elevated status.[4]

So rather than focusing on the money, let's think about what's going on inside the thoughts, beliefs, and feelings of a Mindful Millionaire.

A LIFE OF PROSPERITY

Over the years I've composed list after list about prosperity and what it is. Realizing that none of what I write down is set in stone but that the lists give us an idea of what's going on behind the scenes, of what helps people create abundance for themselves. I'm certain many millionaires have applied these principles to their lives and likely credited them for some of their success. As you read through this list, give the ideas time to soak in so they can permeate your thoughts and inspire you to create what you most want for yourself.

Keep in mind that you don't have to be living each of these principles right now—in fact, the goal of diving into part 2 of this book is to guide you gradually through a process where you will learn how to bring these ideas into reality.

- Prosperity arises by knowing and accepting yourself fully.
- Prosperity correlates to the relationship you have with yourself, not the relationship you have with stuff.
- Prosperity is a natural state of being and can arise spontaneously without cause.
- Prosperity is infinite, without limits.
- Prosperity is not synonymous with having lots of money.
- Prosperity is closely aligned with gratefulness.
- Prosperity is about the inner rewards, far more than the external ones.
- Prosperity is "curvy," flexible, creative, and never absolute.
- Prosperity is what allows you to stay with the bumps and shakes in life while giving up expectations of how life "should" be.

- Prosperity is about living in balance. Balance is looking at the whole picture and then figuring out what is right for you given all the considerations of family, profession, health, environment, money, and your own self.
- Prosperity is holistic.
- Prosperity is custom-fit just for you. What's right for you isn't always right for the next person, and success comes in many shapes and sizes. We all want different things in life, so prosperity arises out of that which is most important to you—a loving family, health, money, fame, success—you name it; you make the final call.
- Prosperity arises when you have a strong sense of purpose and passion. Simon Sinek, author of *Start With Why*, says, "Working hard for something we don't care about is called stress; working hard for something we love is called passion."[5] Prosperity and passion are close friends.
- Prosperity is realizing that while lots of money can be a blessing, it can also be a curse. Money is just a tool; it is never awful and it is never to be avoided. Money is also not something you need to chase. Having money can be great, but having very little money is fine, too. It all comes down to what you are here to do and what tools you need to accomplish your goals.
- Prosperity is about playing full-out in life. It is about showing up and being engaged in whatever you are involved in. After my mom knew she was sick, no matter what ideas I suggested about trips we could take together or events we could attend, her answer was always yes. Her attitude was 100 percent focused on making the most of every single day. We can all learn something from this perspective.
- Prosperity means that if you want to have more money, you figure out how to make more. If you want to spend more time with your family, you create a business and

lifestyle that allows you to do that. If you want to spend more time on vacation, you create that too.

- Prosperity is about feeling so full that you cannot help but give; your time, money, and other precious resources are the vehicles you use to share how you feel.
- Prosperity is what you become by living a life that matters.

Regardless of how long it takes to create prosperity in your life, the rewards are worth it.

THE EVOLUTION OF PROSPERITY

The seven prosperities I am about to share with you comprise a framework for discovering where you are in your own personal evolution of moving from scarcity to wholeness as it pertains to money. By starting at the bottom and working your way up, you can identify the areas where you are currently learning, testing, and solidifying.

The ultimate goal is to be able to live inside of these states of awareness, with each being mastered before you continue to the next. Each builds upon the others as you work your way up the ladder.

Mastering each state of prosperity is a gradual process that can take many years to fully realize, as it relies upon your ability to integrate and live from inside of each truth. As you move through each stage of awareness, you are making conscious choices about who you are and what you believe about yourself and all of life. This is also great training for living deliberately, because the stages teach you just how much power you have to create the life you really want to be living.

I've used the context of what it means to be a Mindful Millionaire to help guide the discussion so we can consider what we know about millionaires and how they are approaching these areas of their lives differently.

THE PROSPERITY LADDER™

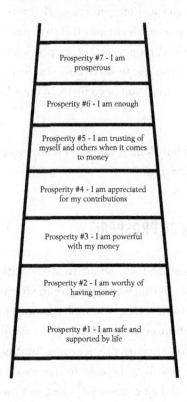

Prosperity #7 - I am prosperous

Prosperity #6 - I am enough

Prosperity #5 - I am trusting of myself and others when it comes to money

Prosperity #4 - I am appreciated for my contributions

Prosperity #3 - I am powerful with my money

Prosperity #2 - I am worthy of having money

Prosperity #1 - I am safe and supported by life

Prosperity 1—I Am Safe and Supported by Life

Instead of getting stuck in the weeds when it comes to worrying about not feeling safe and supported, Mindful Millionaires establish a consistent and reliable income so they feel confident in their ability to take good care of themselves and their families. To accomplish this goal, they know their risk tolerance and are willing to take calculated risks to achieve their goals. The purpose of financial planning isn't to accumulate the biggest pile of money possible. It's to decide what you want out of life, calculate how much money you need to reach those goals, and then choose an investment strategy that will deliver the appropriate returns.

Many millionaires end up holding steady and reliable jobs that allow them to take greater risk when it comes to building wealth. This ensures they won't be forced to be too conservative while building their long-term plans. It is far more difficult to deal with the risk associated with investing and business ownership when you are resource-strapped and stressed about the bottom falling out beneath you. Mindful Millionaires know there is danger in playing it too safe and not taking enough risk to reach their goals. This leads them to take a slightly more aggressive position to realize better returns over the long haul.

My friend Tom Corley has conducted extensive research around the habits of the wealthy,[6] and one of the things he found in his research was that millionaires often have at least three streams of income, thereby diversifying their dependence upon any one stream.[7] In the same way, millionaires also set up insurance to protect their finances from unexpected losses.

Prosperity 2—I Am Worthy of Having Money

Instead of struggling with feelings of unworthiness, Mindful Millionaires dig deep to understand themselves and know their gifts and talents better than anyone. Even if unconscious belief patterns were a problem in the past, they no longer have them buried under the surface causing them to acquire more debt and hinder their ability to save. They've also figured out how to stop ignoring their feelings by allowing themselves to feel a variety of emotions without judging them to be good or bad and right or wrong.

When it comes to managing their money, Mindful Millionaires find ways to live within their means, often choosing to live frugally rather than lavishly. Millionaires typically save at least 20 percent of their income[8] and live in homes currently valued at an average of $320,000 (in 2010).[9] It is likely surprising to learn that eighty-six percent of millionaires are self-made and one in three funded their college educations without debt.[10]

Further, Ramsey Solutions conducted a study[11] of over ten thousand millionaires and found that 94 percent said they live on less than they make, and nearly 75 percent had never carried a credit card balance in their lives. They also found that millionaires spend on average $200 or less each month on restaurants, and 93 percent use coupons all or some of the time when shopping.

Prosperity 3—I Am Powerful with My Money

Instead of fighting off feelings of powerlessness, Mindful Millionaires realize the importance of taking control of their lives and their money. Knowing that financial independence is something they are eager to experience, millionaires are wholeheartedly focused on achieving their goals, and they work hard to get there. Hustling to make things happen is something they learned early in life, and they're able to readily respond to challenges as they arise. Patience is seen as part of the process, and having everything always go their way has nothing to do with how powerful they see themselves.

In his research, Tom Corley found that 86 percent of millionaires who work full-time each put in fifty hours a week or more at their careers.[12] He also found that they watched less than one hour of television daily and spent less than one hour surfing the internet. This gave them more time to focus on personal self-development and self-care, like eating well, sleeping at least seven hours, and exercising on a regular basis.

Tom's research about millionaires ultimately led him to write a book titled *Rich Habits: The Daily Success Habits of Wealthy Individuals*, because he could see that those who were the wealthiest were also the ones with the most positive habits. The habits of the wealthy included things like committing to daily habits, goal setting, and daily self-improvement. Tom took what he learned from his research and applied it to his own life and saw radical improvements as a result. He was able to lose weight, improve his relationships, grow his business, and feel a greater sense of peace about life. Tom said it best when he told me, "Successful people do not rely on chance. They proactively shape the course of their lives. When they look into their mirror, they see the future version of themselves, and that puts a smile on their reflections." I know he is speaking about the person he sees reflecting back to himself in the mirror every morning.

Prosperity 4—I Am Appreciated for My Contributions

Instead of feeling underpaid and unappreciated, Mindful Millionaires develop ways to ensure they are well paid for their efforts. For some, this means starting a business where they are in charge of their own financial destiny, with about 50 percent of millionaires being self-employed or owning a business.[13]

Most importantly, those wishing to become millionaires figure out how to create substantial value in the marketplace, whether they are employed by others or not. This means diving deep into researching and developing valuable solutions the world is seeking and finding ways to use one's talents, knowledge, and gifts to fill these greatest needs. Either way it is about creating so much value that others want to buy from you or have you work for them because they appreciate what you are creating. In this case money, acting as a medium of exchange, naturally flows toward those who provide substantial benefits to others. By taking responsibility for yourself and your ability to create value in the world, you are creating a positive feedback loop that results in receiving money back in return.

Prosperity 5—I Am Trusting of Myself and Others When It Comes to Money

Instead of feeling like they cannot trust anyone, Mindful Millionaires learn all that they need to know about money and investing so they're confident in their own knowledge and can take strategic advantage of the options available. In their research on millionaires, Ramsey Solutions also found that 80 percent invested in their company's 401(k) plan, and 75 percent also invested outside of company plans. Additionally, 75 percent of those surveyed said the reason they had reached the millionaire mark was because they had consistently invested over a long period of time.

A study completed by Spectrum Group showed how wealthier households tend to put greater stock in being financially literate concerning financial products and investments. When asked how important their financial knowledge is to them, 50 percent of millionaires surveyed responded that it was "extremely important," compared with just 27 percent of households with a net worth of less than $100,000.[14]

To become more trusting of your ability to invest requires that you try it and stick with it over time. Taking classes, reading books, talking with friends who invest are all requirements for becoming a skilled money manager. If you are going to have money, this is your responsibility and you cannot abdicate it to others. No one will ever care as much about your money as you do. Your ability to trust others always starts with trusting yourself first.

Eventually, as you become more mindful and conscious about stewarding your money and investing, it is likely you'll also find yourself paying closer attention to the kinds of companies you are investing in, choosing to invest in conscious companies that, for example, are interested in taking good care of their employees and/or preserving the environment. This allows you to feel like you are in alignment with who you really are and with how your money is being used in the world.

Prosperity 6—I Am Enough

Instead of feeling like they are not enough to have what they most want in life, Mindful Millionaires know themselves and know what they are capable of creating. They know that thoughts about not having enough and not being enough are traps they no longer get caught up in. They've become so consistent with their financial behaviors and practices that they find themselves readily able to trust their intuition and wisdom when making financial decisions. They no longer have to worry about unconscious beliefs snagging their attention and causing them to make poor decisions. Now they're focused on spending less time with their money and more time living their lives—while knowing their money is creating a legacy that extends far beyond their limited sense of self. They are also now in a position of regularly giving to causes they believe in and wish to support.

Prosperity 7—I Am Prosperous

Instead of feeling like anything is missing in life, Mindful Millionaires realize that they've always had access to everything they needed. This is because by having a sense of one's own completeness and wholeness, you cannot help but recognize the limitless, boundless, and abundant nature of reality.

By the time you've gone through all seven prosperities and have become a Mindful Millionaire, you've reached a state of grace and radiance that beneficially influences the world around you. Money has become a tool of self-understanding, compassion, and connection with others. The more you're living in flow with yourself, the easier it is to create a more prosperous and supportive world around you.

MY STORY OF PROSPERITY

Less than a year after my scarcity breakthrough in my office, my husband and I decided to overhaul our lives. As part of this decision, we sold or gave away most of our possessions, which we'd collected over the previous thirty years together, and we sold the new home that my husband had custom-designed and built for our family. We escorted my daughter off to her first year of college and pulled my son out of sixth grade for a year. We put our remaining possessions in storage and packed what was left into three small suitcases, embarking on a one-year journey to live freely without economic pressures. We started our trip by moving to the Hawaiian Islands and then spent several months living with my in-laws, where we took turns delighting each other with our culinary skills on a nightly basis.

Before the year was up, we found a home in Sedona, Arizona, and began creating a new life in a new state. By the time we were settled, we were living in a home one-third the size of our previous one, with no debt, no mortgage, and very low monthly expenses. We then built a guesthouse, which, as a rental, brings in more than what it costs for us to live. Through our experiences with money, we've learned that prosperity, to us, means living a simple life that allows us to feel financial independence on a daily basis.

This has given us the freedom to choose how we spend our time and what we nurture in our lives. I am not forced to make choices from a place of scarcity. If, for any reason, my business turns out not to be in service of my values, I can walk away and start something else. If I want to earn less while spending five years to research and write the contents of this book, like I did, I can. If I wish to charge less in order to touch more people with my work, I can. My sense is that this work has become a reflection of my lack of scarcity in creating it.

I think all of us want to be in this kind of position someday, preferably before we are so worn out that we no longer have the energy to create what we most want. If you're not there yet, you can get there. Ask yourself, "How do I rid all forms of scarcity from my life so that I can just show up, be exactly who I want to be, work with the people I want to work with, and not put up with the BS that life can bring?" Ask, "What do I need to do next to ensure I am bringing my most prosperous self into the world?"

When you learn how to embrace and reclaim your prosperity, you experience it in everything around you. I once heard that the difference between poetry and science is that with science, what matters most is having lots of facts so you can offer a solution. With poetry, what matters most is having lots of answers without the need for a solution. For that reason, prosperity is far more like poetry than science: there are limitless answers and no need to shoehorn them into a standardized, hard-and-fast, or preconceived "solution." Prosperity is about custom-fitting your life so it is made just for you.

INFINITE POTENTIAL

The magician David Blaine once said, "We are all capable of infinitely more than we believe. We are stronger and more resourceful than we know, and we can endure much more than we think we can. The only restrictions on our capacity to astonish ourselves and each other are imposed by our own minds."[15]

The process of healing your relationship with money is not necessarily sequential; instead, it relies on you to determine the areas that are most strongly out of balance and to trust that whatever is happening in your life is exactly what you are meant to be paying greater attention to. No matter where you wish to begin, trust that your conditions are appearing perfectly for you to explore what you are ready to let go of so you can see the greater truth of yourself.

Start with knowing you are safe and then work your way up to feeling like not only are you enough, you are whole and complete as designed. When you learn how to embrace and take full ownership of prosperity, you can't help but see it reflected back at you everywhere.

7

YOUR MIND AND YOUR MONEY

Knowing yourself is the beginning of all wisdom.
—ARISTOTLE

Change and inner growth are both dependent upon believing you can do whatever you put your mind to. Confidence (and sometimes, desperation!) is what allows you to sit still, look inside, and recognize the part of you that may be conflicted. Since problems cannot be solved while you are lost inside of their energy, becoming the witness to your mind is critical to being able to approach uncomfortable feelings with an open mind and a patient attitude.

THE BRAIN AND MONEY

The mind has evolved substantially as the brain has developed in human beings over the past tens of thousands of years. As the main organ of the nervous system, the brain manages most of the body's activities. It is responsible for processing information received from both outside and inside the body and is the seat of our emotions and cognitive abilities, including thought, long- and short-term memory, and decision-making.

By gaining a better understanding of how your brain functions at a basic level, you become better able to know the reasons behind why you react and respond to financial situations the way you do. What follows is a simplified explanation in hopes that you can use it to become more mindful and less reactive with your money.

There are three main areas of the brain, and we will examine each of them.

The Reptilian Brain

The oldest of the three areas of the brain is the reptilian brain, named after its similarity to the brain of reptiles, which includes the brain stem and the cerebellum. This area tends to be reliable, rigid, and compulsive. This part of the brain is oriented to keeping you alive more than anything else.

This is the area that releases adrenaline into the body as a result of stress and anxiety. Adrenaline is a hormone produced by the adrenal gland in the body, and because of how it works, adrenaline is something that people can become addicted to. It stimulates the heart rate, dilates the blood vessels and air passages, and creates the sensation that we most associate with physically exhilarating situations. "Fight or flight" is often used to characterize the circumstances under which adrenaline is released into the body. It is an early adaptation that allows animals, as well as humans, to better cope with dangerous and unexpected situations.

This is the part of the brain that gets activated when you become afraid of what might happen to you and your family due to problems with money. When adrenaline is released into the body, we become reactive and more likely to take risks without thinking through all of our options. We instinctively wish to avoid unpleasant conditions and actively seek the path of least resistance. For example, it might cause us to reactively pay for things with a credit card in stressful situations rather than figuring out alternative options.

The Limbic System

The second main area of the brain is the limbic system. The limbic system records memories of behaviors that produce agreeable and disagreeable experiences. The limbic brain includes the hippocampus, amygdala, and hypothalamus and is the seat of value and belief-oriented judgments we make, often unconsciously, that affect our behavior.

This area of the brain releases hormones, like dopamine, cortisol, and endorphins, into the body as a result of excitement, pain, aggression, suffering, love, and sexual activity, among other things. Because these hormones are often associated with highly pleasurable activities, they can also be habit-forming, which explains addictions to sex, love, shopping, and food consumption.

The most obvious way that the limbic system shows up related to money has to do with the hormones that get released when we are spending money, especially on things that we think will make us feel good. The more we spend the more hormones get released and the better we temporarily feel. This may explain why we end up spending more than planned on a shopping excursion and then later decide to return things when the hormones are no longer affecting us.

Another way the limbic system affects money decisions has to do with making choices merely to feel better even when those choices can be counterproductive to your goals. This happens when you're deciding where to invest your money based on the success of past returns. Chasing "hot hands" and getting on the latest bandwagon for where to invest often leads to dismal returns in the long run, but in the short term the limbic system makes us feel good.

Another way that the hormones released by the limbic system can affect us has to do with how we deal with stress. The assumption is that most people are in "glad" mode most of the time, with fear being on the side. If a stressful situation arises, endorphins get released to help a person feel better and then return to a glad state. It is not unusual to unconsciously get into stressful situations with the goal of receiving natural shots of endorphins to make you feel better, thereby returning you to a happy state.

As shocking as it may seem, I've come to see how people often unknowingly get themselves into stressful situations with money merely to receive the hits of hormonal "juice" that come from facing stress.[1] The more stress a person feels, the more likely he or she will experience the release of hormones that will make that person feel better. After a while of this happening over and over again, even if the adrenaline, dopamine, and endorphins don't get released, there is, strangely enough, a sense of satisfaction that still comes as a result of experiencing stress. This is very similar to what happened to Pavlov's dogs when they no longer needed the stimulus to salivate for food. Many people who struggle with stress and anxiety about money can become addicted to behaving in certain ways with money just to receive the feel-good hormones that they think are coming to save them. Plus, when we are stressed there is a higher likelihood that we will make poor choices when it comes to our finances.[2] This is because stress causes us to overestimate the positive potential outcomes while diminishing the negative risks associated with our decisions.

Of course, it doesn't make much sense for people to become addicted to their own suffering. And yet we can see that as a society, we are far more interested in pain and suffering in the headlines than we are about feel-good stories. Marketers know that when their advertisements focus on the negative, they sell stuff. Internet media companies know that when they share negative headlines, far more people click on those articles than if the headlines were less provocative. When we go to see movies, more often than not they are filled with pain, suffering, and violence. When you go to a sports game, you see people focused on the drama and struggles that occur, even more than winning or losing. As hard as it is to face, we are a society addicted to suffering, and the more honest we are about our own tendencies, the easier it becomes to separate ourselves from our addictions.

The Neocortex

The third area of the brain with the greatest amount of recent evolutionary change is the neocortex. This area has two large cerebral hemispheres that are responsible for thought, language, imagination, and consciousness. These two parts of the brain operate codependently with each other through their numerous interconnections, and although they have different specialties, they function best when they are firing together. The neural interconnections between the two hemispheres make us who we are today.

The two hemispheres are called the left brain and right brain. The left brain is good at dealing with facts and details—tending to focus on logical reasoning, organizing, structuring, analysis, and sequences. The right brain, on the other hand, is good at synthesizing, contextualizing, seeing the big picture, emotional expression, social behaviors, and seeing many things at once. Of course, we need both approaches to create fulfilling and productive lives, but oftentimes it is believed that money, because of its connection to numbers, is a more left- than right-brained activity. Similar to the "Yin and Yang of Money" discussion in chapter 5, I do not think this is true. Rather, we want both parts of the brain to be active when we are dealing with money—so that we can make decisions that integrate both the rational and methodical with the touchy-feely "heart-based" ways of thinking. As the most highly developed and advanced part of the brain, the neocortex is what helps us do exactly this. Plus, when we are operating in this way, we become far less reactionary in our decision-making, so we can make better decisions.

When it comes to money, it is not uncommon to find ourselves "overstrengthening" one side of our brains at the expense of the other, similar to what can happen to a tennis player who has one strong and coordinated arm and another that is weak and uncoordinated. Brain-imaging studies have shown that highly successful and creative people are using a much more balanced approach to their decisions which is why we want to talk more about the power of meditation.

A 2012 UCLA School of Medicine study[3] found that the corpus callosum, which is like a cable of nerves cross-linking the brain hemispheres, was remarkably stronger and thicker in the brains of people who are regular meditation practitioners. The same thing goes for other studies, which have shown the hippocampus increasing in thickness as a result of meditation. The hippocampus has been proven to increase learning and memory functioning while also regulating how we feel. The stronger and more developed the hippocampus, the smarter we are and the less depressed we feel.

You can see where this is heading. This book is, after all, called *The Mindful Millionaire*. My own experience of regular meditation practices over the past twenty years has shown me the power of what happens to the brain when we meditate. While there is extensive research available, the one thing I do know is that mind training is serious stuff.

Unfortunately, meditation is also not the magic cure-all pill that some claim. Instead, the real payoffs come with a sincere and devoted practice that helps you alter your understanding of your view of self. My hope is that you are gaining tools throughout this book to show you how to begin tapping into the long-term benefits that come from establishing a dedicated meditation practice. Let's begin by talking a little bit more about the mind and meditation.

THE MIND

The mind is an evolutionary aspect of your body that continues to expand as you live your life. Within the context of this book, "mind" is the vehicle through which we interact with our human experience. Many times when people refer to the mind, they are only referring to one's thoughts, but in this case, the mind includes our brain, our thoughts, and our emotional states.

In learning how to gain better control of your mind, you acquire the keys to the toolbox that helps you orient your life in whatever way you wish. This means the more you know about how your mind works, the more you can counteract your negative and unsupportive behaviors when it comes to money.

Study after study show the transformational effects of meditation and its benefits on not just the brain but on all parts of our bodies and on our overall well-being.[4] Twenty years ago when I first became adept at meditation, I thought I had found the Holy Grail and could not understand why more people didn't do it. Since then, research has continued to provide evidence that mindfulness practice can transform our lives and impact us personally, financially, and professionally, including the following:

- improved stress-management skills
- improved cognitive function and concentration
- increased creativity
- improved decision-making
- increased focus
- improved health
- improved well-being, positive emotions, and life satisfaction
- increased resilience
- decreased loneliness and depression

- decreased PTSD symptoms
- counteraction of the effects of age on the brain

Plus, when breath work is added to your meditation practice, similar to what you will be learning in part 2, reactivity lessens even more.[5]

After nearly twenty years of teaching meditation, I've found that one of the most beneficial skills we can develop is that of concentration—the ability to focus the mind on a single area of attention without wandering. This can be done by focusing on the breath for five to ten minutes and through repetition of visualizations and mantras for longer periods of time. This type of meditation is not always easy, for many reasons—including the fact that when you first learn how to be still and begin trying to focus your mind without distraction, your mind wants to do everything but pay attention to the task at hand. The more distracted you become, the more frustrated you feel and the more difficult it is to continue meditating.

It is helpful to consider that even highly advanced meditators are keeping their minds fixated on only one object of attention for anywhere from three to five minutes. Which means that keeping your mind fixated on an object of focus, like your breath, for fifteen to thirty seconds at a time is going to be difficult no matter who you are. Gradually your abilities improve and it gets easier, as long as you don't become self-critical while you are meditating. The key to meditation is practicing, no matter how you feel and no matter how hard it is and no matter what your mind tries to do. Just doing it over and over again without expectation keeps you going until you realize it has become a natural process. Your abilities to meditate can dramatically improve with more time, attention, and focus devoted to your practice.

As previously noted, most of the time we are operating in a state of awareness that is partially conscious and partially unconscious. This means we are noticing some of the things going on around us but not everything. The more beliefs that are controlling us and the more autopilot mode we are reacting from, the less conscious we are of our surroundings, feelings, impulses, desires, and thoughts.

Through meditation practices and by becoming more "meta-aware," which is where a person is thinking about their thinking, we learn how to recognize awareness itself, which helps us monitor our minds without being swept away by what we are noticing. From here we can notice when our minds have wandered off from something we want to focus on and bring it back to the task at hand. This level of mind control is what gives us the ability to be highly effective and creatively inspired within our activities.

Most of us have very short attention spans, and so we find ourselves gravitating to meditations that do not require us to bring our minds back to the objects of focus. While guided meditations can help you feel more relaxed and calm, it is important to know that not all meditations are created equal when it comes to developing your concentration. Eventually you will want to include silent meditation practice if you wish to improve your concentration skills. My hope in sharing these tips with you is that you will be more patient with yourself as you learn to meditate, so you give yourself the benefit of time and commitment without expecting too much of yourself.

It is also helpful to note that multitasking and "app checking" are testing our brain's ability to stay focused and undistracted. Clifford Nass is a Stanford professor and researcher whose pioneering research[6] into how humans interact with technology found that the increasingly screen-saturated, multitasking modern world was not nurturing the ability to concentrate, analyze, or feel empathy. He explained how multitaskers are "suckers for irrelevancy," which hampers their ability to focus on the problems at hand.

Meditation is not something you can do for a short period of time and then expect the benefits to last. Researchers have found that you must continue your practice on a regular basis in order to keep up its benefits.[7] While you can see benefits quickly in many cases, without regular practice, many of the improvements go away after a certain amount of time and you risk finding yourself back to living a life of distraction.

Learning how to "catch" your feelings midstream before they cause you to create havoc with your money is a powerful practice that can be improved through meditation. Additionally, when you can slow down, take stock of situations with a clear mind, and take responsibility for your own experiences, you no longer have to assume that when something bad happens, you must quickly react to it.

THE EGO

Much has been written about the ego, and for the purposes of this book, we're going to limit the discussion to the idea that the ego is a form of self-identity that includes a collection of beliefs about oneself oriented to answer the question "Who am I?" It includes the past (who you were in the past), present (who you are today), and future selves (who you are in the future).

It is thought that our ideas of self-identity get formed in child-hood, but there is much debate about exactly when this happens. After several years of guiding people through their early childhood memories, I've come to think that we begin developing the self concept from the moment we are born, possibly even from a mid-stage in the womb. All that said, I have seen an amplification of the ego for those of us who have experienced strong feelings around fear from an early age.

For purposes of this work, let's consider how a healthy ego is one that allows us to grow up with a loving sense of self, feelings of resiliency, the ability to solve problems creatively, the capacity to develop meaningful relationships, and a sense of meaning for our lives. This is what most everyone wants, and yet far too few end up having. Instead, many of us find ourselves dealing with what I would call an unhealthy ego.

An unhealthy ego is a form of self-deception that emphasizes feelings of isolation and separation from the rest of the world. The formation of an unhealthy ego has a lot to do with things that happened in our youth. If, during our young years, we encountered a lot of disappointments, difficulties, or we didn't get what we needed on a regular basis, our egos can become damaged. If we don't have the opportunity to heal in a healthy way, the wounded ego learns to compensate and protect the painful parts of the psyche in defensive, reactive, and dysfunctional ways. Acting like a shield, its goal is to protect us from the outside world. At the same time, because it is so caught up in fear, it also prevents us from getting to know and love our truest selves.

The unhealthy ego is reactionary and maintains its strength by confusing and distracting the mind. It is wired to convince us that we need to suffer in order to get what we want. It is rooted in fear, doubt, anxiety, limiting beliefs, and toxic thinking patterns and believes it is the only thing that is keeping us out of harm's way. The unhealthy ego gains its power by drawing the mind's attention away from self-understanding and self-compassion and is the reason why we can find ourselves struggling so much with money. By clinging tightly to fear, lack, and scarcity, the unhealthy ego reinforces that you are incapable of handling things that could happen to you, and so it justifies its role to protect you at all costs.

As a child I worried about my own personal safety on a regular basis. I've come to see how it was partly my environment but more about the way I am naturally predisposed. It's also why I've devoted so much of my life to helping people deal with their fears. I know I am not alone in fearing for my own security and survival, which is why I can so closely relate to the parts of us that hold back out of fear.

When fear is such a prominent emotion, you can't help but listen to this voice inside of your head as if it were the voice of God.

Yet this voice doesn't warrant that sort of revering, because it is merely a collection of conditioned beliefs that are telling you to survive rather than to thrive. It is not telling you to listen to reason, nor to your highest purpose. It is just trying to keep you safe and secure, and for that reason it is taking you down the road most traveled rather than the one you really want to be traveling down.

In order to take care of myself growing up, I attempted to develop a protective and foolproof sense of self. I did this by getting good grades in school, being highly social, climbing up the career ladder, earning lots of money, and doing the "right" things. This approach worked well enough for many years, but the more mindful I became, the more I could see how it prevented me from becoming more intimate with all of life.

Understanding the ego is a great way to learn about all the defensive tactics we're applying to life when we are not in touch with ourselves. When we aren't feeling into our experiences, we don't really know ourselves. Consequently, we struggle to understand the why's behind what we do with our money. Letting go of deep-seated patterns of self-protection allows us to access and deal with our deeper feelings so that they no longer have unconscious control over our lives and our money.

SELF-CRITICISM

What many don't realize, especially in the face of challenges, is that self-criticism—a hallmark of the unhealthy ego—has a nasty way of turning failure into despair by activating your sympathetic nervous system and elevating your stress. It can become so severe that it keeps you from learning and being resilient in the face of failure. The impact can also be heightened when you have been raised in a home with a lot of emotional upsets.

Research has shown that self-criticism can easily make you weaker in the face of failure, more emotional and less likely to assimilate lessons from your failures.[8] The alternative to self-criticism is self-compassion: instead of engaging in harsh self-judgment, you shift your focus toward kindness and understanding. Although it may seem self-indulgent or perhaps even like weakness, self-compassion has been proven to help you become more resilient, stronger, and more enthusiastic about meeting life's challenges head on. Surprisingly, self-compassion has also been shown to help you learn from your mistakes and solve problems in the face of severe uncertainty.

When we feel money shame and money guilt, we have a tendency to self-criticize, to believe that if you aren't where you want to be with money, you're a failure in some way. This is particularly destructive because of the power it has to cause you to give up hope. In my practice, I see people who are so worn down by their own negative criticism that they have a hard time thinking anything positive about themselves. Their money failures are overshadowing all of the good things they've done and preventing them from feeling motivated and inspired about their futures.

Combining self-compassion together with understanding money helps you avoid the downward spiral that can occur when things don't work out as planned. By reminding yourself that you are not alone in your feelings of failure and that mistakes are part of what it means to be intrinsically human, you are extending kindness rather than criticism to yourself. It is helpful to remember that the problems at hand are connected to your feelings of inadequateness rather than your worthiness as a human being.

Here's what one of my clients shared with me about this:

> I didn't know that in neglecting my relationship with money I
> was neglecting a part of myself. I've been on a healing journey
> for thirty-plus years and finally realized how healing my rela-

tionship with money can heal a deeply wounded place inside of me. As with all challenging relationships, healing takes a lot of time, self-compassion, and soul-searching. Now I'm giving it the time and attention that any important relationship deserves. It's some of the deepest and most profound growth work I have ever done and is bringing me to a new level of freedom and clarity of purpose. It is opening doors to new opportunities and allowing me to serve more people and have a greater positive impact in the world.

THE INNER TRIAD

To combat feelings of self-criticism, I've found the following teachings and practices to significantly improve one's chances of negating the unhealthy ego.

Calling Out Your Inner Critic

The inner critic is a concept, used in popular psychology, that explains an internalized voice that judges and demeans people by telling themselves they're bad, wrong, inadequate, worthless, and guilty. The inner critic is often, but not always, inspired by the voice of one or more of your parents, and for that reason it is sometimes called the "inner parent."

One way I can quickly identify my inner critic is by noticing how it speaks to me. While much of the time I am moving through life with a smile on my face, that is not the case when the inner critic has my attention, because all I feel is sadness and dissatisfaction with myself. When I first started meditating and paying closer attention to my thoughts, I came up with the image of there being two people on my shoulder telling me what to do: one person was benevolent, kind, and supportive, while the other, my inner critic, was shouting derogatory and often-angry judgments. Once I "caught" the inner critic, I knew that whatever it was espousing was only trying to make me feel ashamed, guilty, and belittled.

It was interesting to learn many years ago that the Dalai Lama was very surprised by the fact that someone could ever have low self-esteem. It did not make any sense to him, because this is almost unheard of in the culture of Tibetan Buddhism.

My sense is that there are other, remote cultures in the world where this could also be the case, but in the West low self-esteem is commonplace. A big reason for why this is the case has to do with how common it is to have a hyperactive inner critic. After I've worked with people for several sessions, there comes a moment when they all of a sudden share, "Oh my gosh, it's me! I am the one causing my own feelings of shame, guilt, and low self-esteem. It's my own doing!!" This realization gives them great comfort because all of a sudden they've gained some degree of power over it just through the act of calling it out.

The more you understand your inner critic, the greater chance you have to overhaul the way it treats you. No longer willing to listen to the stories of how bad you are with money, how stupid you are for making past mistakes, and how much better it would be if you gave up on your dreams, now you can think to yourself, "Here comes slugger; I'm not going to let him lead the way this time."

When the inner critic is in control of your life and your money your personal self-transformation doesn't stand much chance. While many think it is best to ignore and avoid the voice, I recommend befriending it so you can change the way it talks to you. When you are friends with your inner critic, it is more likely to listen to what you say. This can happen by embracing and accepting it as a natural part of your life. By loving it and appreciating its qualities of being your "helper," your entire way of being shifts. With that, your ego doesn't have to run the show as much as it wants and can just be in service to whatever situation is appearing.

There is a fine balance between the ego helping you and hurting you. Essentially, your job is to let go of trying to grasp tightly to the ego while, at the same time, learning how to allow life to unfold from a new dimension of self-understanding. To do this you must stop your own cycles of blame, guilt, and shame and surrender to what lies beyond, particularly that which nourishes you.

Connecting with Your Inner Child

The "inner child" is another concept used in psychology that explains our childlike aspects, including all that we've learned and experienced before puberty. John Bradshaw, a self-help movement leader, famously used the term "inner child" to point to unresolved childhood experiences and the lingering effects of childhood dysfunction.[9] As you read through the money transformation stories provided in part 2, you will notice just how much the inner child comes up when a person is awakening to their own self-understanding. This has a lot to do with how your experiences and feelings about money go way back to early childhood, as pointed out earlier, and when you start looking inside of your feelings, the memories of situations come flooding back in. Through witnessing, honoring, and loving your inner child, you gain awareness and understanding of situations that were beyond your comprehension at the time.

As a child you just wanted to be free, but instead, as a result of being fragile and vulnerable, you likely found yourself in situations where you were neither sufficiently prepared nor mature enough to handle the challenges presented. Without the emotional and intellectual ability to fully understand the scope of what was happening, you most likely did your best to process and make meaning of the situation. Unfortunately, when we were young we might have taken on responsibility that was way beyond our understanding. When this happened, especially in emotional situations, we may have ended up feeling responsible for things we did not cause or at the very least feeling defenseless and confused. Later in life these tendencies can cause us to feel fear, guilt, and shame around things that we have no reason to feel this way about—and yet we do.

The inner critic and the inner child don't play nicely together most of the time, especially when you consider how the child is always going to be doing things she really wants to do—like going on a shopping spree or flying off to an exotic location at the last minute (and paying extra-high rates as a result), while the inner critic, who is also likely to be acting like a parent, is telling you what an idiot you were for your bad judgment. The trick with helping them get along is first noticing who is in control and where they are coming from. Many times the inner child is just wanting attention and to be loved and accepted for who she is—a spontaneous and fun-loving person. When the parent can have compassion for the child, there is an opportunity to find a balance in which all parts of you are served without anyone being wrong or right.

Oftentimes it takes returning to memories from the past to get fully in touch with one's inner child so you can witness her through the lens of understanding and compassion. It also unleashes the child within, who may have had to grow up a lot faster than planned. Doing so allows this beautiful part of you to engage once again with a joyous and playful spirit that imbues a lightness of being.

The awakening of your inner child is something that many people never forget. The world around you starts to radiate at a brighter intensity; your senses of taste, sound, and touch become far more sensitive; and your awareness of the playfulness waiting for you in all of life reappears. It is like you are reawakening from a very long slumber only to witness a whole new world. By integrating memories into your current reality and accepting the parts of your inner child that became splintered, you are no longer caught in a cycle of pain, suppression, and resistance toward yourself and your money.

Welcoming Your Adult

As you gain greater awareness of who you are and how you wish to be living your life, you become an adult in your life. This is the wise part of you that stays in the here and now and objectively evaluates reality as life unfolds. Your inner adult is the part of you who can skillfully navigate the emotions of the inner child alongside of the harshness of the inner parent. Nurturing both aspects so they feel seen, heard, and honored. From this vantage point, the inner adult feels empowered to make the best decisions because it is capable of making the best possible decisions because it has become "meta-aware" of what's happening around you and is taking into consideration all the facts. The more mindful you become and the more you awaken to yourself, the more the inner adult becomes a powerful guiding force in your life and with your money.

THE PATH OF MONEY CONSCIOUSNESS

Science illuminates the fact that our bodies have unlimited potential to grow, adapt, and heal in ways that are still far too complex to fully understand. In a similar way, changing your reactions when it comes to money can result in significant changes for how you feel about yourself and your ability to manage money. Getting to this point takes time but is well worth your effort, especially because now you know that there are a multitude of influences that come together in shaping why we do what we do with money.

8

KNOWING YOU'RE ON THE RIGHT PATH

A journey of a thousand miles begins with a single step.
—TAO TE CHING, LAO-TZU

To live a prosperous life you must believe you deserve to have all that fulfills you. Knowing yourself and remembering that you are always doing the best you can helps you stay on track and give yourself time to allow the process to do its magic.

The analogy of peeling back the layers of an onion can be used to describe the transformation taking place beneath this process. At first there's a crusty layer of protection that is shed away and reveals more-vulnerable skin underneath. As each layer is shed, you're shown new aspects of yourself that expose your desires and wishes, your kindness, your vulnerability, your desires, and your dreams. Early on you might not be pleased with what you see, because the years of building up walls of protection may have caused you to act in ways that create more harm than good. This is when self-honesty gets tough, because seeing your own flaws can be excruciating—so much so that you may feel compelled along the way to put down the book and nurture your soul until you feel strong enough to continue. You'll know when you're ready to pick it back up again and continue.

JULIE'S STORY

Julie, a successful business owner, was running a million-dollar e-commerce business when we first started working together. A lifetime of negative self-talk had caused her to be consumed by all the things that weren't working in her life. Her family relationships were suffering and she didn't have many close friends. The ongoing self-bullying commentary inside of her head caused her to doubt herself and her abilities. She craved greater connection and yet couldn't figure out how to improve her relationships. Instead, business and money consumed her thinking, and she thought that if only she were making more money, everything would turn around for the better.

Interestingly, Julie and her husband were at the time both big spenders, and no matter how much they earned they never had much left over at the end of the month. It's helpful to know that Julie came from an abusive family in which her parents often fought about money. Her father was very loose with money and didn't save anything, while her mother hoarded away every penny. She saw her mother as being very cheap and going without, to the point of neglect. This neglect showed up in many ways, including the fact that her mom would buy only cheap food: canned rather than fresh, junk rather than healthy, and so on. This caused Julie to associate saving money with being cheap, which became a highly triggering event whenever she tried to save money. Since all of this was hidden away and unconscious, Julie didn't know it was the reason for her overzealous spending behavior as well as her strong resistance to saving.

By engaging in the mindfulness practices featured in part 2, Julie slowly began to change how she spoke to herself, starting with noticing when she was criticizing herself and how that made her feel. By paying greater attention to her feelings, she realized that her lifelong pattern of avoiding her feelings was the crux of the problem. Until she was willing to feel her feelings, she would not be motivated enough to change her behavior.

It turns out that every feeling we have derives from thousands of thoughts. When we become accustomed to repressing, suppressing, and trying to escape our feelings, the energy accumulates and seeks expression through things like emotional distress, bodily disorders, and problems with our money, to name a few. It is only through the elimination of suppressed emotions and the patterns that are causing us to suppress them that we can fully heal ourselves. This elimination increases the flow of energy into and through the nervous system and helps the body return to optimal functioning. It progressively decreases anxiety and negative emotions, causing less need for escapism via alcohol, drugs, and entertainment, while leading to an increase in vitality, vigor, energy, and well-being.

Realizing this pattern gave Julie an incentive to allow her feelings to come forth. The more she felt, the more aware she became of her inner narrative, which helped her "catch" the negative comments and begin a new and more positive conversation with herself. Instead of thinking, "I'm not worthy," she'd try to change the thought to, "I am worthy." There were plenty of times when her negative thoughts would come sweeping back in, but the more she practiced, the less this would occur. Gradually her conversations became more neutral and then eventually more positive and upbeat.

One of the biggest boosts of self-esteem came by way of changing her thoughts from "I am not a saver" to "I am a saver." This thought gradually became a habit in which instead of just telling herself an affirmation, she started saving, moving money from the couple's checking account into a personal savings account on a weekly basis. After modeling this habit for several months she was able to pay off all of their debt and save a sizable amount of money, so much so that she and her husband were able to buy a home in a very expensive part of the country. The newfound confidence created a huge shift in the way they were engaging, not just with their money but also with their business. Which led to increased profits as a result of better inventory management and money tracking.

Julie enjoyed working now more than ever and even found time to help other businesses with their finances. Her income from these side jobs more than doubled within a year as she began owning the value she was bringing to her clients. With each passing success, Julie celebrated her sense of being able to contribute far more than she dreamed possible. This caused her to feel empowered in ways beyond work and that transferred into her family relationships, which strengthened in communication and connection.

Julie was now officially on the pathway to creating the life she always wanted for herself and her family. At the same time, it's important to note there were plenty of times when Julie would question whether or not the process was working, because the shifts were so subtle and gradual. Looking back, she can see how each step led to the next, similar to what happens when you build a house or a business. It takes time, patience, and a very strong commitment for reaching a positive outcome to get there.

DARK NIGHT OF THE SOUL

While Julie was going through the steps of the Mindful Millionaire process, she experienced not one but two horrific events within her family that led her into what I call a "dark night of the soul" experience. The term derives from a poem written by the sixteenth-century Spanish mystic and poet Saint John of the Cross. In the poem, now titled "Dark Night of the Soul,"[1] Saint John chronicles the depths of his own spiritual depression, in which he faces a crisis of faith and a questioning of the purpose of his life.

Facing the suicide of her brother and then, two months later to the day, the death of her stepfather, Julie found herself facing a dark night of the soul, one that lasted for over a year. During that time, Julie and I worked together to help her drop many of her conceptual ideas about life, at least the ideas that had been formed during a childhood filled with great pain. This dissolution created an opening for her to embrace life in a new way that allowed her to question all of her assumptions. Ultimately she realized that it was her choice as to how she interpreted the events, people, and experiences of her past, present, and future.

This kind of spiritual crisis, which can feel similar to depression, strips away the foundational framework you've been living within, taking with it the meaning you've been giving to your life. From this hollowness, it can feel like there is nothing left to live for, which can lead to a collapse of the unhealthy ego and its way of being. While terrifying for most, this experience is what helps us shed our concepts of reality by dying to the old ways of thinking and being. What gets awakened in its place is a new and deeper understanding of life that focuses on loving connection and purpose above all else.

A dark night of the soul can help you reinvent yourself through trial and tragedy so that you can come out on the other side as your True Self. Not the person that you've been conditioned to become but the person you really are.

A powerful example of how dark nights of the soul can lead to huge shifts in the world is what happened to Abraham Lincoln. Here was a man who endured great suffering for much of his life—dealing with lifelong depression, anxiety, and the loss of not one but two of his sons. As a result he was pulled into darkness again and again to face extreme grief and uncertainty. From experiencing the darkness of his soul too many times to count, Lincoln would eventually rise up to face one of the greatest challenges the United States has ever faced and see it through to the best of his ability. He was able to lead the country through severe darkness because he, himself, had moved through facing his own dark night of the soul, and from that he knew the country could do the same and ultimately recover.

Similar to Lincoln, Julie found the darkest of days stripping away the false sense of who she thought she was so she could awaken to her True Self and create her life from that place of awareness.

THE MAGIC BEHIND PROSPERITY

The awakening that occurs whenever we are stripping away the old sense of self leads us back home to a sense of love. The deeper the transformation, the more the love becomes unconditional—both for ourselves and for others. True prosperity arises from feelings of unconditional love. The reason it is so powerful is because love is the foundation of life and is what makes life worth living. Love is what allows us to feel at home in the world and relax deeply into the experience of being. Even without having a dark-night-of-the-soul experience, the process you'll be guided through, starting in the next chapter, is designed to help you reach greater clarity when it comes to unconditional love.

As you learn how to emotionally detach from the stories and challenges of the past, you naturally drift away from anything that doesn't serve your best interests, anything that is not love—the jobs that drain you, the people that don't trust you nor treat you well, toxic environments—anything that causes you to feel less than who you really are. In its place are newly created habits that replace the energetic drain of what used to take lots of willpower to execute. This shift can be both refreshing and frightening because you aren't sure if by letting go, you're going to be okay and yet you have evidence that life could be taking a turn for the better. Where the fear of breaking free to live life on your terms used to worry you, now you are surrendering into a completely new way of being.

To be clear, making this transition isn't always easy. It's like you've jumped into a river with the intention of surrendering to the current. However, once you jump in, you can get cold feet and find yourself holding on to the side of the embankment for dear life. You know that if you let go, you're going to have a blast, but you also worry about the loss of control. Eventually you begin cajoling yourself to let go and trust that everything is going to be okay. It is only in the moment you surrender to the river's current that you fully realize the support the water provides. Going down the path to transformation is not all that different, as you are coming to the realization that life is truly wanting to love and support you along your journey.

In these times you may wish to ask for assistance beyond your limited ego identification. This is likely the time when your True Self, the part of you that has all the wisdom you could ever hope for, meets you where you are and shows you that your fears are not real. It also knows that until you test your wings and fly on your own, you won't be able to live your best life possible. Your True Self is here to help you do just that.

THE JOYS OF YOUR TRUE SELF

The True Self, which some people call the "soul," is often hidden deep inside and knows the truth of all you are and all you've always been. Empowered by love, it sees you as whole and complete. Rather than thinking about the self as you in your body and in this lifetime, the True Self is your connection to everything—including nature, matter, and other living beings. It is one with the grass, the trees, birds, insects, drizzling rain, clouds, tree trunks, rocks, and so on.

Some think of the True Self as our connection to God, Holy Spirit, Allah, Buddha, Krishna, Mother Nature, Source, or Divine Spirit. To me they are embodied representations of the same energy and source that can be found within each of us. They're here to serve in your awakening to a silent, unified, all-encompassing Oneness. When the True Self has the mind's allegiance, you feel supported, loved, and accepted for all you are, and as a result you cannot help but feel peace, joy, and love.

Learning about this aspect of yourself does not require any formal understanding of religion. Of course, many people find great solace and comfort through organized religion, but the point is that it is not a requirement. It is a part of you that is not owned by anyone or anything; it is yours to learn about and nurture. All that matters is finding the answers you're seeking that help you live with greater peace, understanding, and joy.

THE DISCOVERY OF MY TRUE SELF

After I got the news of my father's death, I was drawn to Buddhism the way I would have been to a glass of water in the middle of a hot, arid desert. My craving for meaning ushered in an eleven-year apprenticeship in which I applied the teachings of Buddha to learn how to control my mind and to let go of the pain of the past. Here, my True Self knew exactly what I needed in order to begin my journey, and later it would guide me to make whatever changes were necessary for me to stay the course.

After eleven years of studying and practicing Buddhism, I'm certain it was my True Self that guided me to question aspects of a religious organization I had been training and teaching with. This ultimately caused me to walk away and leave behind my teachers and close friends, which threw me into a painful and emotional tailspin. That was, until one day I was awakened in the middle of the night by a very strong voice that literally shouted out to me, "Corinthians!" The voice was so strong and forceful that I laid in bed wondering what had just happened. I knew so little about Christianity that I wasn't even sure it was a part of the Bible, but I could feel a surge of intensity pushing me to explore it further.

I proceeded to ask a friend who was a Bible scholar to meet with me so I could get his thoughts. The shock of hearing voices that were dictating instructions for what to do next was not something I was accustomed to. My friend assured me that what was happening was a natural progression of my inner work—to not be alarmed and to follow my heart more than anything.

He then gave me a Bible and encouraged me to begin the process of deciphering Corinthians. From there I learned about the story of Paul writing a letter to the church, discussing the many ways in which the "community" had lost its way. I noted how the people had become blinded by their pursuit of and attachment to money, social status, personal disputes, as well as physical and sexual pleasures. Their attachments had become so strong that they were no longer interested in their connection with a higher power.

To say I had chills all over my body would be an understatement. In this case my chills had chills. This one section of the Bible summarized everything I had been learning about money and life. I knew we, as a society, had lost our way and were living in times of great confusion about the meaning of our lives—not knowing why we are here and what we need to do to overcome the tremendous amount of suffering that life often entails. I also knew that for many of us, we are so skeptical of organized religion that we throw everything out the window rather than figure out how to use the teachings without getting caught up in the dogma. I felt like this message was telling me to forge a new pathway for myself and that eventually it would allow me to help others do the same.

PEELING BACK THE LAYERS OF FEAR

The evolution of this process comes down to learning how to break free of the deep attachments to money, success, and the other things that are commonly used to validate one's value in society. To do this for myself I had to confront my fears about what would happen when I no longer fixated on the money—and my survival, for that matter. I also knew I needed new tools and a greater vision for the future beyond the idea that "he who dies with the most, wins." I knew it was time to stop thinking about money as a god and instead recognize money as merely a tool that supports life and our highest calling.

Becoming more mindful about money involves having greater clarity of intent. When you are living intentionally you're directing your energy so that your power is fully brought to bear upon the focus of your will. In contrast, when you are confused you have a limited perspective of reality. This is why many people find it difficult to materialize the things they most want. It is their lack of clarity that stops them. They don't know what they want or what will bring them the happiness they seek. Yet, without clarity, prosperity, fulfillment, and peace of mind are all outside of your reach.

Similar to finding yourself in a room that is full to the brim with lots of furniture and boxes, it becomes very hard to find the things you're looking for. As long as you're living with great amounts of clutter and filling your life up with many things to do, it's hard to know yourself and what brings you the greatest joy. Clarity is what provides the seeds to create a vision for life. Clarity precedes vision, and without it, we run the risk of focusing on the details rather than what life can become.

A HIGHER VISION

My son and I are big comic-character movie fans, especially when it comes to superheroes like Iron Man, Doctor Strange, and Wonder Woman. When you think about these characters, there are the superpowers that everyone gets excited about and there is also, behind their powers, the vision that has great meaning. It is this vision that makes all the difference in why we see them as superheroes.

In the case of Wonder Woman, she has incredible superhuman strength that allows her to save the day when needed, yet without her "higher vision" she could very well use her powers in ways that are not all good. And so it is Wonder Woman's ability to see a vision for the way she wants the world to be that captivates our attention and causes us to believe in her potential. Different from other comic book characters, Wonder Woman is known for her emotional intelligence, belief in love, empathy, compassion, and having a strong social conscience. These traits come together and create a clear vision for an idealistic world, and when Wonder Woman goes out on a mission, you know that is what she is striving for with all of her actions. It is her vision that guides her powerful nature. It is her vision that prevents fear from controlling her.

By knowing yourself and setting a clear vision, you strip away the clutter and all the things that are holding you back from what you most want so you can live deliberately and powerfully in the world. From the standpoint of your vision, you can then tune in to the world and use your wisdom to decide what to focus on and what to leave to others. This is the ultimate path homeward, where you utilize your most sacred gifts consistently and continuously.

This is what happens inside the connection between the intellectual self and the True Self. The more open you become to yourself and the messages that are always available to you, the easier life becomes. It was through this connection that I discovered the power of my own intuitive abilities. By clearing out the clutter of the past and learning how to appreciate my own strengths, then surrendering to the possibility of knowing more than my mind could explain, I gained intuitive powers that continue to amaze and astonish me with their accuracy and diplomacy.

This, combined with meditation, is what allows you to penetrate and ultimately understand your feelings, emotions, and motivations. Being mindful allows you to "read" yourself, your money, and all the various messages you are receiving far more succinctly.

As you journey through part 2, you will be guided through exercises designed to help you do all of this for yourself, and you'll be emptying out that which blocks you from understanding, allowing, and embracing your own enoughness. You'll begin to see the perfection of all things and how everything works out for the good.

You can go at your own pace. There is no rush or reason to ever push yourself beyond what you are ready to explore. It has taken me twenty years to get here, and so remember that when you get frustrated at feeling like you are stuck in the washing machine going around and around.

As I moved along my own pathway to understanding I'd get stuck from time to time, so I allowed the process to guide me rather than having my mind force its way through. Along the way I knew that it was critical to keep trudging along even in the face of great uncertainty. I hope by reading part 1 of this book, you've come to realize that you have no reason to be hard on yourself and that you have limitless potential to create all that you want for yourself. Talking down to yourself, not believing in your potential, and sabotaging your own endeavors only create unnecessary constraints.

When you realize you are a whole, complex, and powerful person, you will place great value in your thoughts and your actions with money and everything else, for that matter. From here you'll know when it's time to focus on money and when it is time to focus on yourself. You'll know when putting yourself first will benefit everyone and when you're ready to focus on being of service to others.

Knowing who you really are means knowing when it's time to pick yourself up because you've fallen down again. It also means knowing when to speak words of love and support to your heart. It means understanding the flaws of your humanness while giving yourself loving acceptance no matter what is happening. It means recognizing your true value—body, mind, and soul.

My wish is for you to see how many of the struggles that have brought you to this book have also become your greatest teachings.

Your money struggles and everything else—all of it is divine and perfectly organized to bring you here right now so that you can engage in the next part of this book.

I am excited for the life you are about to begin—one that is free from much of the suffering you've endured in the past—primarily because you are making a commitment to become more of your True Self. This means you are ready to be less of your "small self" while stepping into your own infinite nature. In turn, this means you will also start to see the world around you, including things like money and other people, in the same way. This is what it takes to truly set yourself up for a life of prosperity. It won't necessarily be easy, but the process you are about to learn will help you in countless ways to begin the transformation.

PART II

THE IPROSPER® PROCESS

The eight-step process you are about to begin will show you how to become more of your True Self when it comes to money. This method shows you the exact steps to help you drop away fear, uncertainty, and scarcity so you can live in greater prosperity. What you will find is that this process encourages you to put everything on the table, to review your beliefs, thoughts, emotions, and feelings, so you can ask the question "Why am I agreeing to this way of being, thinking, and doing?"

Only when you question your assumptions about life and money and move out of automatic agreement with all you've been taught can you claim what you truly want from life. Right now you are operating from countless limiting beliefs that are repeatedly confirming a restricted nature of reality. This is creating a conceptual understanding that governs how you engage in life, one that we're calling the small self. The more you drop away attachment to this small self, the more you realize your true nature.

In order to stop deciding how you think, feel, and act from the small self's perspective, you will need to go through a process that shows you how to change your interpretations of the past. The teachings are leading you through a reconfiguration process by changing the lens from which you experience life so that you're making more enlightened financial decisions for yourself, your family, and the world at large.

9

A WAYFINDING GUIDE FOR YOUR JOURNEY

A wayfinder is any sort of marker that aids travelers in navigation so they can determine their positions and directions. The guidance provided here will help you remain steadfast in your intent as you move through the IPROSPER process. It contains explanations and answers to the many questions that may arise. These points can be reviewed whenever you feel unclear, confused, or wonder "What is happening to me?" or "Should this be happening?" Consider bookmarking these pages for future reference.

NINETEEN RULES FOR THE ROAD

1. Circumstances may come up that prevent you from doing your daily practices, meditation, breathing exercises, and journaling. Keep in mind that this is to be expected and is not an occasion to beat up on yourself. Interruptions happen for many reasons and could be signs of needing to slow

down and become more mindful of the process. Whatever happens, just notice that it gives you a chance to respond to whatever comes up, and you can choose what you wish to do going forward. Take it easy, rely on your intention to carry you through, and know that everything happening is for your ultimate benefit.

2. During this process you may find yourself tempted to judge—yourself, this book, the questions, the author, or other people. It takes courage to recognize this tendency, and so the more you know about it, the easier it will be to deal with it when it comes up. Judgment is a stress response to a condition that is occurring in your environment. Judgment is a symptom of the unhealthy ego, and when you catch it happening you can stop it in its tracks before it takes over your mind and emotions. Remind yourself that the only reason you want to judge is because there is a pain inside of you that wants to feel better; this helps dissipate the stressful energy. By following these instructions to the best of your ability, you can receive the experience even when you don't think it will be helpful to you.

3. The more you can give yourself and others in your life unconditional love as you go through the process, the easier the process will become. As deeply unconscious and long-suppressed memories start to surface, you may feel resistance to this experience. Only through unconditional love and acceptance can we begin to integrate these uncomfortable past occurrences. If things seem like they are "spiraling out of control," simply remind yourself that this is a positive indication that the process is having a profound and causal impact. By persevering and remaining steadfast through whatever resistance arises, you will gain the capacity to move through it and break through to the other side.

4. Sometimes all you can do is surrender. Depending upon your beliefs, the idea of "Let go and let God" may be all you can do to keep moving forward. Letting go and allowing are beautiful responses that can help you in the most trying of times. It is during these times you realize the joy of not having to "figure everything out" and "make things happen." Instead, you can rely on your loving heart and your intention to guide you. Your intention is what draws what you want toward you, not your mind. When you let go, you are allowing things to unfold on their own in perfect timing.

5. Depending on when you decide to do your breath work, meditation, and journaling, you will likely find it far more effective and transformational to do these practices before you drink caffeinated beverages. Caffeine ramps up the left-brain activity and decreases relaxation and creativity, which means it counteracts the exact benefits you are seeking to gain. By allowing your right brain to be stronger while engaging in these practices, you will experience greater benefits.

6. Breath work stimulates detoxification, and so it is recommended that you drink three to four liters of water a day, and to pay close attention to the foods you are ingesting, including the limitation of sugary and salty foods, particularly before you engage in breath work and meditation. The more you do the work, the more your eating habits will naturally change to your benefit, which is expected as you become more aware of food and its effect on your well-being.

7. As much as possible, abstain from medications that cause drowsiness prior to breath work. You may also find it beneficial to not consume alcohol, marijuana, or other mind-altering drugs for the duration of this process. Alcohol,

even in small quantities, decreases authenticity and increases disruptive thoughts. Marijuana can decrease and inhibit awareness. The reasons for avoiding these substances becomes more obvious after you begin breath work and as you start to become more familiar with being in the present moment. Being sober is a prerequisite for awakening authenticity and awareness.

8. You can only do this work for yourself; you cannot do it because someone asked you to do it. If you are here because you were asked to be, then take time before you proceed to take ownership of this process for yourself. We cannot develop inner awareness to satisfy someone else's needs and demands. Do it for yourself.

9. People, especially those you've known for a long time and are very close to you, are likely to act differently toward you during this process. This is a sign that you are changing and that it is being reflected back at you. This can be positive and somewhat challenging, especially when old patterns are being released and recontextualized. You are doing this process to live with greater joy, peace, and prosperity, and oftentimes our relationships need to shift in order to allow these feelings to become more present.

10. Keep going no matter what. Resistance can and will occur. Keep showing up and you will be rewarded in countless ways for your tenacity. Being present to whatever is occurring, even when you don't want to do it, is all you can ask of yourself. Feeling grumpy, irritated, frustrated, pissed off, and sleepy are all normal reactions. Avoiding how you feel is very different from being present and letting things happen of their own accord. Avoiding is a reaction; learn how to notice the difference in your behavior when you are reacting versus responding. Also note that feeling

your feelings is not the same as taking your feelings out on others; we always try to do that as little as possible.

11. Everything happening is in your favor and best interests. By setting this as your intention, you will be clear about your motives and objectives for this process. The more deliberately you live, the more this will make sense to you. Because our capacity to suppress memories is so well developed, unconscious memories don't always surface as images in our mind, but as external circumstances. Whatever is happening with your money while going through this process is helping you practice what you are learning here.

12. You are perfect just the way you are—no fixing, no adjusting; nothing is needed by you or anyone else. All you need now is to reclaim this truth for yourself. The realization of your own perfection can take a long time or it can happen in seconds. While you may feel like you are getting nowhere, it is helpful to remember this program takes time. You will not always know where you are in the process, and that is okay.

13. There will be days when you feel distracted and confused. This occurs because you are gaining new awareness about your life and surroundings. Agree to think there is nothing wrong with feeling this way, and it will pass as the integration occurs.

14. Things that were important to you in the past may no longer capture your attention and interest. This is fine because it reveals that you are moving into a new flow of being. As your priorities shift, you become more present to the flow of life. The more present you become, the more responsibility you take for your own life and the less desire you'll have when it comes to controlling the lives of others. Stay in your own lane at all times.

15. As you become more in tune with yourself, you may find yourself speaking up in situations where you would not have done so before. Learning how to deeply listen to yourself—your mind, your heart, your feelings, your emotions, your gut, your intuition—means your inner voice is becoming stronger and louder. Whether you are saying yes or no, either way, it's good to know it is coming from deep inside and is worthy of your attention.

16. Your financial situation will likely undergo some changes during this process. Windfalls may appear out of nowhere, or it may seem like resources are diminishing. Either way, it is helpful to remember that money is a reflection of your own flow of energy and provides insight into the movement of whatever is shifting inside of you. By focusing on your inner experiences rather than what is happening with money, you are shifting gradually toward greater prosperity and abundance. Dropping attachment to certain outcomes allows new possibilities to emerge.

17. Unexplainable synchronicities may occur. Delight in all that appears. People you haven't spoken to in many years might reach out, new opportunities might be offered up, conversations might happen out of the blue, and information that comes into your awareness might lead you in new directions. When we transform the conditions of our charged emotions, our entire world shifts. Opportunities appear that allow us to make amends and take responsibility for past actions; you might witness profound shifts occurring for others or be in situations that beg for unconditional love and so on. All of these things occur to help you integrate and clear the past. More than anything, trust the process.

18. It will likely become increasingly difficult to explain this experience to others. When this occurs, trust that who

you are becoming is more important than trying to explain it. Because the mind is no longer controlling the process, it isn't able to fully understand what is taking place. Instead, your feeling awareness is growing, which is more difficult to explain than mental shifts. Feeling awareness is what increases your psychic abilities and intuitive sense, which take time to integrate and speak about. For this reason, those not going through this process will be challenged to understand.

19. Complete the process. As much as you may want to stop along the way, it is best to instead take a break and then return to where you left off. By completing the process, you're trained in an art form that equips you with insight, tools, financial understanding, and in practices that allow you to integrate your emotions and transform your relationship with money. This capacity removes stress, anxiety, and attachment from your experience and gives you a sense of happiness and joy about your future.

Before completing this chapter—please review, adjust, and copy into your journal the following contract:

IPROSPER CONTRACT

I, _____,
understand that I am pursuing an intensive and guided exploration into my money story. I promise to engage fully in the eight-step course and commit to doing my daily meditation practices, readings, journaling, money dates, and other designated tasks. I understand that this course will raise issues and emotions for me that I will need to pay attention to and deal with. I am willing to reach out to others whenever I have questions or concerns that I am not able to deal with on my

own. I will also reach out to those who support me in pursuing my goals and dreams, including friends, family, spiritual teachers, and therapists who I believe can help support me through this process. I commit myself to excellent self-care, sleep, diet, exercise/yoga, and things that make me feel really, really, really good for the entire duration of the course and beyond. It is my responsibility to take excellent care of and pay attention to my inner voice at all times.

Initials: _____

Date: _____

You are now prepared for the IPROSPER process. As you embark upon this journey, be comforted and encouraged by your intention, commitment, and willingness, as that is more than enough to carry you through.

10

STEP 1—I IS FOR INTENTION

Our intention creates our reality.
—WAYNE DYER

This step initiates the process of financial-wellness recovery. It's designed to help you create your money mindfulness practice and set intentions for what you wish to explore, understand, and integrate during the IPROSPER process.

Building wealth is commonly equated with becoming richer in ways that leverage time and money, while being better skilled, smarter, and more capable than others. These are all thought to be good and necessary to become more powerful and successful in the world. True prosperity, as we've been learning, is not about those things at all. Instead, it is about the process of inner transformation that brings forth personal liberation.

This approach involves turning how you see the world upside down so you can overhaul your assumptions, values, and belief systems. Prosperity from this level of understanding lies in embracing a new paradigm with which you reclaim your power as a whole, complete, and abundant being. From this place of transformation, you begin to operate as the creator of your life, choosing to be in a world where love and peace of mind is everything.

Deep inside you have known this is your destiny, and yet the wealth, health, and happiness you've sought probably haven't come all that easily. While there is no magic pill for instant recovery, there is a teachable, trackable process we can follow to get there, and IPROSPER is designed to help you do just that. It is structured in such a way that it becomes completely unique to your own individuality and provides recognizable and methodical practices to guide you through it.

TWO WAYS TO GO THROUGH IPROSPER

As mentioned at the beginning of the book, you can approach this part of the book in one of two ways—introductorily or experientially.

The introductory approach is simple: you continue reading this text as though it were a novel. You don't do the practices or apply the tools. You read through it as if you were working through chapters in a book. You are focused on absorbing the material mentally rather than engaging in the conscious experiential process. You will still receive insight and benefit from this approach, and it will help you transform the way you interact with your experiences with money. Once you have completed the introductory approach, you can return to the beginning and take the experiential approach when you're ready. It will not lessen the outcome; instead, it can enhance your experience and give you time to integrate key learnings.

The experiential approach guides you through the process mentally, physically, and emotionally. It will show you mindfulness practices, breathing techniques, journaling practices, and breakthrough exercises. After each time you complete the entire process, you can take a one-month break from the deliberate work to allow for integration. During the breaks, you'll want to continue your breathing practices and mindfulness practices; you may also wish to continue journaling. All three of these practices are something you will likely want to continue way beyond your experiences with this book.

ESTABLISHING YOUR INTENTION

To begin, the first thing you want to do is set your intention. This is a heartfelt and sincere request for how you want to be feeling by the time you finish this process and beyond. It may be that you set an intention that will take more time to accomplish than the amount of time you'll be doing this process, but that doesn't mean you can set a long-term intention right now. What do you want to be feeling and experiencing in your life as a result of what you'll be doing here?

Take a moment to write down what you're thinking about. Here are a few examples of what people who've done this process have set as intentions for themselves:

> "I am happy, free of worries and self-doubt. I believe in myself and have found my true joy and bliss."
>
> "I have a bulging bank account, zero debt, and I own a beautiful home by the sea."
>
> "I've discovered my purpose and feel truly grateful and excited to wake up and begin each new day."
>
> "I am in a relationship that is committed, loving, and special. I am truly and deeply in love with and loved by someone who wants the same things I do."
>
> "I have wonderful health and incredible fitness and energy."

As you walk through the following eight steps, you will be creating a new way of being for yourself and your money. You have the potential to gain many realizations through the process. Potential is like a handful of seeds in the field of your mind, and your breath work, meditation, and journaling practices are the actions you'll be doing to cultivate these seeds that you are planting now.

In the spirit of holism, this next step of the process is designed to ensure that you have the tools you need to improve the ecosystem of your life. Similar to when a farmer wants to grow crops in his fields, he goes through a process of preparing the ground to ensure that the seeds he plants will thrive. In this case, what follows is designed to help you prepare your mind for the journey ahead.

PREPARATORY PRACTICES

Preparatory practices are things I learned from my Buddhist teacher many years ago. They are what you do before you "go within," so that your environment, your schedule, and your own self-care are organized in such a way that you are set up for success. These practices help make everything you will be doing over the next few months easier and more effective.

Creating Your Prosperity Shrine

You'll want to set up a place in your home or office where you will be practicing the IPROSPER process. It should have a place to sit quietly for meditation and contemplation, as well as have a place to journal. Once you've selected a place for your practice, it is helpful to make sure it is softly lit, clean, and free of clutter. You may want to create a shrine that includes representations of your intentions, your dreams, and your spiritual guides. Flowers, incense, crystals, candles, and beautiful images will help remind you of your highest intentions throughout the process.

Creating Your Schedule

You'll want to establish boundaries for your practice, making time for when you are going to engage in the meditations, contemplations, and journaling exercises. If you will need to wake up earlier to ensure you have sufficient time, then decide that now and change the alarm on your phone or clock. You may also need to set calendar reminders for what time you need to go to bed to ensure you get sufficient sleep.

Taking Good Care of You

As noted in the introduction to part 2, you'll want to be sure to get plenty of exercise and make a point of focusing on the care of your body during this process. Yoga, stretching, walking, weight lifting, and running will all help you because they can assist in calming your mind. The more energy you bring to the surface through the contemplative exercises, the more your body will want to be moving and releasing energy.

Setting Boundaries for Your Success

During this process you may find that you wish to be less social, or perhaps you'll feel more picky about whom you want to spend your time with. Know that you may be more sensitive to what others say and do during this process. Spend some time thinking about how to create boundaries that are going to be loving, supportive, and make you feel good.

This process is about thinking about yourself and how to ensure you are placing yourself in the best environment possible. By doing this, you will help yourself learn about patterns and behaviors that you may wish to continue beyond the course. So use this time as a practice run for the life you are creating.

DAILY MINDFULNESS RITUALS

Now let's talk about the rituals that will help you get the most from your efforts—before, during, and after your daily practice.

Get Comfortable

Find a position where you are most comfortable and yet won't be tempted to fall asleep. Sit upright with a straight back and comfortable sit bones. Consider placing your feet firmly on the ground and uncrossing your legs and arms.

Use Your Breath to Settle and Calm the Mind

Take three nice deep and slow breaths. If you are feeling tired, you can focus on longer inhalations. If you are feeling distracted you can focus on longer exhalations. If you are fine as is, then make your inhales and exhales even.

Get Grounded and Connected into Your Body

Take a few seconds to tighten your body, including clenching both your hands and feet. As you exhale, you can release the clench and imagine that a cord starts at the base of your spine and goes down into the earth, where it mixes into the ground beneath you, touching the rocks, dampness, and roots of the plants. If you are still feeling distracted, you can imagine that the cord descends all the way to the center of the earth, where it hooks lightly and allows you to feel a complete connection to Mother Earth. Breathe into that connection and return to your body to find how connected you feel to your feet, hands, heart, and head, perhaps even fluttering your eyes to notice that you are fully here in your body now.

Set Your Intentions

Take a moment to set an intention for your daily practice. If your problems are overtaking your thoughts, you can gently invite them to release and allow yourself to focus on the meditation and journaling at hand. Ask them to wait for you to return later, and witness the energy leaving your body.

Request Assistance from the Divine

Depending upon your spiritual beliefs, now is the time to welcome in higher awareness and guidance beyond your conscious awareness. This can be in the form of divine awareness, God, Jesus, Buddha, Allah, Krishna, divine love, universal energy, angels, or guides, and welcome in this energy to infuse love, support, and assistance into your practice.

Practice Schedule

- 5 minutes of breath work
- 5–10 minutes of meditation
- 20–40 minutes of journaling

Gratitude and Dedication

This final step can be used to celebrate the grace in your life and to dedicate the merits of your practice to those closest to you as well as all living beings. An example of a dedication could be: "May all living beings experience lasting happiness and abundance. May all beings be free from their suffering. May I be free from my suffering, and may I experience lasting joy and abundance."

. . .

You will want to go through this preparatory process each time you engage in practice. It will help ensure that the time you spend is focused, effective, and highly rewarding. You may even want to compare what happens in your journaling practices when you leave the other parts out, to see the benefits for yourself. My sense is that you will notice how much clearer and more focused your energy is by going through the preparatory practices every day. They only take a few minutes and are well worth the added effort.

BREATH-WORK PRACTICE

If this is your first time using breath work, it is helpful to note that focused and consciously connected breathing helps you uncover, isolate, and identify those areas in your consciousness that are unresolved so that you can release them. The breathing practices that you will be learning here are meant to help you relax and use rhythmical breathing to cleanse the body and the mind. When a person breathes normally, fully, and freely, it automatically produces many beneficial changes in the body, mind, and feeling sense. Repetitive and rhythmical breathing empties the negative mental energies out of your body and enables you to incorporate life energy into your body instead. Much of the pain and fear we are holding on to is a result of clinging to negative thoughts. By letting go of these fear-based thoughts through breath work, you can release much of what you are storing inside. Similar to when a person takes the garbage out and does not feel the need to examine all the trash before putting it into the garbage bin, in this case when you engage in breath work you can carry your trash out and let it go swiftly without overthinking it.

To get started, we begin breathing naturally and rhythmically. It is best to find a seated position that allows your back to be upright so that you aren't tempted to fall asleep. You can close your eyes or keep them open slightly. I've found I am much better able to stay focused with my eyes closed. Breathe in and out through the nostrils whenever possible. Try to remain as calm and still as you can throughout the practice. Your breathing becomes an automatic process in which you are breathing in and out without pausing. It is very important to continue breathing without interruptions. Notice how in each moment that you are focused on your breath, you are also focused on the present moment. The intention is to not pause between breaths for the entire session. This can be tricky to do at first, as the mind will likely try to tell you to stop breathing in and out without pausing between breaths. The goal is to continue breathing past these thoughts. You can choose how deeply you wish to breathe. In the beginning you may wish to engage in more shallow breathing, and as you gain familiarity with the process, find that your breath deepens naturally. The more oxygenated you become, the more your thirst for oxygen will increase.

It's fascinating to consider how often we unconsciously hold our breath during the day—when we are frightened, when we are thinking and listening deeply, when we are exercising or doing a particularly challenging task—and yet this deprives the body of energy that could help us become more responsive and less reactive. The same thing goes for shallow versus deep rhythmic breathing. I've personally seen dramatic shifts in my capacity for taking deep breaths and how much better I feel when I am taking long, deeper breaths. All said, when we are less present, our breathing isn't as connected and our lives end up becoming a reflection of this disconnection.

As you continue to breathe you may come up against various forms of resistance that tell you, "I don't want to do this, because it is too hard" or "I don't want to do this because it isn't doing anything" or "I don't need to do this because I already feel good enough." Watching these thoughts appear and then releasing them with your breath is the best way to continue through it. Your only goal is to continue with connected breathing again and again. Gradually you will start to notice that the voices diminish and aren't as tempting to follow. Continuing with your breath work allows your mind to anchor into the present moment instead of being pulled into the past or projected into the future. You may find yourself getting sleepy, which is normal. Until you have more experience in the present moment, you are going to feel more accustomed to residing in waves of unconsciousness, which feels like sleepwalking to the awakened mind. The process of breathing is pulling you out of this unconsciousness, and as you recover your awareness, sleepiness can arise as an attempt to bring you back into your comfort zone.

To aid in the process of rhythmic breathing, you may find it helpful to repeat a mantra or positive statement at the same time as you breathe in and out. Repeat the words "I am prosperous" as you breathe in and as you breathe out. Repeating the mantra for the five minutes that you are engaged in breath work may help keep your mind focused. You may also wish to set a timer to keep track of how long you are engaged in focused breathing. At first it might seem as if time is going by very quickly, or you might be tempted to check the clock along the way, which can cause you to stop breathing rhythmically. Reminding yourself that you are just practicing and not expecting perfection will help you return your attention to your breath. As you become more seasoned, you may find yourself breathing rhythmically for longer periods of time, which is perfectly acceptable.

If at any time you feel any sense of hyperventilation or numbness in your hands and feet, mindfully decrease the depth of your breathing and the speed at which you are breathing. There are other more advanced breath-work techniques that can be done, but that is not the focus for this book. Instead, it is about gentle, easy breathing that does not create external effects beyond feeling more oxygenated and relaxed.

Through consistent daily attention to breathing, you will find yourself progressively anchoring into the present moment, which can lead to substantial benefits in your life. Additionally, the gentle energy release you receive through the rhythmic process gives you a sense of connection to your body, your personal safety, your mind, and your spirit.

MEDITATION PRACTICE

After completion of the breath-work practice is a great time to spend five to ten minutes sitting quietly without movement. Here you will be able to notice with greater awareness how you feel as a result of the breath work, as well as your mental state. You may choose to think about those you love and hold dear. As you feel love in your heart, you will want to continue focusing on this feeling for as long as possible. When your mind wanders, you'll bring it back to the feelings of relaxation and love and then sit with that focus. Again, when your mind wanders, you'll catch it and bring it back. You may have to do this ten, twenty, thirty, or fifty times. Nothing matters other than bringing your mind back to the feelings of relaxation, peace, and love. Judgment is not your friend, so do your best to let any of those sorts of thoughts go as soon as they appear. Then just return back to your breath and your feelings.

By remaining as physically and mentally present as possible during meditation, we are training ourselves to remain present throughout the day. This helps us respond rather than react to whatever we are integrating. It also helps us to dissolve distraction and confusion, which can arise when hidden emotional pain is coming to the surface. Through our meditation practice, when challenging events occur, we can "be" with our feelings without trying to control them.

Once you get the hang of doing this type of meditation, you can then begin to listen to the guided meditations I've created to support the various steps of the process.[1] These guided meditations are meant to further deepen your understanding of the teachings and how they relate to patterns of scarcity.

A NOTE ABOUT MINDFULNESS

Mindfulness (the practice of meditation) is the ability to be mentally focused in the present moment without judgment. By practicing various meditation techniques we can slow down and pay attention to what is happening inside and outside of our bodies and minds. Meditators learn how to quiet the mind's constant chatter of thoughts, anxieties, and regrets by focusing on the present moment. It can be done when we are relaxing our bodies, as well as when we are eating, exercising, working, or even paying bills. The most common practice is sitting meditation, during which you sit in a comfortable position, eyes lightly closed, and focus on the awareness of your breath and other sensations. When thoughts come, you gently let them go without judgment and return to focus on the breath. Over time, this helps you connect with a deeper, calmer part of yourself and retrains the brain to not get stuck in useless rumination of the past or upsetting scenarios of the future that would otherwise leave you feeling stressed, anxious, or depressed.

The reason the present moment is so powerful is because it is the only moment of truth that you can ever fully experience. As we've been discussing, our interpretations of the past and the future are likely to be distorted reflections and projections of reality. However, when you are fully present to the experience of the present moment, you have the ability to drop away beliefs, judgments, and projections and just be. This ability is substantially heightened through the practice of mindfulness and meditation.

JOURNALING PRACTICE

Journaling is an incredible tool for self-understanding. By getting your thoughts down on paper, preferably through long handwriting rather than typing, you gain valuable insights about yourself. For example, writing this book has been a journaling practice for me—it was amazing to realize just how much was stored inside of my mind—both consciously and unconsciously. The healing effects of bringing things out onto paper are incredibly profound. What you will likely find here if you've ever struggled with maintaining a regular journaling practice, is that IPROSPER will make it easier, thanks to the many writing prompts you are given along the way.

As you go through the "Mindful Moments of Reflection" at the end of each step, take your time to journal following the various prompts. At any time if you don't want to respond to a question, move to the next one. Doing the journaling and other exercises will help you achieve deeper insight than thought alone can reach.

In the beginning of your journaling session, you may find it helpful to start by putting pen to paper and just writing without thinking. The reason we do this is to let everything and anything come out that is waiting to be heard, felt, and witnessed. This can be a conscious exercise, in which you already know what you need to write about, or a very unconscious one, in which you put the pen to paper and allow the messages to come through without any thought. Either way is perfect, and you may find yourself playing with both.

A Note About Habitual and Devotional Practices

As you engage in meditation and journaling practices on a daily basis, my hope is that your rituals eventually become habitual and devotional.

Habits are formed by repetition and commitment: the more you repeat the rituals, the more likely you are to create a mindfulness habit. Habits are powerful tools to help you stay on track with achieving your intentions: they remind you to continue your practices without having to think too much.

However, habits are not as profound and uplifting as when you add in devotional practices. Devotion gives your habits great meaning at the soul level through the incorporation of kindness, unconditional love, and enthusiasm for a person, cause, or activity. Devotion is about bringing forth that which inspires and fulfills you at the deepest level of your being. Devotion is what happens when you feel connected, supported, and most aligned with the world around you. Devotional practices may include love for others, giving, your connection to religious and inspiring figures, to sacred concepts, or to Mother Nature—anything that fills your soul.

For myself I am completely inspired whenever I connect to the "energy" of spiritual teachers like Buddha, Jesus, Mother Teresa, and others who evidenced great kindness and love toward the world.

Take a moment to think about someone in your life who does this for you—a child, a spiritual teacher, a partner, a parent—and allow yourself to feel affection and unconditional love toward that person. Notice what happens for you in this awareness. This inspired feeling of love and appreciation is what you are wanting to bring into your daily awareness when it comes to managing your money. Even something like balancing your checkbook can become an act of great devotion if you see it as a form of love for yourself and your family. With this practice, we're taking something that was unfamiliar—in this case infusing love into money—and then creating a new habit out of our awareness so that it changes how we engage with money. From there, when you go to pay bills or ask to be paid, you realize that money can serve as an exchange of love. No one but you needs to know this is even happening behind the scenes. All that matters is that you have transformed money into something meaningful and enjoyable.

WEEKLY TASKS

These tasks are meant to help you solidify what you are learning in each of the process steps:

Belief Notebook

Create a small notebook solely for writing down the beliefs you find yourself discovering when it comes to money, scarcity, relationships, abundance, and anything else. Perhaps it can be divided into two sections. The first can have all the limiting and negative beliefs you come across throughout this process. The second section can include all the positive and uplifting beliefs you have and are wanting to create

Take a Money Date

This is inspired by the work of Julia Cameron in her book *The Artist's Way*,[2] in which she encourages readers to take an "artist date" at least once a week. In this case, I am asking you to take at least one money date per week for the duration of the course. This can be anything that has to do with money, including the following: buying a cup of coffee for the person behind you in line at Starbucks, giving money away, asking for money from someone, increasing your price on something you sell, buying a gift for yourself, decreasing your price on something you sell, asking for assistance when thinking about a big money decision, taking a class about investing or budgeting, and so on. These money dates can be things that take only a few minutes or they can take a few hours; you decide what you want to do, and after you do it, write a few sentences about how it made you feel and if you learned anything through the process.

One of the reasons money dates are so effective is because they encourage you to try things you wouldn't normally do. Plus, if you want to increase the chances of having what you do become a normal part of your life, you can take a moment to share your money dates in the Mindful Millionaire Community on Facebook. When we share our stories with others, they become bigger parts of our learning experience, so don't be shy, and share away!

Money Experiences

Write about one of your past negative or positive experiences with money—something that you feel a great deal of pleasure about *or* a lot of shame or guilt about. When you are done, take a few moments to feel deep gratitude for what happened and all that you learned through the experience. If you wrote about something that made you feel good, no other actions are necessary. If you wrote about something that was painful, then offer forgiveness to yourself and anyone else involved in the process. If for any reason you feel like it would help you release negative experiences from the past, you can tear up or burn what you have written. Trust whatever comes to you through this process, especially when you are getting started.

Gratitude Notes

Along the way you will likely find yourself wanting to write about gratitude. This will come about spontaneously and will likely grow over time. This is just a reminder that when you want to write about thankfulness and how you feel about your life, your journaling is awaiting you!

DAILY PRACTICES FOR I IS FOR INTENTION

1. Engage in process of preparatory practices
2. Breath-work practice—5 minutes
3. Meditation practice—5 minutes
4. Journaling practice—20–40 minutes
5. Dedication and gratitude

MINDFUL MOMENTS OF REFLECTION

For your daily journaling practice, here are some suggestions for prompts that you will want to complete inside of your journal:

1. Review the "Daily Mindfulness Rituals" found in this chapter, and journal about how you feel about them—things you want to try, skip, spend more time on, and so on.

2. Take a piece of paper and draw a line down the middle. On the left side write the words "In My Money Comfort Zone" and on the right side, write the words "Outside My Money Comfort Zone." Next, write down in each column the things that are in or outside of your comfort zone when it comes to money. You may also choose to write about feelings that you are not comfortable expressing when it comes to money. This helps you notice exactly where you are today. Remember when I was sharing the need for un-bridled self-honesty? This is one of those times. Then take time to sit and review what you've written down. You may wish to journal about your discoveries.

3. List ten of your favorite things to spend money on and ten of your least favorite things to spend money on. Favorite things might include clothes, trips, coffee, smoothies, and organic food. Least favorite things might include your electricity bill, clothes, gas, food, parking fees, and so forth. The goal is to notice how you feel about engaging with your money.

4. Write about your dreams and inspirations when it comes to money.

5. Write about your mindset. Consider what it means to have a growth-oriented mindset and a fixed mindset. After studying the behavior of thousands of children[3] Dr. Carol S. Dweck coined the terms "fixed mindset"

and "growth mindset" to describe the underlying be- liefs people have about learning and intelligence. When students believe they can get smarter, they understand that effort makes them stronger. Therefore they put in extra time and effort, and that leads to higher achieve- ment. The opposite is the case when you have a fixed (or closed) mindset, in which you don't believe you can change.

What parts of you are most open and growth oriented? Which parts are more fixed? What can you learn about yourself, and how does it apply to changing your relation- ship with money? Notice your willingness to change and also the ways in which you are unwilling to change (which can be every bit as powerful to acknowledge).

6. Write down all the changes you are wanting to make and those you are unwilling to make when it comes to your money. Start with small changes and move toward the larger changes.

MINDFUL MOMENTS OF ACTION

Take time to review how you've progressed through step 1 with these four questions.

1. How many days did you do your practices?
2. How was the experience for you?
3. What did you struggle with completing?
4. Is there anything else you would like to note for this step—things to revisit in the future, areas of focus, ques- tions you'd like to have answered?

SUMMARY OF STEP 1—I IS FOR INTENTION

Your intention is what matters more than anything as you embark on this journey. By setting a purposeful intention, you begin the process of drawing what you want most toward you. Your intention becomes your North Star—the guiding principle for why you are doing what you are doing. It also helps you shift out of living in the past. It helps you recognize the importance of knowing where you want to go rather than thinking about where you've been. I have seen many people change their lives for the better just by getting the right messages established in their minds and consistently focusing on those messages. All of a sudden the difficulty of your circumstances don't seem as important as they used to. Now you are focusing on what you really, really want to create for yourself, and it is just a matter of time and effort before you bring it into your life.

11

STEP 2—P IS FOR PATTERN

A human being is a part of the whole, called by us "Universe,"
a part limited in time and space. He experiences himself,
his thoughts and feelings as something separated from the
rest—a kind of optical delusion of his consciousness.
—ALBERT EINSTEIN

This step initiates awareness of the scarcity patterns that have been working against you when it comes to money. The exercises and stories are aimed at helping you better understand your past money behaviors and teaching you how to apply my framework based on the "Seven Sacred Truths" into your relationship with money.

One of the core needs we have as human beings is to be supported. Without support, not only do we find ourselves questioning our ability to survive, we question the rational behind life itself. The same thing can occur when we do not feel worthy, powerful, loved, or trustworthy. These scarcity-oriented patterns, when trapped in our psyches, can cause us to create an "optical delusion of consciousness," just like Albert Einstein referred to.

Within this step, you will be learning about seven centers of energy, known as the "chakras," which serve as portals between your inner world of emotions, feelings, and unconscious beliefs, and your external world of relationships, the physical body, your work, your environment, and your money. Once understood, even from a basic level, these portals have the potential to transform how you experience life by guiding you away from patterns of scarcity into a world of prosperity. Even if you've already studied in other ways what I am about to share, I want to encourage you to be open to new discoveries, because oftentimes the context in which you are learning can change everything. This way of interpreting the chakras and money is unique to what I teach and based on years of study, meditation, contemplation, and many realizations, both for myself and for my clients.

A SACRED PATHWAY TO FINANCIAL WELLNESS

I'd like to start by inviting you into yourself—into your inner world of being. Just like if I were to take you to a place you'd never visited before, I'd first show you a map to be sure you can easily get around and not get lost. Here I will be walking you through one of the most powerful maps of your inner world that has ever been documented and that has inspired millions of people since its creation over three thousand years ago. Since then it has inspired spiritual leaders, political figures, philosophers, and people like Abraham Maslow, who used it to create his "hierarchy of needs,"[1] and Joseph Campbell, who used it within the context of the classic "hero's journey."[2]

Here I am sharing my own interpretation of how this map, otherwise known as the seven-chakras system, applies to money. I have taken creative liberties based upon many years of working with the chakras, especially when it comes to money, scarcity, and abundance. You may have different reactions from those I explain, and that is perfectly fine; none of what I am sharing are absolute truths—instead, they are works in progress, and your own truth is what matters more than anything. As you try these practices for yourself and then verify the validity of what is shared, you will have the opportunity to determine what makes the most sense for you, and I ask that you trust that above everything else.

The map is a vertically aligned depiction of the process of your individual maturation through seven distinct energetic phases, starting at the base of the spine and rising upward to the crown of the skull. This process of spiritual "adulting" is used to explain the movement of energy that takes place, most often, by ascending toward the Divine as a result of gradually mastering the physical world. At each stage you gain greater self-understanding and appreciation for your own ability to create in physical form and eventually to channel the Divine.

In addition to helping you understand your own evolution, each of the seven chakras can help you notice and release the "bruises" that you have accumulated throughout your life and beyond. That's because the chakra system helps you engage in energetic self-evaluation by revealing how your thoughts, feelings, memories, and beliefs are stored in one of these seven energy centers.

The more energetic bruises you've collected, the more likely it is for them to negatively affect you by causing you to engage in fearful and avoidant behaviors. This is why having a map to use in the identification and release of these bruises is such powerful work. Further, I've found that for those of us who have experienced a lot of bruises, we do not always have a strong navigation system for dealing with conditions that trigger fear, which makes it harder to heal ourselves. The chakras, as they are explored in this chapter, can help you to not only notice where you are stuck in limiting patterns as a result of scarcity beliefs but also to heal those patterns once and for all. For this reason, even with an elementary understanding of the chakras combined with daily mindfulness practices, you can find yourself living with greater harmony and peace in all areas of life.

Knowledge of the chakras is most comprehensively found in the science behind the practice of yoga and was first formulated by the physician-sage Patanjali. Chakra centers each govern specific aspects of your physical, psychological, and spiritual being and can be truly discovered only through personal experience in working with them. A state of balance between them is the key to the health of the various body systems that they govern. In other words, imbalance, damage, or blockage of these centers can lead to problems in the physical, psychological, or spiritual aspect of our being. By learning about the chakras, you are learning how to repair, balance, and clear your own personal energy system.

Before I began integrating the chakras into my money practices and teachings, I had no idea of the powerful benefits that would be gained by my clients who put them into use. Within a few weeks of creating the first of many different chakra meditations, my clients began to share the dramatic impact they were having on their financial psyches. Feedback included the following: "For the first time ever I am no longer worrying incessantly about money." "I feel so peaceful, and I'm getting more done that I can ever remember." "I'm finally feeling called to change my money habits." The more I heard, the more I knew it was important to continue researching and developing this body of work.

By using my chakra meditations[3] on a regular basis, my clients were, quite remarkably, able to hold the space for their money struggles without falling into fits of blame, judgment, and/or avoidance. This helped them go deeper into healing than ever before without running into obstacles that had prevented their recovery in the past.

Through my research in having thousands of people practice the meditations and provide me with feedback, I was able to confirm the ways in which scarcity gets trapped both physically and metaphysically within. One way to explain how it works is to imagine that the chakras are like lenses on glasses that get fogged up as a result of our emotional imbalances and blockages. The "fog" is a symptom of the unconscious patterns of fear, guilt, and shame we're holding on to as a result of our past. This fog then prevents us from seeing life as it truly is and creates a distorted reality in which, instead of seeing prosperity and abundance, we see scarcity and lack. This makes us think we, ourselves, are a reflection of scarcity, which ends up showing itself in different money patterns according to the energy center where we feel most stuck.

In order to understand how this works, practically speaking, we must dive even deeper into the chakras and the framework I've developed that gives context to how the chakras and our relationship with money go together.

THE SEVEN SACRED TRUTHS

To begin, it is helpful to see how each chakra acts as a lens for one central theme in your life. The list below depicts this connection.

The root chakra is your security lens.
The sacral chakra is your desire lens.
The solar plexus chakra is your power lens.
The heart chakra is your love lens.
The throat chakra is your expression lens.
The brow chakra is your integrative lens.
The crown chakra is your vision lens.

By learning more about how the chakras regulate and manage the physical, emotional, mental, and spiritual aspects of life, you gain the ability to govern your life with greater clarity. This awareness can lead to the removal of the fog of scarcity, which allows you to approach life from the perspective of prosperity.

To help you do this, I will next be guiding you through each of the chakra lenses so you can apply them to your own life and discover where you are out of balance and therefore looking through the lens of scarcity. By learning how this works, you'll be able to tune in to information about where your patterns came from and how they are affecting your money behaviors. In later steps, you'll be gaining practices that help you rebalance, repair, and unblock your energy centers so that you no longer view life through "foggy" lenses.

THE SEVEN MONEY STORIES

At the end of each chakra-lens section you will find a money story based upon the work I've completed with my clients. Each story is related to one of the seven chakras and is meant to inspire you to better understand your own money story. The details of these stories have been changed to protect the identity of those featured, who also granted their permission for their stories to be included in this book.

Your goal is to use the stories to help you discover the lowest chakra that awakens feelings about where you are with money. You may feel like you relate to one story more than the others, or you may not relate to any of them. You have access to all seven of these money stories,[4] including the narrative behind the money breakthroughs that took place while we were working together.

Further, by giving you real life examples of how this work has been applied by others, these stories are meant to help you better understand how your scarcity patterns coincide with a specific energy center in your body. As you read about how money and the chakras come together, you'll notice that the issues arising with money are often located in the first four chakras—and that is where we end up spending most of our energy, especially when we are struggling with money. Mastering these four areas, before moving onto the fifth, sixth, and seventh chakras, are a powerful practice for anyone who wishes to drastically improve their relationship with money.

Before I discovered the scarcity patterns that are highlighted in this next section, it was difficult to not get lost inside of my own and others' money stories. There were just too many moving parts, and it was hard to pinpoint the root causes surrounding people's money struggles. As a result of this framework, however, everything came into focus and provided a way for me to help my clients in profoundly effective ways. In the same way, by learning this methodology you will have a much easier time figuring out the core issues behind your own limiting patterns and what can be done to bring them into balance.

The process of healing your relationship with money, as you move through the following seven chakras, is not necessarily sequential; instead, it relies on determining the areas that are most strongly out of balance, trusting that whatever is coming up at the present moment is exactly what you are meant to be paying attention to. In the end, the goal, if you can call it that, is to have all of your chakras balanced and humming harmoniously in the background of your life, which creates feelings of well-being and peace of mind.

The Root Chakra—Your Security Lens

The first chakra lens regulates your sense of safety and security. If you are struggling with this chakra, you are afraid of not being able to take care of your most basic needs, including food, shelter, and clothing. This chakra is located at the base of the spine, in the area of the perineum, and is represented by the color red. When you have money, you may feel a sense of temporary relief, but when you don't, all hell breaks loose inside and your fears can consume all of your thoughts, which leads to "tunneling," as previously discussed in chapter 1.

When you are looking at life through a warped security lens, there is a strong chance that the game you are playing with money is called "playing not to lose," rather than "playing to win." Playing not to lose is about avoiding your fears surrounding lack. These fears start very early in life. One memory that plagued me for many years involves an archetypical story.

I was in fourth grade and I had saved some money up that I kept in my purse. My parents took us to a neighborhood concert in Berkeley, California, for the day, and I was excited to bring my purse with me. I remember playing in a park on the swings and slides and having the time of my life listening to music. At some point we walked around the nearby shops and I came across a necklace I wanted to buy with my money. I looked down to open my purse and realized it was gone. I immediately started running back to the park, instinctively knowing I had left it there.

Upon reaching the park I saw my purse laying in the dirt, and as I picked it up I could see that it was open and the money was gone. The devastation I felt about losing my money was tremendous. I knew it was my fault and I vowed to never lose money again due to my carelessness. Sure enough, I've lost my purse or wallet only a few other times since then, and when it happens I'm immediately brought back to my childhood feelings. Funny enough, I think this affected me far beyond losing my purse and transferred into an unreasonable fear of losing my money in any situation.

Thankfully, this fear does not have to be your reality. As the root chakra comes into balance, you feel a sense of grounded strength that translates into your relationship with money. This helps you be both flexible and consistent in your money-making activities so you can take more risk, which helps you to dynamically move through life. As a result, you feel stronger and more capable when it comes to earning money consistently and sufficiently, so your fears about security and safety no longer cause you to avoid situations in which you might lose or fail, thereby shifting into a play-to-win mentality.

When Your Security Lens Is Clouded by Scarcity

You may feel: extreme financial fears no matter how much money you have in the bank, "bag lady" syndrome, obsession with work and earning money, unable to walk away from a reliable job to follow your passion, extreme risk aversion, lack of financial accountability, and/or financial codependency.

You may believe things like: "I've always had money problems, so I always will"; "I am not a part of that club"; "I have to work hard, like really hard, to make money"; "I don't have the ability to earn more"; "There's no such thing as a free lunch"; "If I make more money, they'll just take it"; "If you're born poor, you'll die poor."

As a child, you may have faced situations in which: there was a fear of or actual abandonment (physical and/or emotional), womb/birth trauma, poor connection with parents/mother, inherited fears, physical abuse, and/or moderate to severe family-related financial loss.

As an adult, you may have faced situations in which: you went through bankruptcy and/or lost significant resources or wealth with a divorce that caused severe hardships. Other events that can cause strong fear about survival and safety would include active military combat, surviving a terrorist attack, or witnessing or being injured in a mass shooting or other dangerous situation.

If any or all of those are part of your pattern, you may find the following prosperity affirmations helpful to say out loud or integrate into your meditation practice:

- I am safe.
- I am strong.
- I am supported.
- I am capable of financially taking care of myself.
- I see the presence of the universe supporting my existence.

A Root Chakra Money Story

Danielle operates a successful hair salon, and appeared (on the outside) to be both cheerful and happy. The truth, though, was that Danielle, now divorced, was buried in debt and struggled to attract and develop healthy romantic relationships. Growing up, Danielle's mother and father were abusive alcoholics. Her mother, in an effort to keep Danielle and her siblings safe, left her father in the middle of the night. Sadly, though, her mother developed a new relationship with someone equally toxic. As Danielle matured, she too married someone who was emotionally abusive and financially unstable.

Reflecting on her past, Danielle recognized her problems with money and relationships stemmed from past experiences of abandonment and lack of security. As such, she didn't believe she was capable of financial or romantic success.

Going through the IPROSPER process, Danielle sought to identify and release past issues around abandonment and not feeling safe. By releasing these negative thought patterns, Danielle learned to trust her ability to care for herself and ensured that her business and relationships support the life she wants to be living. Danielle's story provides an example to those of us who struggle with our sense of security, demonstrating how to break free of those patterns so we can live with greater freedom and prosperity.

The Sacral Chakra—Your Feeling Lens

The second chakra regulates how you feel about money, desire, and pleasure. If you are struggling with the sacral chakra, you are afraid of being emotionally hurt, indirectly or directly, while attempting to have your needs met. The residual effect of this fear, as it pertains to money, is a concern that you will never be able to feel worthy enough to get your spending and debt under control. The sacral chakra is located in the area of the lower abdomen and sexual organs of the body, and it is represented by the color orange. In addition to feelings of unworthiness, it is connected to your relationships and personal sensitivities. Similar to what happens with the root chakra, if our warning systems are put on high alert early in life, we're far more likely to avoid situations in which our sense of worthiness might be threatened. The problem is that disconnecting with your money (and whatever challenges you're dealing with) only further compounds your financial problems.

When we are very young and going through the "terrible twos," we are learning how to crawl, walk, and explore the world on our own for the first time. During this time there is a good chance we are causing a lot of disruption in our homes and pushing the limits of our parents' patience—some more than others. One moment we're getting into something we're not supposed to, and in the next we're having a temper tantrum about not getting what we want. Depending upon our personality, we might cry, scream, or emote in other ways, and if, during this time, we are chastised, criticized, and/or talked down to for expressing our feelings, there is a good chance we'll adopt the belief that our feelings are not acceptable. Yet as babies, how we feel is everything. It is how we communicate to the external world, and so when we are hungry, tired, or want something, we express feelings that will help us get those things. When our feelings are nurtured by our caregivers, we gain a well-rounded emotional life. When they are not, we can find ourselves negating our own feelings later in life.

Add to this challenge that if we were reprimanded with shaming techniques a lot as a child, we might struggle with feelings of shame and guilt throughout our lives. To be clear, shame gets used as a behavior modification technique to get children to stop crying or to pay attention and do what they are told. When used in this way, shaming is telling a child he or she is bad rather than that the behavior is bad. Because of the intensity of how shame is received, the practice works well in the short run but takes a toll in the long term on the psyche of the individual. When shaming and ridiculing are used to change behavior, rather than taking the time to explain what isn't working, the child can end up feeling like he or she is not worthy or good enough for the things most wanted. When we believe our feelings are bad or wrong, we end up with an unconscious desire to prove that we, ourselves, are not worthy.

When the sacral chakra is balanced, you feel a strong sense of emotional intelligence. This helps you be in touch with your feelings while also nurturing others. You have healthy boundaries in place for how you engage with others and how to avoid situations of codependency, and you can easily enjoy physical pleasure. As a result you're able to be vulnerable with others while feeling a strong sense of your own worth and value in the world. These aspects get reflected in how easily you can save money, pay off debt, and better manage your money.

When Your Feeling Lens Is Clouded by Scarcity

You may feel: fear of having and holding on to money, coming up with lots of ideas for making money but never taking the time to flesh them out, consumed by other people making lots of money, a tendency to be manipulated or taken advantage of while in pursuit of money. *Or you may experience:* emotional avoidance of money, excessive spending and debt accumulation, physical ailments as a result of money problems, and/or self-sabotage with money activities.

You may believe things like: "I don't deserve money"; "Money is not important"; "There's no such thing as a free lunch"; "You cannot get everything you want in life"; "When I have money, I let it slip through my fingers"; "I'm not worthy of earning more"; "I've always had money problems, so I always will."

As a child, you may have faced situations in which: you felt ashamed of your feelings, experienced sexual, emotional, or physical abuse, manipulation by caregivers, alcoholism in a parent or caregiver. You may even have faced sexual traumas that happened to one or both of your parents, which were passed down to you indirectly.

As an adult, you may have faced situations in which: you experienced financial manipulation, rape, sexual abuse and/or manipulation, rejection/lack of acceptance by parents and other mentors, emotional distress caused by overspending, debt accumulation and/or financial mismanagement.

If any or all of those are part of your pattern, you may find the following prosperity affirmations helpful to say out loud or integrate into your meditation practice:

- I honor and appreciate how I feel.
- I listen to my feelings about money.
- I appreciate and allow my desires to inspire me.
- I am worthy of a healthy relationship with money.

Sacral Chakra Money Story

Barbara, working as a pediatric nurse, had a history of disastrous family finances and toxic romantic relationships. Her mother, who was buried in emotional pain, neglected herself and her family, while her father vacillated between intense bouts of rage and generous states of giving.

Going through the IPROSPER process, Barbara learned how to identify and release the beliefs and habits that had kept her stuck in financial hardship. After releasing these negative patterns, Barbara embarked on a new journey to take far greater responsibility over the family's finances. Ushering in a new level of awareness around the importance of living within her means meant Barbara persuaded her husband to downsize their entire household and lower their monthly expenses. As a result, she created a sense of peace and clarity about her and her family's future and put them on the road to financial recovery.

The Solar Plexus Chakra—Your Power Lens

The third chakra regulates your feelings of power and control over your life. If you are struggling with this chakra, you worry about not being in control of your money. The power chakra is located in the area of your navel near the solar plexus and corresponds to the stomach, which means you may feel imbalances in your gut and suffer digestive problems as a result. It is yellow in color. The need to feel powerful is connected to our sense of integrity. When we give away our power, by allowing other forces (even our beliefs) to control us, our sense of self is diminished. This lack of being in control of our financial lives weakens our fortitude to manage our money wisely. By regaining balance in the power chakra, you develop greater inner honesty and purity, which helps you modify the nature of your interactions with money so that you engage with it out of cooperation rather than disempowerment.

Once we've learned how to communicate at a basic level, as children we begin to actively explore the world around us. We are curious and readily seek to understand how things work, how people treat us, and how powerful we are. Depending upon the responses we receive from our closest relationships, we form opinions about ourselves and others. If we find a lot of support, we adopt beliefs that confirm our ability to be effective in the world at creating what we want. If the responses come across as harsh and judgmental, we'll likely conclude that we are not powerful.

Later, when it comes time to become empowered with money, there may be resistance to step into one's own power because you don't feel powerful to begin with. This is especially because our culture has laden money with many negative ideas surrounding power and the responsibilities that come with having it.

If you don't feel powerful with money, you may not try very hard to earn it, or you become tightfisted with it. You don't want to spend it, you don't want to give it away, you hold back on spending it on things you enjoy. You may find yourself, quite unconsciously, settling for a lower standard of living than you truly wish to be living—buying an older car than you want, living in not as nice a neighborhood, buying lower quality food, buying lots of cheaper things instead of investing in higher quality items. Or you may do the exact opposite and live beyond your income or become obsessed with having lots of money regardless of the toll it takes on you and your family.

When the power chakra is balanced, you feel a strong sense of self-esteem and effective will. This helps you feel able to meet whatever challenges come your way with money. You may find yourself feeling a playful sense of humor that comes by feeling confident in your abilities and skills. As a result you're able to easily manage your money to ensure it is fulfilling your goals.

When Your Power Lens Is Clouded by Scarcity

You may feel: a tendency to make financial decisions without taking all details into consideration; needing to have the final word; seeking power and control, using force if necessary; heavy risk taking; a compulsive need to prove yourself. *Or you may experience:* procrastination, fear of failure, fear of ridicule, fear of being seen as an imposter, fear of being victimized, low self-esteem, passivity in business and financial dealings, unreliability and inconsistency with money matters, and poor follow-up.

You may believe things like: "I've made too many mistakes with money and don't deserve more"; "I'm doomed to repeat my parents' money beliefs"; "What I have is because of other people"; "I wouldn't know what to do with it if I had more"; "It's too late to become a millionaire"; Or you believe things like, "It takes money to make money"; "Money makes the world go around"; "I need to control other people to get what I want"; "All that matters is the money"; "This is business not personal."

As a child, you may have faced situations in which: you experienced divorce and family estrangement, authoritarianism, and invalidation by parents or other caregivers; exploitation (e.g., childhood fame); being demeaned or bullied by others; over- or underparenting—too little or too much responsibility given as a child; inherited authority issues (your parent's parents were too harsh in parenting); racial, sexual, or financial discrimination.

As an adult, you may have faced situations in which: you needed to constantly prove yourself as a powerful person; you were blindsided in a career or with financial matters or in relationships when financial matters were also at stake; you experienced business failures or dealing with the effects of poor financial decisions; you were a victim of financial manipulation.

If any or all of those are part of your pattern, you may find the following prosperity affirmations helpful to say out loud or integrate into your meditation practice:

- I honor the power within me.
- I finish whatever I begin.
- I seek to find the middle ground free from extremes.
- I strive for excellence in all that I do (without needing to have it be perfect).
- I am diligent and capable.

Power Chakra Money Story

Hemant, who was born to affluent, loving parents, learned the value of hard work from childhood. Quickly earning more than $200,000 per year fresh out of college, Hemant rarely had money concerns—that is, until he decided to partner in a technology start-up that required continuous inflows of funding that he had to borrow from his parents. Reaching over $50,000 in credit card debt and hundreds of thousands owed to his parents, Hemant endured an upsetting divorce and a company on the brink of disaster. Having thought of himself in the past as capable, Hemant realized that he was powerless to turn his financial situation around by himself.

Reflecting on a childhood memory, Hemant identified and then released the belief that he was irresponsible with money. Working through the IPROSPER process, Hemant tackled his debt by taking a job outside of the start-up. By working evenings on the start-up, he avoided having to request additional cash injections from his parents. After six months, he was able to pay off his credit card debt, and his company was able to secure external financing that helped him repay a portion of what he owed his parents. Hemant was left feeling empowered, and his relationship with money was positively changed forever.

The Heart Chakra—Your Love Lens

The fourth chakra regulates feelings of being loved and appreciated for one's contributions. The money fear that gets activated is the belief that you are not able to ask for and receive what you most want. This area also governs feelings related to being cared for physically and emotionally. It is located in the area of the heart, is green in color, and is symbolic of the crossing between the personal and the universal. The lower chakras represent our animal natures and instincts, while the heart begins the journey toward the spiritual realm. Below the diaphragm, your consciousness is centered on "you," and above that you move into the universal consciousness of "we." The heart ties into your feelings of being able to fully give of yourself and to fully receive nurturing. The more these are in balance with each other, the more joy you feel in your heart. However, whenever giving and receiving are not in balance for long periods of time, you eventually find yourself feeling a sense of depletion or selfishness. All things in life want to find harmony, and the heart is where harmony finds itself most welcome. This is because the more you feel in balance with giving and receiving, the more you can expand your own personal reach and create what you most want.

Before the age of seven we are creating beliefs about our relationships, love, our heart's innermost desires, and universal principles around giving and receiving. If during this time we learn the power of love and its many forms, including forgiveness, compassion, generosity, kindness, and caring for oneself and others, we naturally understand relationships and how to love and protect ourselves. However, if our relationships were inhibited by experiences and beliefs that disrupted the natural forces surrounding nurturing, our dreams, wants, and needs can become stunted and diminished.

The awakening of the heart chakra means a rising upward into an experience of unity with all of life. Love is the path of the heart that trusts that everything will work out in the physical world. For that reason, love is an action of faith that tells you it is okay to not be operating from defense, protection, and fear, that all will turn out in the end, even if you have no conceptual understanding as to the "'how." To create an abundant life requires you to believe in the possibility of goodness regardless of the circumstances you are experiencing in the present moment. It is a very elevated state of consciousness, and it makes sense that you have to navigate through the root, sacral, and solar plexus chakras before you can comfortably and enjoyably stroll through the awarenesses that come through the heart chakra.

The process of understanding love, compassion, and acceptance begins within one's tribe—often the family unit—and then extends out into the greater world. Depending upon what has happened in our homes or within our closest relationships, we may or may not feel secure in our own sense of self-love.

When the heart chakra is balanced, you feel a strong sense of compassionate love toward others and you become self-sustaining. This helps you feel empathy for others' conditions while also taking good care of yourself. Establishing a sense of intimacy with all of life is what happens when love is strong and flowing inside. The result of this is being paid commensurate to the value you are creating through your efforts in the world.

When Your Love Lens Is Clouded by Scarcity

You may feel: codependency; lack of strong boundaries when it comes to money; "comparitis" and jealousy toward others' financial conditions; a sense that success is determined solely by financial payments/rewards or net worth; little to no focus on giving. *Or you may experience:* isolation regarding money troubles, overgiving, undercharging, inability to let go of finished relationships.

You may believe things like: "It is wrong to have more than others"; "If I have more, then someone has less"; "People will think I'm greedy if I want to make a lot of money"; "Money is the root of all evil"; "Money will give my life meaning and validation."

As a child you may have faced situations in which: you witnessed the divorce and/or the death of a loved one; you experienced shaming and criticism, love with strings attached, betrayal from those closest to you, a lack of hugging, nurturing, and appropriate touching; you were deprived of hearing and feeling how much you are loved and accepted.

As an adult you may have faced situations in which: you experienced betrayal, conditional love, divorce and partner breakups, loss of a child; financial hardships, including bankruptcy; upsets that remind you of being separate (rather than connected) to those you love dearly.

If any or all of those are part of your pattern, you may find the following prosperity affirmations helpful to say out loud or integrate into your meditation practice:

- I am worthy of love.
- I am deeply connected to others.
- I am empathetic to my own needs as well as the needs of others.
- I am well paid for my contributions.

Heart Chakra Money Story

Leanne faced physical abuse and emotional neglect in her home at the hands of her parents until the age of thirteen. The resulting challenges impacted her relationships, including her right-out-of-college marriage to her high school sweetheart, in which they financially struggled for many years. As an adult, Leanne runs a successful virtual staffing business. Her business and the resulting additional income eventually gave her the strength to leave her marriage. Sadly, though, her past financial problems followed her with debt skyrocketing to over $200,000. Although her business revenue is strong, her expenses are equally high. She is barely breaking even.

Through an exploration of her childhood, Leanne discovered the belief that she was not loved, and she was unable to have a partner relationship without severe hardship. Through the IPROSPER process, Leanne identified and healed her childhood pain that surrounded an event with her mother. Her improved emotional state helped her see how she'd been undercharging her clients for many years.

From this new vantage point, she successfully and confidently increased her prices, which netted her an income ten times the amount she was earning previously, and her business rapidly started to grow. Further, she started to receive requests for speaking and consulting opportunities. Leanne's story exemplifies how a damaged relationship with money can stem from a lack of feeling loved and appreciated and shows what can happen when limiting beliefs such as those are released.

The Throat Chakra—Your Expression Lens

The fifth chakra regulates how you feel about your own significance. If you are struggling with this chakra, you may worry about your ability to act in your best interests when it comes to money. You are also likely to be experiencing one of two extremes—lack of trusting yourself and others or overly trusting your own judgment or the judgment of others without proper vetting. Located at the base of the throat, it is mostly sky blue in color, and it corresponds to the thyroid and the lungs. This chakra also regulates creative expression. While this chakra can be a challenge for many people, it is important to focus on mastering the lower chakras before trying to tackle this one as it requires you to be in a strong connection with the first three chakras to fully integrate.

As this chakra comes into balance, you start wanting to trust yourself more while aligning your core values and beliefs with your money. This in turn may result in the desire to invest your time and money according to your values. This transformative process can lead to the selection of strategic partners and advisors who are aligned with your values so as to best help you achieve your highest goals.

During adolescence we're learning how to integrate the beliefs and experiences of our early childhood. Through this process we articulate what we want and do not want based on how much we know of our own needs and desires and how worthy we feel of receiving them. During this time we are called to use our words to express and create, yet if we feel inhibition toward our innermost feelings, we may find ourselves repressing more than expressing. Adding to these blocks, we may also come up against pressures to be seen as highly competent and responsible, which causes us to want to adapt our needs and wants to fit in and comply rather that stick out.

Somewhere along the way, you may have lost connection with your own needs for recognition, self-esteem, and authority. This phase of evolution and understanding has a lot to do with fully stepping into your own sense of yourself and your power as a creative and expressive being who can do whatever you set out to do. It is about creating greater confidence about yourself, your own voice, and your ability to competently manage your money wisely.

Once you are able to see your life through the lens that anything others have accomplished is simply evidence that you too can accomplish it, no matter what your past or current circumstances are, your life shifts. To be able to do this however you must accept full responsibility for your life and be sure to speak your truth, even if that truth is about your desire to provide a meaningful contribution to the process of managing your money. The more you do this, the more power you'll gain to create that which is most important to you.

When the throat chakra is balanced, you feel a healthy sense of significance and responsibility. This helps you say yes to life's opportunities and possibilities and no to that which isn't important to you. You are a good listener as well as someone who speaks clearly and concisely. As a result you're able to trust yourself and others when it comes to money, knowing that you are good at doing due diligence so that you make decisions intuitively and from a strong mental understanding of your options.

When Your Expression Lens Is Clouded by Scarcity

You may feel: a dominating approach to money, acting like you know everything; an urge to seek out "drama" when it comes to money; an inability to listen to advisors, feeling overly responsible to take care of your problems without asking for help. *Or you may experience:* fear of speaking your truth, fear of asking questions, and/or fear of losing your money in the stock market (so you don't invest).

You may believe things like: "It's not nice to talk about money"; "I wouldn't know what to do with it if I did make a lot of money"; "I'd probably invest in the wrong thing and lose it if I invested"; "I'm too trusting and gullible": "There's a secret language I never learned and never will"; Or, you may believe, "Investing is for rich people"; "All wealthy people must've gotten there by dishonest means"; "I don't trust other people with my money"; "If I can't invest by myself, I won't do it."

As a child, you may have faced situations in which: you experienced lack of trust from your parents or, the opposite, you did not trust them; the death of a parent that caused the remaining parent to "check out" on parental duties; harsh criticism; fear of being taken advantage by others (may be indirectly evidenced by parents' beliefs).

As an adult, you may have faced situations in which: you were financially betrayed by someone you trusted; you lied or were manipulated by yourself or by those you love; financial secrets were kept from you (and the shock of discovering them); a financial advisor abused or manipulated you.

If any or all of those are part of your pattern, you may find the following prosperity affirmations helpful to say out loud or integrate into your meditation practice:

- I trust myself.
- When I don't know something, I set out to learn about it.

- I seek to surround myself with people I trust.
- I am clearly expressing my desires and wishes.
- I am significant.

Throat Chakra Money Story

Rod, a life coach, led a life filled with financial mishaps. He experienced bankruptcy, the loss of two businesses, the burden of extreme debt, including the painful breakup of various relationships. Rod knew that unhealed sexual abuse during his childhood, at the hands of his father, was perpetuating his financial problems, but he didn't know how to stop the pattern. The resulting emotional damage wreaked havoc on his life and his confidence in himself.

Moving through the IPROSPER process, Rod learned how to identify and release limiting beliefs and negative habits, including forgiving his father for the past. Upon releasing the past, Rod built a new business and overhauled his finances. He also got engaged to the love of his life.

The Brow Chakra—Your Integrative Lens

The sixth chakra regulates a sense of being enough and having enough. Here you are guided by the highest and most profound aspects of yourself so you can live fully and freely. If you are struggling with this chakra, you may have trouble going beyond the small-self ego state and accessing your True Self. Located behind the eyebrows at the center of your forehead, this chakra corresponds to your eyes and pituitary gland and the integration of your intuition with all other areas of your awareness. It is mostly indigo in color. Activating this chakra strengthens your intuition and sensitivity to the higher planes of existence by becoming open to a new dimension of what it means to live fully. Of greatest importance is ensuring that your money is used to serve the highest good.

During your preteens, you are developing your self-image for its unveiling at around the time of puberty. During this time, when you are maturing sexually, you are also learning about how you feel about yourself, your gender, your sexuality, your intellect, and your intuitive abilities. If you are able to ultimately see, understand, and accept your truths from a place of love, you gain the ability to set goals and solve problems from this place of understanding. However, if the opposite occurs, you may find yourself being continually challenged when it comes to creating all that you wish for.

One of the ways this translates into your relationship with money is by replaying rhetoric around which part of yourself is most worthy (and accurate) when making decisions with money. Your heart speaks to the importance of following your gut and intuition with money decisions, while your mind encourages you to pay attention to the facts, numbers, and spreadsheets. This back-and-forth conversation can make it very difficult to decide what to do next. This may result in complacency or decisions that lack introspective thought and/or intellectual understanding, which creates money decisions that do not reflect all parts of what it means to be human.

For many years, it has been thought that emotional and intuitive energy weakens our ability to make decisions that affect us economically, and that intellectual capabilities weaken our ability to make decisions that affect us emotionally. However within the past fifty years the thought has been growing that when the heart and the head come together, we're able to make more balanced and unified decisions than otherwise. The problem is that we're still figuring out how to do this for ourselves. The trick is to learn how to make decisions that include all parts of you.

When the brow chakra is balanced, you feel a strong sense of intuitive and perceptive guidance when it comes to your money. This helps you be in touch with your "sixth" sense, which allows you to visualize the outcomes of your decisions before you even make them. This becomes reflected in how you easily are able to make financial decisions that serve your mind, heart, and soul.

When Your Intuitive Lens Is Clouded by Scarcity

You may feel: obsessive about money, business, relationships; difficulty in concentrating on tasks at hand, especially those that remind you of painful events in your life; disturbed by nightmares or spiritual "emergencies"; obsessive about self-care practices. *Or you may experience:* insensitivity to others' financial conditions, poor memory about money plans, denial of important financial issues, difficulty meditating, difficulty visualizing, lack of consistency with self-care practices, difficulty in making big money decisions.

You may believe things like: "There will never be enough money"; "Surely I should be taking care of humanity before I take care of my own feelings of abundance"; "Everything I do to make money must come from my (spiritual) guides"; "All of my decisions must make sense financially and/or practically."

As a child, you may have faced situations in which: there was miscommunication about realities of life, invalidation of intuition and psychic abilities, invalidation of science and financial principles, unhealed parental trauma that got projected onto you.

As an adult, you may have faced situations in which: past decisions caused financial trouble in either extreme—as a result of trusting intuition over mind or mind over intuition.

If any or all of this is part of your pattern, you may find the following prosperity affirmations helpful to say out loud or integrate into your meditation practice:

- I am open to the wisdom and guidance that comes from within.
- I am open to the science of financial methodology.
- I can create a vision and bring it into reality.
- I am worthy of my own council with money and appreciate paying attention to both my heart and my mind.

Brow Chakra Money Story

Caroline, working as a healer, failed to ever earn more than $48,000 a year. Although she had no debt, she struggled to increase her earnings and to feel well-compensated for her services. Reflecting on her life, Caroline recognized her pattern of always putting others before herself. Rarely receiving, Caroline couldn't help but give her time and energy to others without being compensated for her time.

Working her way through the IPROSPER process, Caroline identified and released her perpetual need to help others in the absence of caring for herself. This was significant because it was a turning point in helping her write and publish a book about her life, as well as start charging for her services, particularly the ones she most enjoyed doing.

The Crown Chakra—Your Divine Lens

The seventh chakra regulates how you see yourself in relation to the Divine. If you are struggling with this chakra, you may be in conflict when it comes to merging your humanness with your Divine connection, which causes you to question your wholeness. This chakra is located at the crown of the head and is luminous shades of lavender and fuchsia with specks of white. This chakra has to do with learning and integrating an understanding of what it means to be a spiritual being in a human body—sensing that all parts of you are perfect as designed and then integrating these parts into one state of being. As you embody and integrate your sense of wholeness, your life begins to reflect this back at you. Your money is a reflection of what it means to be in the world but not of it.

Living with a balanced crown chakra allows you to feel solidly connected to the cosmos and your human body—the infinite areas of space and time. This means you have reached a state of grace and radiance that cannot help but have a profound and beneficial influence upon those around you. By restoring the wounds brought about by many years of stripping away the spiritual meanings of life, you feel a stronger sense of purpose, meaning, and direction, which gets channeled into your relationship with money.

However, when the crown chakra is out of balance and scarcity is present, there is a tendency to do one of two things:

1. Engage in economic bypassing, in which you treat money as mundane and unnecessary. This can cause a person to always be struggling financially. Yet being able to take care of your humanity (by earning, saving, spending, and investing money) while living in a very aware state of consciousness is worthy of reverence. In this case, money becomes a tool of understanding, compassion, and social connection, and the more that those with balanced crown chakras are in flow with their money, the more easily we can create a loving world that complies with our highest goals and wishes.

2. The second possibility is to engage in spiritual bypassing, in which a person tends to overanalyze to the point of

negating any possibility of a higher power. Although my sense is that very few people would be interested in this book if they did not have some faith beyond the here and now, there is a good chance you know of others who fit this description. In this case, doubt, which is sometimes accompanied by extreme pessimism, causes a person to intellectualize everything to the point where there is no possibility other than cause and effect. When someone is spiritually skeptical, doubt often plays a big theme in their way of seeing the world, and that prevents one from seeing his or her own potential for abundance and prosperity.

From the teen years to early twenties, we are busy creating beliefs about how we fit into the world—our roles, capabilities, capacities, spiritual connections, and expectations for the future. Depending upon what happened to us throughout our childhood as part of the six other stages, we may find ourselves struggling through this time of our lives. While it is possible to have a sense of enoughness at the core of our being, many people have not gained the awareness of how to even begin to explore this development. When aspects of ourselves have not developed due to blocks that occurred earlier in life, we'll struggle with making peace with ourselves and our past to the point where we cannot complete the process of maturation. Rather than this phase of life being filled with excitement and creative purpose based on our own individuality, instead, we find ourselves questioning the ways in which we can fit in with others.

Unfortunately, it is easy to become hijacked by the goal of fitting in rather than experiencing individuation, which is the ideal state of maturing. Without a strong sense of self-awareness and one's own guiding principles, it is difficult to create a sense of feeling like you are enough. Instead, you end up feeling like you can never be enough, especially when you're comparing yourself to others and focused on what it will take to fit in to their ideals rather than your own.

It is during this phase of development when you have the capacity to generate devotion, inspiration, and prophetic thoughts that transcend the limited nature of physical reality. However, in this time of social media and an extreme focus on fitting in, few have the mental space in which to engage in finding themselves and following the guidance within. It can also be a time when, at the other end of the spectrum, the individual relinquishes the practical human experience to the spiritual without regard of the physical realm. Neither is ideal, because as a human being, the goal is to learn as much from our human experience as possible so that we can live in harmony with the world around us.

When the crown chakra is balanced, you feel open to the idea of undoing the known and dropping away the old so you can become something new. From this way of being, you feel a strong spiritual connection while at the same time confident in your wisdom as a result of study and contemplation. This leads to creating and living by beliefs that support prosperity and abundance while promoting a sense of freedom. These are often spiritual leaders who are consistently walking their talk and are not ashamed of their ability to create financial prosperity. At the same time, they enjoy being of service to others far more than serving themselves, and so what prosperity they have is shared freely with others in hopes of relieving their suffering. An example of this was Mother Teresa, who devoted her life to serving the poor and providing them with a clean place to die in dignity. During her lifetime, she channeled millions of dollars through her charities with the goal of treating people, especially those who had been marginalized by society, as if they were Christ themselves.

When Your Divine Lens Is Clouded by Scarcity

You may feel: part of a rigid belief system, focused on spiritual connection without minding your own responsibilities to take care of yourself financially, spiritual addictions, disassociation from the body. *Or you may experience:* at the other end of the spectrum, spiritual cynicism and doubt, overintellectualism, and/or apathy toward spiritual thought.

You may believe: "If I am good, God will supply all my needs"; "If I am bad, I will be poor"; "There is nothing beyond what I see with my own two eyes"; "If I don't take care of myself, no one will."

As a child, you may have faced situations in which: you experienced withholding of information and invalidation of one's spiritual beliefs, forced religiosity, manipulation and abuse by religious figureheads, parents engaged in blind obedience to a religious group without questioning assumptions, spiritual bypassing, spiritual hypocrisy. Or you may have been taught that nothing is real unless it is provable through science and thinking anything other than that is irresponsible.

As an adult, you may have faced situations in which: you experienced feelings of deep separation from any concept of God or divine beings; belonging to religious organizations that try to control what you believe; being taught to surrender all sense of self to a master, guru, or specific concept of God.

If any or all of this is part of your pattern, you may find the following prosperity affirmations helpful to say out loud or integrate into your meditation practice:

- I am prosperous.
- I am abundant.
- I am free.
- I am divinely connected.

Crown Chakra Money Story

Growing up, Sheila was poor, not because her family lacked money but because her parents prioritized contributions to their church over most anything else. With tattered clothing and ongoing feelings of deprivation and hunger, Sheila did not learn how to take care of herself in the world; instead, she believed that it was up to the man of the home (and God). As an adult, she was incapable of taking care of herself without severe struggle. She experienced bouts of hunger and homelessness over the course of several years. In time she earned enough money to better care for herself, but she got physically shaken up whenever she had to give any thought to money management.

Applying the IPROSPER work to her life, Sheila recognized a destructive pattern—her habit of moving from one controlling person to the next while failing to recognize her capabilities and her responsibility to herself. Sheila's story exemplifies the importance of knowing how to care for one's practical needs while balancing the real world with the heavenly realm of Divine Spirit.

OVERCOMING YOUR MONEY PATTERNS

Before we wrap up this step, I want to explain one additional detail about the chakra lenses and how they can help you with your money transformation. Up until now your experiences with money have served as a reflection of your previously defined realities. Now, after reading this chapter and going through the "Mindful Moments of Reflection" that follow, you are invited to begin questioning your assumptions whenever you notice scarcity-oriented beliefs coming to mind. This will help you build awareness of your patterns so you can be more mindful about how your beliefs are affecting your present and future realities. Gradually this will help you create a new reality based on principles of prosperity rather than scarcity.

In his book *The One Thing*, Gary Keller[5] shares that in order to be successful in life, it is advantageous to focus on one thing at a time so as to not get distracted from your top priority. As you work through the IPROSPER process, the one thing you want to focus on is the chakra that carries the most emotional charge for you. By picking one of the seven chakra themes highlighted in this chapter and keeping it in the back of your mind as you move through the remaining steps, you'll gain far greater understanding about yourself, the patterns you are ready to release, and what can be done to improve how you engage with your money.

If you have trouble deciding which one is most applicable to you, then start with the root chakra and work your way up accordingly. If the root chakra is absolutely not the most relevant to you, then move to the sacral and so on until you settle at one. You will most likely be going through the IPROSPER process several times, which will give you the opportunity to approach the process from other chakra lenses in the future.

Once you get to the Permission, Evidence, and Reinvent steps (chapters 15, 16, and 17), you'll be applying what you've learned as you create a financial plan that is customized just for where you are with your money.

In the end, this process of awakening to your old patterns and creating a new version of reality comes down to being in agreement with your truest version of yourself. Your work here with the chakras is helping you better understand who you really are and how to create your reality from that place.

WEEKLY TASKS

1. Belief Notebook

Continue to write down the beliefs you find yourself discovering when it comes to money, scarcity, relationships, abundance, and anything else.

2. Take a Money Date

Get out into the world and do something with your money that you've never done before or know you'd like to do more of. This isn't about spending a lot of money; it's about trying different things with money to see how it makes you feel. Buy lunch for a stranger, send a friend an unexpected gift, treat yourself to something fun. Go outside of your comfort zone and see what gets awakened in the process.

3. Money Experiences

Journal about at least one of your past experiences with money that remains vivid in your mind.

4. Gratitude Notes

Take a few minutes to journal about what you are grateful for every day.

Daily Practices for P Is for Pattern

1. Engage in process of preparatory practices
2. Breath-work practice—5 minutes
3. Meditation practice—5 minutes
4. Journaling practice—20–40 minutes
5. Dedication and gratitude

Mindful Moments of Reflection

Take time to reflect on each of the seven chakra lens patterns explored in this step by answering the following questions for each chakra.

Root Chakra

When Your Security Lens Is Clouded by Scarcity

Does this pattern apply to you? (yes or no)

Indicate on a scale of 0 to 10—0 being no emotional resonance and 10 being a very high emotional resonance: How do you rate your own challenges with fear around feeling secure and safe?

If you rated yourself as 6 or higher, complete the following questions as you review the commentary provided about the root chakra:

> What feelings noted apply to you, if any?
>
> What beliefs noted apply to you, if any?
>
> What situations from childhood overlap or are similar to what's been noted?
>
> What situations from adulthood overlap or are similar to what's been highlighted?
>
> What other feelings, emotions, and memories came up when reading or writing about the root chakra? Do you feel sadness, shame, guilt, or something else?

Sacral Chakra

When Your Feeling Lens Is Clouded by Scarcity

Does this pattern apply to you? (yes or no)

Indicate on a scale of 0 to 10—0 being no emotional resonance and 10 being a very high emotional resonance: How do you rate your own challenges with limitation surrounding feeling, desire, and pleasure?

If you rated yourself as 6 or higher, complete the following questions as you review the commentary provided about the sacral chakra:

What feelings noted apply to you, if any?

What beliefs noted apply to you, if any?

What situations from childhood overlap or are similar to what's been highlighted?

What situations from adulthood overlap or are similar to what's been highlighted?

What other feelings, emotions, and memories came up when reading or writing about the sacral chakra? Do you feel sadness, shame, guilt, or something else?

Solar Plexus Chakra

When Your Power Lens Is Clouded by Scarcity

Does this pattern apply to you? (yes or no)

Indicate on a scale of 0 to 10—0 being no emotional resonance and 10 being a very high emotional resonance: How do you rate your own challenges with limitation surrounding your own power?

If you rated yourself as 6 or higher, complete the following questions as you review the commentary provided about the solar plexus chakra:

What feelings noted apply to you, if any?

What beliefs noted apply to you, if any?

What situations from childhood overlap or are similar to what's been highlighted?

What situations from adulthood overlap or are similar to what's been highlighted?

What other feelings, emotions, and memories came up when reading or writing about the solar plexus chakra? Do you feel sadness, shame, guilt, or something else?

Heart Chakra

When Your Love Lens Is Clouded by Scarcity

Does this pattern apply to you? (yes or no)

Indicate on a scale of 0 to 10—0 being no emotional resonance and 10 being a very high emotional resonance: How do you rate your own challenges with limitation surrounding love and being appreciated?

If you rated yourself as 6 or higher, complete the following questions as you review the commentary provided about the heart chakra:

What feelings noted apply to you, if any?

What beliefs noted apply to you, if any?

What situations from childhood overlap or are similar to what's been highlighted?

What situations from adulthood overlap or are similar to what's been highlighted?

What other feelings, emotions, and memories came up when reading or writing about the heart chakra? Do you feel sadness, shame, guilt, or something else?

Throat Chakra

When Your Expression Lens Is Clouded by Scarcity

Does this pattern apply to you? (yes or no)

Indicate on a scale of 0 to 10—0 being no emotional resonance and 10 being a very high emotional resonance: How do you rate your feelings of limitation surrounding your own expression?

If you rated yourself as 6 or higher, complete the following questions as you review the commentary provided about the throat chakra:

What feelings noted apply to you, if any?

What beliefs noted apply to you, if any?

What situations from childhood overlap or are similar to what's been highlighted?

What situations from adulthood overlap or are similar to what's been highlighted?

What other feelings, emotions, and memories came up when reading or writing about the throat chakra? Do you feel sadness, shame, guilt, or something else?

Brow Chakra

When Your Intuitive Lens Is Clouded by Scarcity

Does this pattern apply to you? (yes or no)

Indicate on a scale of 0 to 10—0 being no emotional resonance and 10 being a very high emotional resonance: How do you rate your feelings of limitation surrounding your own intuition?

If you rated yourself as 6 or higher, complete the following questions as you review the commentary provided about the brow chakra:

What feelings noted apply to you, if any?

What beliefs noted apply to you, if any?

What situations from childhood overlap or are similar to what's been highlighted?

What situations from adulthood overlap or are similar to what's been highlighted?

What other feelings, emotions, and memories came up when reading or writing about the brow chakra? Do you feel sadness, shame, guilt, or something else?

Crown Chakra

When Your Divine Lens Is Clouded by Scarcity

Does this pattern apply to you? (yes or no)

Indicate on a scale of 0 to 10—0 being no emotional resonance and 10 being a very high emotional resonance: How do you rate your feelings of limitation surrounding the Divine?

If you rated yourself as 6 or higher, complete the following questions as you review the commentary provided about the crown chakra:

What feelings noted apply to you, if any?

What beliefs noted apply to you, if any?

What situations from childhood overlap or are similar to what's been highlighted?

What situations from adulthood overlap or are similar to what's been highlighted?

What other feelings, emotions, and memories came up when reading or writing about the crown chakra? Do you feel sadness, shame, guilt, or something else?

DAILY PRACTICES FOR P IS FOR PATTERN

1. Engage in process of preparatory practices
2. Breath-work practice—5 minutes
3. Meditation practice—5 minutes
4. Journaling practice—20–40 minutes
5. Dedication and gratitude

MINDFUL MOMENTS OF ACTION

1. How many days did you do your practices?
2. What was the experience like for you?

3. What did you struggle with completing?
4. Is there anything else you would like to note for this step—things to revisit in the future, areas of focus, questions you'd like to have answered?

SUMMARY OF STEP 2—P IS FOR PATTERN

Learning how to rewire the patterns you've established when it comes to money is not easy. You've spent a lifetime learning how to do things a certain way. Just because you've become aware of the challenges doesn't mean they will automatically change by themselves. Knowing where some of your patterns got started and why they've been tough to let go of helps you become more compassionate rather than critical of yourself, which is necessary to begin shifting your behaviors.

It also helps to notice that just because the past has been a certain way, you do not have to live this way for the rest of your life. A beautiful quote from the Bible is from Romans 12:2, which says, "be transformed by the renewing of your mind." As you move through this process, you will begin to see your mind transforming mentally, emotionally, and spiritually. Life is not about who you have been in the past; it is about who you decide to be in this present moment and the next.

12

STEP 3—R IS FOR RECLAIMING YOUR FEELINGS

We think too much and feel too little.
—CHARLIE CHAPLIN

This step addresses the importance of getting in touch with your feelings and coming into your power as an intuitive being. You will be invited to reveal new dimensions of insight through the journaling exercises.

OPENING UP TO YOURSELF

To help you get in touch with the deepest parts of yourself, you'll need to begin releasing some of the "layers" of protection that have built up over the years. This allows you to ultimately discover who you are and who you are not. This takes time and is not always an easy process. Right now there is a good chance your ego is kicking up some resistance, and I just want you to know that is normal and to keep moving through it. It is merely F.E.A.R—"false evidence appearing real"—and your job is to not let it stop you. Instead, all you need to do is notice it, befriend it, and then continue moving forward toward a life in which fear and resistance no longer control you.

To move into your "feeling" sense, you'll need to become more vulnerable with yourself. This isn't always easy to do, especially when you are first starting out. That's because the mind is wired to control everything, which lessens our ability to feel what's going on under the surface of our mind.

PROTECTING YOURSELF

Prior to doing IPROSPER, I felt the need to hide myself and my thoughts and feelings whenever possible. One way I did this was to carry an imaginary shield of protection around with me. The shield helped ensure that people did not get too close unless I wanted to let them in. It also helped me navigate life without worrying about people hurting me. While it did a good job of keeping me safe, it also kept a lot of people out of my life. That's because even if we can't physically see the shield, people know that something is not quite right. It's like they can feel us being guarded and therefore they don't get too close. Sadly, this lack of intimacy prevents our relationships from becoming as close as we'd like them to be. Even when we think we're close to another person, this shield is still blocking the depths of what the relationship could become.

Anyone who has gone through a lot of challenges and emotional upsets knows how deep these roots of protection go—causing a constant sense of needing to protect yourself at all times. Looking back, I can see now how I had created some very effective mechanisms, always on high alert, to discern whether or not people coming into my sphere were safe or not. This was because I was still holding on to deep-seated fears, left over from my youth, that people I trusted would hurt me. Because this way of holding myself was second nature, I didn't even know it was preventing me from having the sorts of relationships I craved.

THE OTHER SIDE OF FEELING

In 2014, about six months after I started my business, I was invited to participate in a weeklong workshop that would change how I saw all of this. In the beginning of the workshop, similar to what we've been doing together here, we did exercises to help us clear negativity out of our consciousness so that we could make space for our feeling sense to develop. We did this process for a few days, which was mentally exhausting and at the same time highly effective.

To think about all the things you are holding on to when it comes to your family, friends, and yourself—the grudges, frustrations, disappointments, expectations, dreams, regrets—and then to let them go in a few days' time was incredibly freeing. Watching the emotional baggage release from my psyche revealed just how much it had been preventing me from feeling a deeper awareness within myself. It is also interesting to note that this was happening even after I'd been meditating regularly for over 15 years.

As the activities moved into participants' working in pairs on various exercises, I began to let go of my inner critic and just be. The purge of past emotional trauma was so powerful, cleansing my psyche to such a degree that I began to magically sense other people's thoughts and feelings. It was like all of a sudden I had claimed the truth of who I really was, which allowed me to claim the truth of all that is. I could feel truth radiating out in all directions, and from that a sense of peace and freedom arose. I knew the truth in that instant of what unconditional love feels like, and I surrendered into it completely.

From this new awareness, I had the ability to access a whole new dimension of understanding that I had previously been cut off from.

I'll be honest, I didn't completely understand what was happening to me, yet I did know that I had suddenly gained psychic powers that went way beyond anything reason could explain.

LOVE AND ABOVE

As we learn to let go of anything other than unconditional love, the small self recedes in value and importance while the True Self begins to converse with you. It starts with a tiny voice that is so small you barely hear it, and, for me at least, it wasn't so much words that I heard but feelings in my body that began to communicate. This is when I found myself progressively entering a new way of being that invited me to feel the unexplainable energy everywhere. This sixth sense, which is generated through your connection to the True Self, begins to channel another dimension of communication into your awareness.

To engage in this way we need to recognize the difference between our sixth sense and our feelings and emotions. As I mentioned earlier, you've probably created imaginary, emotional barriers to protect yourself, and yet that is what causes you to feel numbness and disconnection between who you think you are and who you really are. You may have thought the imaginary shield would protect you against the pains of the world, but what you probably didn't realize is that it is also preventing you from tapping into this flow of energetic communication.

To learn how to cut through the numbness, we discover the only way through is to turn toward our painful, disfigured, unwanted, and disowned parts so we can cultivate intimate understanding of them. We do this by surrendering our feelings and allowing them to be present without condemning, judging, resisting, or getting caught up inside of them. We simply look at them, observe, and allow them to be, without trying to modify and change them. This willingness gives our reactive responses the ability to dissipate naturally.

Going through this process means letting your heart be open and exposed while becoming more comfortable with your own discomfort. It takes being vulnerable if you want to connect with the deepest parts of yourself—so that you can feel deep compassion for the child self within and also allow yourself to feel compassion toward others' child selves.

It is important to note that you can only be where you are. Your evolution is predicated upon your awakening in your own time. This moment is perfect for you right now, and wherever you are is exactly where you need to be. Even hearing about the freedom that can be gained is enough to attract you toward it. By learning about my experiences, you are being introduced to your own gateway of discovery.

When you know you are free, you see the freedom everywhere around you, including in other people. Your field of awareness begins to not only attract your True Self toward you, it also brings greater prosperity.

TOOLS FOR AWAKENING

The breath work, meditation, and journaling exercises you've been doing since chapter 10, are meant to help you begin the untangling process of releasing suppressed memories and emotional charges. An illustration of how this works is to see a cup of water and oil wherein the water represents who you really are and the oil represents the emotional experiences. When we are living reactively with money, it's similar to stirring the cup vigorously so that it is impossible to see the oil and water apart from each other. Reacting is the shaking and stirring, and responding is allowing the water and oil to be still so they can separate. Only when the oil and water are separated from each other can you see how the memories and emotions are negatively impacting your perspective.

We are not journaling about past memories to reexperience or relive them so much as we are allowing these experiences to flow out of our awareness. As they appear and release, we realize how we've been holding on to these old wounds and at the same time hiding from them. Through this, it becomes apparent how we've been reacting rather than responding when we feel emotionally charged. Our attention becomes fixated on the problem, the event, or the person instead of seeing what's happening as a consequence of our past wounds.

The more you allow your feelings and emotions to naturally dissipate, the easier it becomes to stop getting flustered and upset by money challenges. This is because you see how your endless array of thoughts are causing you to feel the way you do about money. Thoughts are just endless rationalizations of your inner feelings and emotions, and so when you stop following them, you stop being triggered by situations.

Our task for this step is to continue your daily practices of breath work, meditation, and journaling on a daily basis. Journaling prompts you will be guided through are oriented to your past experiences with money. Combining this with the breath work and meditation practices gives you an opportunity to release the surfacing energy with the intention of integration. No matter what comes up through the exercises—mentally, physically, emotionally, and spiritually—keep your intention focused on surrendering the negative feelings as they arise rather than feeling the need to express them.

DAILY PRACTICES FOR R IS FOR RECLAIMING YOUR FEELINGS

1. Engage in process of preparatory practices
2. Breath-work practice—5 minutes

3. Meditation practice—5 minutes
4. Journaling practice—20–40 minutes
5. Dedication and gratitude

MINDFUL MOMENTS OF REFLECTION

Reflect on and complete the following statements:

My earliest experiences with money were . . . (Be sure to explore things like when you first received an allowance, your first jobs for pay, adverse experiences with money, extreme highs or lows, unusual events, vivid memories, painful losses, windfalls, large gifts, and so on.)

Distinctive childhood memories not connected to money were . . . (Include any highly emotional events, highly favorable events and repetitive patterns within your environment, with your health, within your relationships including your family and friends/friends of parents that help you put your past into better context.)

I believed the following things about money growing up:

The way money was treated in my home by my parents growing up was as follows:

My mother believes/believed the following things about money:

My father believes/believed the following things about money:

In my family [include grandparents, aunts, uncles, and cousins if helpful and more expansive than previous responses], money meant . . .

In my family, money was not connected to . . .

My beliefs about money have been influenced the most by . . .

Some of my core money beliefs that are different from what I learned from my family are . . .

Some of my core values [those held as important] that came from my family are . . .

In your journal, list three money experiences that happen to you repeatedly. Now complete these statements:

> Money comes to me as a result of . . .
>
> The area in which I feel the greatest sense of pride and joy with money is . . .
>
> My partner [or past partners] believe the following about money:
>
> In relation to my friends and family, I think I have [how much] money . . . I think this [matters/does not matter] to me because . . .
>
> The areas in my life where I feel the most confident about money are . . .
>
> My biggest regret with money is . . .
>
> What concerns me the most about money is . . .

In your journal, list three actions you have done that caused people to believe certain things about you and your money. Then complete these statements:

> My fears with money have a lot to do with . . .
>
> My struggles with money have a lot to do with . . .
>
> If I had a lot of money, I wouldn't be able to . . .
>
> If I had more money, I would be able to . . .

Before moving on to the next chapter, take a moment to journal or contemplate what you learned in chapter 11 about your scarcity-lens patterns combined with what you've learned here in chapter 12 about your money history. What do you now understand about your relationship with money? What realizations are you having? What feelings are arising, and where are you feeling them in your body? What assumptions are you questioning about your perspective? Is anything else coming up?

MINDFUL MOMENTS OF ACTION

1. How many days did you do your practices?
2. What was the experience like for you?
3. What did you struggle with completing?
4. Is there anything else you would like to note for this step—things to revisit in the future, areas of focus, questions you'd like to have answered?

SUMMARY OF STEP 3—R IS FOR RECLAIMING YOUR FEELINGS

Awakening to how you feel allows you to notice the difference between real and perceived stress. This helps you respond to challenges rather than react to them, which causes you to become more creative and solution-oriented than scarcity oriented. As you gain an understanding of your past conditioning with money, you will note the events in your life differently. One way to think about the process is to imagine that you are watching a scary movie and you decide that it is too much and you need a break from its intensity. Instead of being caught up in the movie, you pay attention for a few minutes to the edges of the movie screen. This allows you to back away and notice that it is only a movie and not real. By pulling back from the emotions you are feeling in that moment, you regain your ability to enjoy the film without getting traumatized by it.

The process of journaling is a great way to help you step back and notice how much you've been caught up in the drama of life. This gives you the chance to remove yourself from the emotional fog brought about by these stories so you can respond rather than react to whatever life is serving up.

13

STEP 4—O IS FOR OPPORTUNITY

The world is not to be put in order; the world is order,
incarnate. It is for us to harmonize with this order.
—HENRY MILLER

This step is about exploring yourself and your belief systems. You'll
be invited to look inside of your fears and dive into the process of
finding balance within your relationship with money, which helps
you step more fully into your own sense of power.

OPPORTUNITY TO LEARN FROM YOUR PAST

One of the biggest barriers to getting your money where you want it
to be is the belief that if it was going to get better, then you'd already
be there by now. Having worked with thousands of people, I know
nothing could be further from the truth, and yet as long as you believe it, it will continue to be your reality.

When I start helping my clients document their money stories,
I can see how deep their belief patterns run and how hard it can
be to notice these patterns on their own. I also see that unless they
learn how to step back and see their stories rather than living inside

of them, they keep getting lost in the minutiae and can't make appropriate changes as a result. Seeing their money stories in writing, however, changes everything. Now they have clarity about why they'd struggled in the past and where they want to be in the future. This makes a huge difference in their mindsets and gives them confidence to take a stand for creating the life they really want to be living.

When situations and stories are written down versus merely swimming around in our heads, they become far more clear, concrete, and real. This "realness" is important because we have a harder time avoiding them. Once written, your story becomes out in the open so you can better understand what happened and how it has affected your life.

The first time I wrote down the story of one of my clients, Leanne, the clarity that arose for both of us about what had been happening for her and her money was astounding. I had been coaching her for nearly two years, and yet much of what she had written had never been explored.

All of a sudden we had newfound clarity about why she was so stuck in her past. Now we could see how her tendencies to avoid money were connected to not wanting to get hurt by loved ones, as well as the patterns of shame she was exposed to from an early age. This gave us clues about the breakthroughs she was ready to have, which further inspired her to remain accountable to personal growth rather than get pulled back into her old story.

FEAR OF THE UNKNOWN

Much of the time the fear of letting go is much scarier than the actual process. Intense fear can be so overwhelming it prevents us from looking into the most destructive areas of our lives. By avoiding the areas that contain the highest emotional charge, we end up identifying with our fears as if they were real.

By giving ourselves unconditional love we develop the capacity to calm our fears and help ourselves and others in an authentic way. The more we do this the easier it becomes to recognize the aspects of ourselves that feel broken and at fault.

Having gone through not one but many dark nights of the soul, I've noticed how shame can play a powerful part in the process of instigating breakthroughs. The feelings of intense self-criticism and scrutiny that shame creates within a person's psyche grow and fester until the pressure becomes so intense that the only possible solution is a breaking down of the egocentric personality. As long as shame remains stuck within us, we are blocking out access to the supreme consciousness and therefore do not have the capacity to live to our fullest potential.

YOUR MONEY STORY

During this chapter, you'll be uncovering ever-greater details behind your money story by journaling through a series of questions. As you move through the process, you're encouraged to embrace your discomfort. The emotions that arise from fear, anger, and grief are meaningful expressions that are ready to be felt without judgment and suppression. By responding with loving attention rather than reacting to the emotions and feelings that arise, you'll develop a greater sense of freedom to be as you are.

Ever since we left childhood behind, our child self has been using physical, emotional, and mental states of discomfort to bring our attention back to that which was never integrated. It does this to encourage us to focus and attend to all that is unresolved.

The journaling exercises are meant to bring your past out into the open so you can recognize that manifesting discomfort with money is merely an effect and not the cause. It is critical at this phase to recognize how limiting this behavior has become so that you can focus on the effect and what you wish to change with your money experiences going forward.

FINDING BALANCE WITH YOUR MONEY

When I was eleven, my father, with the utmost conviction, sat me down to tell me about the principle of yin and yang. It was crucial, he told me, to work toward balance in all aspects of life. He spoke excitedly as he explained the yin and yang symbol and how it could teach us to live in harmony rather than disruption.

He was adamant that someday it would help me better understand the meaning of life. Looking back, I think my dad had the realization in that moment that wholeness was possible for all of us. Granted, he didn't know how to get there at the time but he was deeply inspired by his realization. He knew that when we learn how to integrate all parts of ourselves into wholeness, life cannot help but improve.

Guiding students through one of my first money workshops, I found myself trying to explain how common it is to swing between the extremes when it comes to money—feast or famine, rich or poor, tough or soft, rising or falling, controlling or chaotic, dominating or submissive. One day you're on a spending binge, and the next you aren't willing to spend a penny. One day you're organized and managing your money carefully, and the next you've lost track and can't bear the thought of looking at your account balances. One day everything is copacetic with your partner, and the next you're facing a huge argument over your spending choices. One day the stock market is jubilantly going up, and the next it is in a freefall. While emotions cannot always be avoided when money appears to be generating a never-ending roller coaster of drama, it is possible to learn better responses to our emotions as they arise.

A transformational tool that I've been studying on and off for years involves the principle of yin and yang, which has its roots in Taoism. You may be familiar with the graphic image (shown on the previous page) that is designed to represent two halves coming together in complete wholeness. The yin and yang principle describes how seemingly opposite forces, one light and one dark, are interdependent and are necessary in creating harmony in the natural world. This way of being applies to all of life's interests and teaches us to not fight and oppose but to sustain and maintain harmony by making use of both sides of ourselves.

The yin and yang are two sides of the same coin: the tail is yin, the head is yang. Learning how to balance between the two is important for health, vitality, and peace of mind. When we are stronger in one and deficient in another, we find ourselves feeling unsettled, with low energy and high levels of stress. This is happening because we haven't learned how to integrate the experiences of what it means to be human.

Yin is a very feminine principle (and is not the same as we traditionally think of as gender-specific): it is patient, internal, introspective, contemplative, compassionate, yielding, nurturing, right-brained, intuitive, creative, ambivalent, and soft. Regardless of gender, yin is the mode we go into when we are seeking answers to questions that have been posed by one's circumstances. How this plays out with money is that when we are in yin mode, we tend to be more relaxed and creative and are less likely to focus on how much we are being paid and how much we are earning. Yin energy helps us become more creative and soulful in our approach to life.

Yang, on the other hand, is a masculine principle that is active, external, assertive, dominating, initiating, logical, conscientious, certain, and hard. Yang energy is what causes us to take action and bring things into reality. With money, yang energy is the catalyst that helps us plan, strategize, implement, and sell. It is more common for money to be associated with yang energy because these actions result in people making a lot of money.

Traditionally, it was thought that women would naturally lean toward more feminine (yin) qualities, while men would lean toward masculine (yang) qualities, but as times have changed, the lines have blurred. It isn't quite that simple, but it does help explain why women have gravitated to jobs like nursing and teaching and why more men can be found working on Wall Street as well as on a construction jobsite or in an auto-repair shop. What I've found is that the action of working for money is more often associated with the orientation of yang energy, while yin energy is more oriented to receptivity and nurturing. When I was writing my own money story, I noticed how I've always earned and saved the most money when I was working in yang-oriented environments, but when I started working for myself I became far more yin oriented, which led to a decrease in income.

When we are wanting to create more prosperity in our lives, we are well served by embracing both sides. Through the embodiment of both parts of our wholeness we release any resistance to the parts that have been labeled as not as good, and instead we integrate that which is not as familiar into our bag of tools. Now we're able to command our money in new ways that were being avoided.

For the naturally yin-oriented person who felt like hustling for money was a bad thing, she may start holding herself accountable to achieving several short-term financial goals. For the yang-oriented person, he may find himself meditating and reflecting before making any big financial decisions to ensure they are aligned with his heart and his head. What this means is that inside of this newly perceptive awareness, we can find ourselves moving energy with far less effort and commanding our destiny with greater power than we knew was even possible.

YIN QUALITIES

YIN QUALITIES		EXCESS YIN
Flow	introversion	needy
right brain - intuitive	relaxation	confused
abundant - infinite supply	satisfaction	boundary-less
collaborative	non-linear	martyr
compassion	incubating	depressive
nurturing	persistent	apathetic
creative	loving	emotional
ambivalent	alluring	defensive
empathetic	gentle	self-denying
sensitive	neat	tamed
tolerant	succorance	chaotic
caring	positive	overwhelmed
attentive	imagination	overthinking
deferent	cloudy	sluggish
patient	consuming	laziness
sensual	passive	slow thinking
radiant	shadows	
vulnerable	feminine	
sweetness		
expressive		
sharing		
tenderness		
wisdom		
dependent		

YANG QUALITIES

YANG QUALITIES		EXCESS YANG
active	assertive	forcing
goal directed	independence	rigid
left brain - logical	responsible	too many boundaries
limited/finite supply	humorous	domination
competitive	fiery	anxiety
valor	intellectual	rage
initiating	masculine	blocked
conscientious	fearless	aggressive
certainty	self-assured	greedy
action	cunning	predatory
ambition	calm under pressure	over controlling
extroversion	productive	domination
excitement	confident	reactive
adventurous	tactical	harsh
getting things done	strategic	deference to truth
courageous	calculated	masochistic
tough	prudent	inability to relax
hard	political	insomnia
diplomatic	fatherly	addiction
unexpressive	dependable	frustration
protecting	passionate	end justifies the means
methodical	bold	narcissistic
authority		

To do this you first look at the qualities of both yin and yang to identify which are more similar to how you engage with money. You might also think about what I suggested earlier and consider a time when you were earning the most and least amount of money, and ask yourself the following questions:

Which of the two traits (yin or yang) were you more commonly applying in your work when you were earning the most?

What traits were you applying when you were making the
  least?

In each situation, did it feel draining and overwhelming, or
  did it feel uplifting and confirming?

Going forward, what are you receptive to trying differently
  to better integrate the yin and the yang?

Absent of integration, we gravitate to one extreme or the other.
Yin *or* yang rather than yin *and* yang. Perhaps when we were young
we could push ourselves to do more yang-oriented work, but gradually this wore us down and we found ourselves moving toward yin
activities. It's no surprise that our society has taught us to go out and
strive to achieve and buy and get into debt, and we listened until
one day we couldn't anymore—at least not when it meant sacrificing
ourselves and our lives in pursuit of money.

By learning how to integrate power and balance, we no longer
need to chase the material dream, nor do we need to place false
expectations on ourselves to be anything other than who we are.
Instead, we feel confidence in our own sovereign beingness that allows us to be both our yang and our yin selves, without expectation
of one being better than the other.

For a moment, think about the tone of how you engage with
money. When do you feel most powerful?

- Do you find yourself feeling more powerful when you are
  in yang or yin mode?
- Why do you think that is the case?
- What happens when you approach money with yang
  energy?
- What happens when you approach it with yin energy?
- How do you define your concepts of power as it relates to
  the yin and yang?
- What resistance do you feel toward being more yin?

- What resistance do you feel toward being more yang?
- Reviewing what you've written, do you notice any similarities between yourself and your parents?
- Do your tendencies to gravitate to one side or the other affect your relationship with money? If so, how?

Knowing your yin and yang tendencies allows you to use the methodology to become more versatile in your approach to money. Doing so will help you see when you're falling into a comfort zone that is not helping you create your dreams. There is no right or wrong about any of this, but you will gain the ability to see how you can grow your capacity to move back and forth between the yin and the yang more easily and confidently.

As you look at what you've written down, notice if you're more yin oriented with money, and, if so, what you can do differently to move in the direction of the yang. If you're more yang focused, then look for new ways to explore the yin aspects of your behavior with money.

As you progress through the process, you'll start to notice how good it feels to move back and forth between the two parts of yourself. Noticing how you can move from one stage to the next—from planting seeds (yin) and growing the food (yang), to nurturing the crops (yin) and then harvesting (yang), or from selling the goods (yang) to receiving the money (yin). During this entire life cycle you are working with different parts to create a sense of the whole.

One of the reasons many of us tend to operate from one side or the other is that we get stuck inside of our comfort zones and have trouble changing direction. For example, if we are very yin oriented, we think to ourselves, "I don't want to be greedy, so I am not willing to ask people to buy my products and services." Or, "I don't want to be pushy and aggressive, so I am not going to follow up with my prospects." Or, "I don't want to be too controlling, so I am not going to take charge of the process." Or, on the yang side, we may be thinking to ourselves, "I don't want to be too flexible and accommodating, because people will take advantage of me." Or, "I don't want to be too vulnerable or people won't respect me." Or, "I don't want to be seen as too creative, because people won't think I'm serious."

Our negative self-talk recycles itself because we're afraid of what will happen when we reveal all parts of ourselves to the world. Our fear is what causes us to place a great deal of attention on the extremes and to blow them out of proportion, rather than notice how everything has its limits and just because you come close to them doesn't mean you have to cross over them. When we notice that most of these fears are not reasonable, we learn to question our assumptions and accept that all parts of ourselves are valid. When we do this, we feel more powerful, optimistic and better able to positively impact our finances. Psychologists call this state of being self-efficacy where you believe in yourself and your ability to positively change your own life.

When we're more yin and we begin to play with the yang, we find it to be vibrant and exciting. It tells us to go after the things we most want in life and gives us the power of making things happen. The yang inspires us to take risks and pursue making money, getting organized, and putting systems in place; it is about having fun and being silly, trying and failing, competing for the fun of it, and taking massive action because you can and want to.

When we are more yang and we try being yinlike, we find it to be soulful, nurturing, mindful, and supportive. It tells us we can slow down and relax. It shows us the power of letting things happen on their own timelines without pushing and pulling.

WHAT DOES BALANCE LOOK LIKE FOR YOU?

You can ponder this question in terms of your overall lifestyle. If you are overworked and under a lot of pressure, stress could be breaking you down in more ways than one. By incorporating more yin practice in your life, you can slow down and create more peace.

Just as it has been throughout each step, the goal is to continue doing your daily meditation and breath work practices and allow them to help you open up to new possibilities and opportunities when it comes to money.

Now is a great time to also recognize where and when you have found yourself struggling with money and what you can do differently as a result of embodying more yang qualities in your life. This is the energy that is going to allow you to plan, strategize, and take action more effectively and powerfully when it comes to your financial planning.

Becoming more open to the qualities of the yin and the yang helps you be in better balance with all parts of yourself. By reaching back to your past can you rescue aspects of your child self and shower it with the unconditional love and attention. This "inside" job is the pathway for consciously integrating the unconscious and for releasing the child self from its past so that the adult self can realize peace of mind.

Allow these questions to inspire and guide you, but do not feel limited to the questions themselves. There is no right way to carry out this process; it is about opening communication channels to see what unfolds. Take all the pressure off yourself to do it in a certain way. Feel free to expand, elaborate, and go off into other directions, as you never know what you might find when you unleash the floodgates to your conscious and unconscious thoughts. The whole point is to feel good about yourself without judgment. There is no need to push yourself further than you wish to go, and even reading through each of these steps is already working its magic.

DAILY PRACTICES FOR O IS FOR OPPORTUNITY

1. Engage in process of preparatory practices
2. Breath-work practice—5 minutes

3. Meditation practice—5 minutes
4. Journaling practice—20–40 minutes
5. Dedication and gratitude

MINDFUL MOMENTS OF REFLECTION

This week you'll be continuing in your journaling practice by following the journal prompts, completing the exercises, and answering the questions that are provided.

When it comes to earning money, I do the following:
When it comes to spending money, I do the following:
When it comes to managing my money, I do the following:
When it comes to saving money, I do the following:
When it comes to investing money, I do the following:
When it comes to receiving money, I do the following:
When it comes to giving money, I do the following:

Finally, write a summary about how you engage with money. Be bone-crushingly honest with yourself.

MINDFUL MOMENTS OF ACTION

Money Tracking

Spend the next thirty days tracking everything you spend money on. You can get a journal and set it up so you are tracking all of your personal expenses down to the penny, and if you are a business owner, then you can add a section to track your business expenses in the same way. The goal is to bring the unconscious into consciousness when it comes to your spending. Money tracking is going to allow you to change how you relate to your money one purchase at a time.

As we've been discussing, you cannot change something about yourself and your behaviors until you become aware of it. Money tracking is the only way that you can notice what you are doing now and create the opportunity to save more money in the future.

When I first graduated from college, I worked for a summer at a casino near Lake Tahoe, in Nevada. What I found astounding is that money in casinos is highly tracked—how much each table is bringing in, what the minimum at the tables were set at depending upon the time of day, how many tables were to be open at any given time, and so on. Without any doubt, the reason casinos are so profitable is because they track everything down to the penny. The same thing goes for the success of Olympic athletes, who must track their speed, distance, sleep, food intake, and more so that they know without a shadow of doubt where they are and where they need to be on a daily basis. If you wish to change your life and your money, you must bring your spending into conscious awareness. It is the only way to make changes so that you can meet your goals. It will take only a month or two before you notice that your spending behavior shifts so that you are making new choices and applying better discipline to your spending, and you will have more left over for saving, investing, and for taxes if you are self-employed.

Yin and Yang Exercise

Now it's time to really see where you are with the yin and yang qualities. Review the yin and yang lists provided in this chapter, print them out, and use colored highlighters to indicate different traits as they apply to your practices with money and financial matters.

- Yellow indicates a trait you are doing or being on a regular basis.
- Orange indicates a trait you would like to do or be more of but don't do very often.

- Pink indicates a trait you try to avoid and have not wanted to be or do because it makes you uncomfortable.
- You do not have to mark all of the words, just those that resonate as you answer the questions noted.

Upon completion of these journaling exercises, take time to map out next steps for yourself. Write about the traits you wish to become more familiar with when it comes to money and the ways you can be sure to put those into practice.

An example would be that you notice you are not tapping in to your yang qualities when it comes to sales in your business. Ask yourself in this situation, "What are the behaviors I can do differently?" You may write down things like, "be more proactive with the sales process, follow up on a consistent basis with prospects, create business goals that are tied to my financial goals" and so on. Once you've completed this evaluation, put these goals into practice immediately, and be sure to keep track of your progress.

MINDFUL MOMENTS OF ACTION

1. How many days did you do your practices?
2. What was the experience like for you?
3. What did you struggle with completing?
4. Is there anything else you would like to note for this step—things to revisit in the future, areas of focus, questions you'd like to have answered?

SUMMARY FOR STEP 4—O IS FOR OPPORTUNITY

Making a commitment to create greater balance between the yin and the yang helps you become more powerful and sure-footed in the world. At the very core of your being, you are a spirit having a human experience. When your relationships or the stresses of life become too much, you lose your lightness of being. The most beneficial thing you can do for yourself during these times is to embrace the gap between the softness and the brilliance of your humanness. By coupling your masculine qualities of clarity and decisiveness with your feminine qualities of receiving, you increase your confidence in yourself and your ability to make a difference in your own life. With higher self-efficacy, you're more likely to take actions that help you reach your financial goals. As you stay the course, with repeated effort, no matter how difficult or challenging your circumstances are, you can eventually bring your dreams into reality.

14

STEP 5—S IS FOR STORY

Those who don't know history are destined to repeat it.
—EDMUND BURKE

This step helps you understand the context of your life and how it relates to your money. Here is where you can see not only how your beliefs got created but the choices you've made as a result of those beliefs and how they are affecting your money. I introduce the "hero's journey" as a framework to better understand your past so you can ultimately play a significant role in the creation of what you want your money story to look like in the future.

One of the most difficult tasks a person can face, when they are being brutally honest with themselves, is the question of whether or not they're happy with the life they've been living. As you know with my story, when I asked myself a similar question after my father was killed and then again in the elevator on that fateful day, my answer both times was "not really."

ADMITTING THE TRUTH

It is common to not want to look backward into the past out of fear of what you might find. The challenge is that when we don't understand the past, we have an uncanny way of repeating it. That's because without looking closely at our past, we never get a chance to truly learn from it.

This is one of the reasons why writing your money story can become one of the most powerful stories you'll ever write. As humans, we're wired for story. We seek out and respond to things we hear, watch, and read through storytelling. This happens because storytelling is the language of the brain: we actually think in story, which is why the brain is so good at probing through stories to find meaning and information. In fact, the story is so second nature that we don't even have to think about how it works; once a story grabs your attention, you are hooked. This is why storytelling about ourselves is such a powerful healing tool.

By engaging in the journaling prompts thus far, you've opened a portal of understanding about your past that very few people will ever take the time to complete. Through this work, you're opening a field of awareness so you can better understand your life. I've found that when we learn how to tell our money story through the eyes of the protagonist, we're taking ownership of our life in an entirely new way. Rather than being a victim inside of the story, the process of writing it allows you to organize your thoughts, notice what you've learned and are still learning, as well as see the mistakes, hardships, failures, and celebrations that have taken place along the journey—seeing the whole picture, perhaps for the first time ever. This is why storytelling can be so transformative for both the person telling the story and those who hear it.

By writing your money story, you are projecting unconscious energy of your past outward into a conscious level of awareness.

Thereby bringing forth any and all negativity that is ready to be cleared and cleansed from your psyche. Sometimes this negativity will hurt similar to when you open a scab on your body, other times it will just feel numb. Realizing that both reactions are normal and to be expected helps you explore more deeply what's coming up. To help you in this process, alongside of writing your hero's journey, I've created journaling prompts designed to keep you moving through the suppressed energy. This is important because you want to make sure you are processing the feelings that are arising rather than resisting and resuppressing them.

With painful events of the past, in order to clear and cleanse them from our psyche, we must be able to notice them and forgive ourselves and others wherever we have the strength to do so. Keep in mind that forgiveness is not about condoning bad behavior so much as it is about releasing the energy of resentment and guilt. The more you can drop away the negativity that has been held within, the better able you become to direct your actions so they bring about your true intentions.

YOUR MONEY STORY HOLDS THE KEY

During the process of writing my money story, I learned a great deal about my parents and their backstories before I was born. To understand their lives in this way filled me with compassion for how hard they had to work to keep food on the table and smiles on their faces. Both of them had been deeply traumatized by their youth, and I learned how their pain was often, unconsciously, being passed on to me and my brother. My parents were so torn up inside that they couldn't stop themselves from taking their pain out on each other and on us as their kids. I then grew up without realizing that I had internalized a great deal of their pain and took it on as my own. This caused me to not trust myself, nor did I feel like I could trust others.

It was only by writing my money story that I came to understand their side of the story, which helped me face the feelings I didn't want to feel growing up. By accepting my feelings without internalizing them and allowing them to just be without the need to make myself or them wrong, the negativity I had been holding on to for far too long dissipated. As the energy settled within my psyche, I could accept responsibility for how I had internalized the pain and I became able to forgive both myself and my parents for the past. This ushered in a new understanding of love and compassion for my parents that I could not realize inside of the negativity I had been holding on to.

Writing my money story also helped me understand why I had often felt like a victim who was worried about being hurt by others. Before that, I didn't understand why I struggled so much with feelings of being unlovable. My story also revealed how my need to prove myself worthy of others' love caused me to become obsessed with money as a panacea.

Writing your money story is about being honest with yourself and where you've been so you can heal the conflicts inside and approach money with a fresh start. The more you forgive, the more you own your story, the easier it becomes to set powerful intentions for where you wish to go next. By accepting the truth of your past, you can write the truth of who you really want to be going forward.

THE SEVEN STAGES OF THE HERO'S JOURNEY (ADAPTED FROM JOSEPH CAMPBELL'S *THE HERO'S JOURNEY*)

The hero's journey is the common template for a category of tales that involve a hero who goes on an adventure, encounters challenges along the way, and in a decisive crisis wins a battle, then returns home changed or transformed. *Star Wars* is a perfect example of the hero's journey, where Luke Skywalker takes in his battle against the

The Hero's Journey

"evil empire." The study of the hero's journey began nearly 150 years ago by an anthropologist who wanted to better understand common themes in stories; it was later popularized by Joseph Campbell, who was influenced by C. G. Jung's views of mythology.

I've found that we are each on our own hero's journey, and the more you understand how your story fits into the larger narrative, the easier it is to gain perspective of the process of transformation. By seeing how your own process of liberation is happening in all areas of your life, including your money, you can glean great meaning from your journey without running the risk of getting stuck along the way.

Here are the main stages of the hero's journey:

1. Ordinary money world—This is the way things have been with money in the past including your patterns discovered in step 2, chapter 11.
2. Call to adventure—A conflict or disruption keeps you from continuing in the ordinary money world.

3. Crossing the threshold—This signifies that the hero has finally committed to the journey and is ready to move forward.

4. Pursuit of the pot of gold—Here you are trying to figure out what you really want rather than what others have wanted for you or what you mistakenly thought you wanted.

5. Meeting the enemy and facing the ordeal—This is the part of the story where you have to look at the things you've avoided in the past.

6. Climax: dying to the old and awakening to possibility—This is the moment of letting go of the past, when you are dropping away the beliefs and shadows you've been holding on to. This feels like a death and, eventually, a rebirth.

7. Finding the end of the rainbow and the reward—Here you find the reward you have been seeking for many years, if not your entire life.

8. Resurrection: the road back to the ordinary world, writing your new money story—From here you are free to write the story you really want to be living.

Whenever we are learning something new—especially when it is likely to change our perspectives—it is profoundly helpful to have a guide or a map to follow. The hero's journey serves as your map of understanding so you know where you came from and, hence, where you are heading.

By noticing what has happened in the past for all the key players in your story, you'll gain understanding about how your beliefs were created and why you no longer have a need for them. From this vantage point, you are no longer the victim of your story; instead, you are the protagonist and the witness, who is ready to create a new paradigm for reality.

LIVING IN INTEGRITY

Writing our money story also helps us better understand the world around us. In the face of what we've witnessed for the past several years in popular news, we're seeing our political leaders reveal their true colors, media figures falling from grace, business leaders engaging in deceptive financial practices—and what we are learning is just how important it is to live transparently and with integrity. Each time a famous person gets caught in an act of deception, it serves as a reminder about our own personal deceptions and why it matters to be living truthfully, honestly, consciously, and respectfully within the world. This kind of honest living is exactly what we are now being called into with our money.

When we are not living with integrity ourselves, it is very difficult to do so with others. We will slip up and make mistakes even when we try to avoid them. These could be mild slipups and/or major ones. The most important thing to realize is that as we clear out our past of unresolved emotional pain, negativity and conflicts, we feel naturally drawn to be in greater alignment and truth with all of life.

The same thing applies to breaking free of patterns of scarcity. When we are living from a mindset of lack and not enough, we can't help but engage in deceptive practices with money. This is one of the reasons why money has such a bad reputation, because of how humans engage with it when they are living and expressing "not-enoughness." By writing your hero's journey, you'll become empowered to break free of these patterns and create new ways of being with money that serve not only your own highest good but the highest good of the world around you.

MINDFUL MOMENTS OF REFLECTION

Here is an overview of each of the stages you will be guided through, along with examples that you can follow. To start, you may wish to draw out a depiction of your own hero's journey on a big sheet of paper or take a few minutes to create a chronological list of your big life events (date of birth, the birth of siblings, major changes, big moves, marriages, divorces, death of loved ones, graduations, new jobs, key memories and other important milestones). This process can make what follows far easier by giving you a visual map that helps you walk through your past.

Also keep in mind that you can be going through many different hero's journeys at the same time—they can each feature different aspects of your life—including how money plays out in your career, in your relationships, and with your health. During the five years I've been writing this book, I've taken several journeys which allowed me to write about money in the way it is presented here. Knowing this, my hope is that this process gives you freedom to realize you can start anywhere you want with the exercises. There is no right or wrong way to do this. The goal is to write a story that you've lived through in the past or are living through right now so you can use it as a tool to forgive, let go, and experience what it means to be living with true freedom. The questions provided are oriented to working through a story you are living through right now but you can adapt them for past situations as well.

1. Ordinary Money World

The ordinary world (aka your money story of the past) allows you to get to know yourself as the hero/heroine before the journey begins. You'll likely find it much easier to write the story from the perspective of the witness to the story rather than being inside of it.

The point is to write about your drives, urges, and problems, while revealing your unique characteristics and flaws that make your story more understandable to the audience.

Already you can feel the shift that occurs when you put yourself in the role of the witness of your life. Granted, you cannot help but fall back into your story from time to time, but the more you step back and witness it unfolding from the objective role of witness, the more insight you'll gain about your past. You may find it helpful to go back and review the seven money stories in chapter 11 to gain ideas about your own story.

Example: In Leanne's story, you quickly learn that she is a divorced mother of two boys who experienced a lot of hardship and emotional grief in her childhood and during her marriage. This is the backstory of her life and sets the stage for where she's at before she begins her money transformation.

Write about where you've been with money prior to beginning your money transformation journey.

2. Call to Adventure

The call to money adventure sets the course for why the heroine had to leave the comfort of the status quo and presents the challenge that she feels compelled to undertake. The call throws the ordinary world off balance and establishes the stakes involved if she does not accept the challenge. The call to adventure can take on many forms, including the purchase of a large asset, a bill coming due, a new project needing attention, the arrival of someone who causes problems in your life, or a death of a loved one, to name a few. The heroine may need several calls before she finally realizes that a challenge must be met and that she must begin the journey.

Example: For Leanne, she got to the point where her financial strug- gles could no longer be avoided. She had to find solutions, and when the opportunity came to begin this work through the Mindful Millionaire process, she seized it, feeling like it was her best possible alternative for changing her life.

What money worries were you facing when you knew you had to change your life and do something different? What situation prompted you to know that you had to make a shift? What happens if you don't? Why does it matter to you to change?

Is there anything holding you back from accepting the call? What did (or do) you have to do to help you move forward on the journey?

3. Crossing the Threshold

Crossing the threshold signifies that the hero has finally committed to the journey and is ready to move forward.

Example: The moment Leanne decided to leave her husband and start a new life, she crossed the threshold into the special world.

Write about the turning point that caused you to begin a new pathway with money—even if you didn't know it at the time. See if you can pinpoint a time when you knew you had to make some big changes in your life and you decided to move forward.

4. Pursuit of the Pot of Gold

Having crossed the threshold, the heroine faces tests, encounters allies, confronts enemies, and learns the rules of the special world. The heroine needs to find out who can be trusted. Mentors inspire and help us question assumptions. Allies are earned. A sidekick may appear. An entire team is forged. Enemies and villains are encountered. The heroine must prepare herself for the greater conflicts yet to come and needs to test her skills and powers or perhaps seek further training from her mentor. This part of the journey can take years to unfold and develop. You may return to this part of the process again and again, realizing that you are still working your way through the pursuit.

Example: After leaving her husband, Leanne continued to grow and nurture her business while raising her two sons. She met and worked with several mentors and business coaches who helped her improve her business operations, but her profits remained dismal. She also dated a man who would awaken her ability to love again. Each step of the way helped her develop her skills and powers and led her to begin the IPROSPER process.

Write down the challenges you have already met or expect to encounter along your journey as it pertains to money. What is your mission? Who are your money mentors and people you seek guidance from? What other resources or allies did you or can you enlist to support you? Do you have a sidekick or a team of supporters? If so, how can they help you? Who are your enemies/villains, and why do you see them in this way? What are the skills and strengths you've brought with you? What are your areas of weakness you need to pay close attention to? Summarize and outline what your next steps will be based on what you've learned while pursuing the pot of gold.

5. Meeting the Enemy and Facing the Ordeal

The hero is realizing that he has a problem that isn't going to be easy to remedy. The ways he's been living his life are no longer working. The enemy that appears may be a person or an event that helps him feel the frustration of what it is like to be him. As he continues on his journey, he eventually comes face-to-face with an ordeal, a central life-or-death crisis, during which he faces his greatest fear and confronts his most difficult challenge. His journey wavers on the brink of failure, and the witness wonders whether the hero will survive. The ordeal is the essential stage of any journey. This is about helping you face your own shadows and decide if you have the strength to continue.

Example: At the same time as Leanne was beginning this process, she was also dating a man who brought forth intense emotions ranging from passion to absolute frustration. The intensity of the relationship caused her to dive into the depths of her soul and find strength she didn't even know she had. This experience brought her to her knees. From the dissolution of this relationship, Leanne was ready to look into her past to understand why she was repeatedly drawn to dysfunctional relationships, including the one she had with money. The limiting belief she was finally ready to explore was "I do not feel appreciated nor loved."

Write down the trials you are currently facing and notice if you can see an opportunity, similar to what happened for Leanne, to look deeply inside your own relationships, including the one you have with yourself. Can you see any opportunity to die to the old and begin anew? What limiting beliefs are you ready to let go of that are no longer serving you?

If helpful, you can refer back to the beliefs based on the seven scarcity patterns in chapter 3.

If you feel called to go even deeper, now is the time to take the scarcity pattern you identified in chapter 11 and walk yourself through the following eight questions. These questions were originally inspired by the enquiry practices I've learned from Byron Katie and Holly Riley (see chapter 2) and have been modified to help you specifically with identifying and releasing limiting money beliefs.

1. What are the limiting beliefs that you are holding on to about money? List them, then, working your way down your list one by one, you can ask yourself the following questions for each belief you've written down.

2. How do you feel when you are thinking about this belief? What sensations do you notice in your body, mind, and emotions? Write down all the words and statements that appear.

3. What money stories appear from your past when you think about this belief?

4. What do you gain by holding on to this belief?

5. Has there ever been a time when this belief was not true for you? If so, write about when, where, and how.

6. Do you find yourself acting out in any way to yourself or hurting others when you hold this belief?

7. Is there anyone you'd like to forgive, including yourself, when it comes to how you are feeling about this belief?

8. Without this limiting belief, who are you?

6. Climax—Dying to the Old and Awakening to Possibility

This is the moment when the heroine lets go of the past and experiences a "death." The more she forgives herself and others, the more the past is released. Dropping away the beliefs you've been holding on to allows something new to be birthed in its place. Only through letting go of the past and feeling a sense of compassion for yourself and others can the heroine be reborn. Only then can she experience a resurrection that grants powers or insight to see the journey to the end.

Example: The climax is the breakthrough process highlighted in each of the seven money stories in chapter 11, including the one with Leanne. For Leanne, it was time to see how the story she'd created about herself being unlovable was not true, but before she could let it go, she engaged in the process of forgiving herself and her mother. This allowed her to release the energy that had been stuck inside since she was four years old. This death to her old beliefs allowed her to continue her journey with a bright new perspective about life.

If you've identified opportunities for forgiveness to yourself and to or from others, you can proceed to the next step.

Bring to mind anyone who needs to be forgiven for something that occurred in the past. If there is more than one person, you'll want to do this process with each, one at a time. When you bring the person to mind, take a moment to acknowledge his or her presence and know that if the person frightens you in any way, you are immune to any negativity he or she could project onto you. Know you are safe here.

Ask yourself what you would like to say to that person. Notice how you are not condoning the actions of the past but that you are wanting to let go of the energy and pain the person may have caused you. Confirm the reasons for wanting to forgive him or her and say out loud or in writing what you wish to say to that person.

Notice if there is anything the person wishes to say in return and allow time for silence to see what comes in response to this open-ended question. It may be a feeling, a word, or even a full sentence; notice what was shared. If what you sense is coming from a loving place, you will likely find it easier to forgive. But if not, you may have to sit with it for days or weeks to see what unfolds at its own pace.

From the person's response, you can now state what you wish to say to him or her out loud or in writing. If and when the time is right and you feel the heartfelt desire, you can then offer your forgiveness out loud, mixing your hearts together in a flow of love and releasing them.

Repeat as necessary to include all those you know you are ready to forgive.

Now you can ask yourself if you would like to forgive yourself for any past actions or betrayals (of yourself). If so, what would you like to say to yourself? Once that is complete, you can offer yourself forgiveness out loud.

This may take some time to sit with. Look at what you have written about your past with money, and if necessary write a list of the things you know your soul would appreciate no longer holding the burden of. Even if you do not think you can forgive yourself for something, please write it down anyway. You may be surprised at what becomes possible through the tangibility of writing things down.

There is one last area to address, and that includes asking for the forgiveness of others.

Take a moment to write down the names of those you wish to ask for forgiveness from. Again, you do not have to write down why you need their forgiveness; just allow yourself to write down the names of any people who come to mind.

One at a time, bring each person to mind, say whatever needs to be said, and as you do this, ask for forgiveness. Since you are guiding this process, take the time to see the person offer you forgiveness in response to your request. Focus on seeing him or her affirmatively extend the forgiveness. Notice and make note of anything that comes up in the process. You may feel the need to do this multiple times before you feel completeness with the process.

Notice during forgiveness if anyone or anything else arises, and keep track of it. Notice whether you can feel the death of an old part of yourself and a rebirth of something new in its place.

The forgiveness process is now complete, and you may return to it at any time if other people should come to mind at a later date.

7. Finding the End of the Rainbow—The Reward

By this stage the hero has survived death, overcome his greatest fear, and now earns the reward that was sought. The hero's reward comes in many forms, including greater knowledge or insight and reconciliation with a loved one. No matter the reward, the hero is ready to celebrate. Now the hero can take a breath and celebrate the accomplishments and the resulting lightness of being, before proceeding to the next stage.

Example: At this stage, Leanne is feeling better and better about herself and is ready to increase the prices she charges to her clients—the ultimate reward of being able to have her business support the lifestyle she's always wanted. She goes through the process, and it is a resounding success, including her profits being up by over 50 percent.

Take a moment to journal about the epiphanies and awarenesses you've gained about your relationship with money—noticing where you've found a reward, a great treasure, an important teaching, or a magic potion. If you haven't arrived at this stage of the process, then dream about what you want the reward to be for all the time and energy you've invested into this process. What do you most want your reward to be?

In the context of your money story, the reward could be the secret that has eluded you about your patterns of behavior with money. Be mindful to notice and acknowledge what you need to know so you can avoid repeating patterns that aren't serving you and your money. Write your reward down so you can remind yourself of the lessons learned.

Depending upon what comes up, you may notice yourself easily getting caught in a washing machine–like cycle in which you are saying the same things you've said to yourself in the past—"I am not enough," or "I try lots of things but nothing ever sticks with me" or "I'm hopeless," etc. If you do get caught, then here are the questions to ask yourself: "What inside of me needs to struggle with this thing? What inside of me needs to keep this trait, feeling, action, or belief in place?"

8. Resurrection—The Road Back to the Ordinary World: Writing Your New Money Story

In most stories, the heroine returns with the solution she has always wanted—a sense of knowing who she is and where she is heading in life. Being in greater connection with her True Self, she returns to the known world to engage in the practical application of what she's learned. This completes the cycle of the journey. Story lines have been resolved, balance has been restored to her life, and the heroine may now embark on a new life, forever influenced by the journey traveled.

Example: After getting her money back on track, Leanne began looking into ways to follow her passion around parenting and coaching other parents who are going through difficult divorces like she experienced. She could feel drawn to serving other women such as herself, and her first group course quickly turned into a successful venture. With her money,

Leanne continues to find ways to invest in the growth of her business while steadily paying down her debt. She also continues her journey of self-understanding—realizing that each day brings more opportunity to become more of her True Self.

To complete this final step you can answer a few additional questions:

What do you want your new experiences with money to look and feel like, now that you can see how the past played out?

How do you see yourself continuing forward? What is most important for you to keep in mind?

What key money areas do you need to pay the most attention to right away?

What additional money work needs to still be done? When do you want to work on these?

Congratulations! You've written your money story, which will continue to evolve as you move forward through the remainder of the steps. Keep in mind that you can repeat this process every time you notice another limiting belief arising. We've all lived many different hero's journeys throughout our lives, and this process is something you can continue to use whenever you need it.

DAILY PRACTICES FOR S IS FOR STORY

1. Engage in process of preparatory practices
2. Breath-work practice—5 minutes
3. Meditation practice—5 minutes
4. Journaling practice—20–40 minutes
5. Dedication and gratitude

MINDFUL MOMENTS OF ACTION

1. How many days did you do your practices?
2. What was the experience like for you?
3. What did you struggle with completing?
4. Is there anything else you would like to note for this step—things to revisit in the future, areas of focus, questions you'd like to have answered?

SUMMARY FOR STEP 5—S IS FOR STORY

Christopher Vogler, author of *The Writer's Journey: Mythic Structure for Writers*,[1] explains how the hero's journey represents the universal human condition of being born into this world, growing, learning, struggling to become an individual, and dying. The word "hero" comes from a Greek root that means to "protect and serve." The hero is connected with self-sacrifice. He is the person who transcends ego, but at first, the hero is all ego. Deeply immersed in the ego's journey, the hero is learning how to incorporate all the parts of himself back into the whole.

By writing your own hero's journey, you gain the power to change your story going forward. All it takes is willingness combined with the belief that it is possible. When we refuse to face our own shadow, we relegate this energy to the unconscious, and from there it exerts its power in a negative and projected form. You've been learning about how your shadow has affected your relationship with money, and the more you come to terms with your shadow, the less friction it will create in your life. That's because when your shadow comes into your conscious awareness and you are not trying to make it wrong, the shadow becomes less rigid in its boundaries and more open to possibility and change. Joseph Campbell said it best: "We must let go of the life we have planned, so as to have the life that is waiting for us."

15

STEP 6—P IS FOR PERMISSION

I've learned that making a "living"
is not the same thing as making a "life."
—MAYA ANGELOU

This step turns your attention to giving yourself permission to create what you most want going forward. This is when we get practical about integrating what you've learned about your past, who you really are, and how you want to engage with money. The emphasis is on using holistic financial planning to help you create a foundation for your personal transformation.

A NEW REALITY FOR FINANCIAL PLANNING

Financial planning is not just about money planning, it is about life planning. This step is about giving yourself permission to create what you really want with your money. It's also about holistically applying what you've learned about yourself to create a financial plan for the future.

Through this process we'll be taking a holistic approach to financial planning, which means we will be looking at the "wholes" in which many elements affect each other simultaneously. The notion of holism helps you know what you want to do first and how much of it you will do so the whole appears.

Take a moment to sit back and think about the rest of your life. What do you want for yourself and your family? What are your needs? What are you dreams? Notice that when you are planning your future, eventually you think about how much money you'll need to fund things like your children's education, retirement, health care, travel, vacation homes, RVs, and so on. It is useful to admit we're so conditioned to thinking about the money before the lifestyle, that oftentimes we hold ourselves back from going for what we really want.

So this time we're going to try it differently. We're going to start by helping you gain clarity in your goals. We'll be using holistic management techniques that were originally developed by Allan Savory for better farm and land management,[1] which I've adapted for financial-planning purposes. Finally, we'll spend time exploring some powerful ways to give yourself permission to create what you most want.

GIVING YOURSELF PERMISSION

Permission is a funny thing—when we were kids many of us couldn't wait to be adults so that we no longer had to ask for permission to do what we wanted to do. The sad thing is that even though we're all grown up now, many of us have never fully given ourselves permission to go after what we most want. Or if we did, there is always a sinking feeling that we're going to get caught doing something we aren't supposed to do.

You've come into this life to sing the song that only you can sing. Everything we've been doing thus far is to help you access who you really are outside of your stories of limitation. It is meant to welcome you into greater intimacy with all of life while realizing what you agreed to in the past and how it no longer needs to keep you from being seen, known, and fully accepted. You have always been doing the best you can to learn and grow, and now is the time to create a life that reflects your truth—with your body, relationships, and with your money.

Imagine for a moment that you are in a very safe space where you are embraced with love, compassion, and understanding—feeling into your True Self at the center of your heart and giving yourself permission to know your truth. Realize all that you have withheld from the light and kept in the darkness and how it is time to fully give yourself permission to be seen and witnessed in your fullest expression. As you give yourself this permission, allow the aspects of yourself that have been hidden from view to be realigned in a higher way.

You are capable of great things even when it feels a bit scary to think about what that means for you. Many people are afraid of success and what comes with it—thinking that in order to be successful we're going to lose the ability to have time to ourselves and for our family. While this can happen, it's not something for you to fear as you are connecting more deeply with your True Self.

Similar to everything we've been covering, your financial success is subjective. Going forward, you have the power to define your own criteria for success. No matter what it means to you, now is the time for you to sing your song, and your relationship with money is here to help you light the way. As you make choices about what financial success and abundance mean to you, you'll begin to take meaningful and powerful steps that bring you toward it.

One of the tools that can help you stay in the light is something I created several years ago called the Wealth Flower. Before coming up with the process, I was at a crossroad and wasn't sure what I wanted to do with my life and my business. Out of a desire to become more deliberate in my actions, I started writing out all the things I most wanted for myself and for my family.

For the first time, I went big with my goals and decided I

wouldn't hold back in expressing what I really wanted. I'll admit that I didn't want to share my Wealth Flower with anyone, out of fear of what people, including my husband, would say about what I had written. Yet after a few weeks I got up the courage to share it with my husband, my coach, and my spiritual mentor, which made it all the more real.

The goals that I wrote about in the Wealth Flower included all the main areas of my life—health, relationships, finances, business, environment, and spirituality. I knew it would take time to bring them into reality, but, sure enough, one by one they did. Each would turn out to have teachings associated with it that I needed to receive before moving on to the next. They weren't always easy to accomplish, and some would drop away as I realized they weren't as important to me as I first thought. But what remained and would eventually be achieved were deeply aligned with my wishes for a better life in which I could make a bigger impact in the lives of others. Plus, for the first time, the achievement of the goals that centered around peace of mind were the ones that became far more important than the financial ones.

A few of the biggest goals I set included the selling of our large custom-designed home that my husband had built for us, moving to a warmer climate than where we were living in the Lake Tahoe area of the Sierra Nevada, getting rid of much of our furniture and stuff, getting my daughter well-set financially for college, pulling my son out of school to be with us as we took time off to travel for a year.

Quite surprisingly, within seven months, just about everything had been accomplished, even though it wasn't something that I was forcing into action. Mostly I was focused on helping my husband get on board with why my goals would also help him live his best life, too. Thankfully he acquiesced, and together we began bringing the goals into reality. While I can't say it was an easy time for us, it worked out beyond our wildest dreams in the end.

When you're married and have been raising a family together

for over twenty-eight years, you accumulate a lot of stuff, especially when you have a four-thousand-square-foot home with three garage bays and a storage building on five acres. The amount of physical (and emotional) cleansing that took place was incredible. This clearing process then created the opportunity to put our remaining things in storage and move to Hawaii for several months, where we focused on enjoying life for an extended time without much in the way of economic pressures.

CREATING FLOW

The experience of getting rid of our stuff turned into a symbolic process of death to the old and birth to the new. In the busyness of our lives toward the end of our time in Truckee, I don't think we had time to fully understand what we had done until we arrived in Hawaii. While the first few weeks were just like any other vacation, eventually we started to understand what it meant to live your life without obligation. I'll be honest and share that it wasn't easy to live this way. For so many years we had been going at top speed, and then to put the brakes on life was disconcerting, especially for my husband. He even commented about three weeks into the trip that he was thinking about getting a job in Hawaii because it felt uncomfortable to not be working. Thankfully, just giving words to it helped him see how it was merely the discomfort of not knowing what to do that was bothering him.

About one month into our travels everything came together quite magically. We were attending an infamous haunted house at an old high school near Makawao on the island of Maui, and something happened that evening that finally allowed us to really, really have fun. It was almost like we had been faking the fun up until that day when everything changed.

While walking down the dark path outside of the school as part of the haunting experience that was filled with real human "zombies," we were startled several times so much that I had to rely on my son and my husband to help me through it. My husband, Tim, being his not-so-funny self, decided to scare me from behind. By this time, after seeing so many zombies walking around us, I was already on high alert, and so when he decided to grab me from behind, I screamed louder than I've ever screamed before and even peed my pants. I am not sure which thing bothered me more—the fact that Tim had scared me or that Tim and Aidan were laughing so hard they made me start laughing and I almost did it again.

The joy of being in the moment with each other led us to feel such incredible intimacy, which would carry us through our next several months of traveling together. I think the shift came from letting go of the idea that everything has to be planned out and organized into nice, perfect boxes. In our time together we learned how to be okay with life being messy and us not knowing what was happening from one day to the next. After that we became very fluid, flexible, and in flow with each day as it came.

Looking back, I see that we had to create new beliefs in place of the old we were living within. To do this, Tim and I each had to find new beliefs that motivated us to feel excited about life and eager to continue on our trip. In the end we found common ground that allowed each of us to expand and grow through our traveling experiences in our own unique ways. We stepped into the flow of life while giving ourselves permission to love every moment of it.

To help you get started and give yourself greater permission to create what you most want, let's consider the components that make up your financial plan. Later on, you'll have a chance to complete your own Wealth Flower, but first we'll start by thinking about your finances as an ecosystem that includes a network of interconnected activities.

YOUR FINANCIAL ECOSYSTEM

Your financial ecosystem is composed of five foundational blocks:

- income—the money you receive into your asset accounts
- expenses—the money that is deducted from your asset accounts
- assets—that which you own
- liabilities—that which you owe to others
- life energy—the energy behind all that you are and all that you do

Then there are many types of activities involved in managing your financial ecosystem, which include but are not limited to the following:

- money tracking
- credit-score management
- emergency fund
- debt/liability management
- spending and saving strategy
- personal growth and quality of life
- investing
- time management
- collaboration with financial partners
- insurance planning
- estate planning
- home-mortgage management
- giving and being of service to others
- creation and monitoring of financial plan

Finally, we have the six core determinants that affect your quality of life, which also happen to be the sections you'll be exploring as part of the Wealth Flower:

- health
- finance/money
- business/career
- relationships
- spiritual and emotional health
- environment

The goal, when engaging in holistic financial planning, is to take all of these considerations into mind as you chart your plan. Since not everything will apply to you nor be of great importance, the framework is meant to be a guideline to help you in preparing a plan that custom-fits you.

GUIDELINES TO CONSIDER FOR HOLISTIC FINANCIAL PLANNING

The Whole Is Greater Than the Sum of Its Parts

Taking a holistic approach to financial planning allows you to create a long-term sustainable plan for your future. It is based on the premise, established by the creator of Savory Institute, Allan Savory, "that no whole, be it a family, a business, a community, or a nation, can be managed without looking inward to the lesser wholes that combine to form it, and *outward to the greater wholes of which it is a member.*"[2] He notes how we put a great deal of emphasis on our tasks without reflecting on how we work within a greater whole. Allan's work helps us remember that it is only by looking at the bigger picture that we are likely to take responsibility for the long-term consequences of our actions.

Identify Your Weak Links

Weak links are the areas of your plan where, if anything is going to break down, it will likely happen as a result of these things. By clearly knowing your weakest links, you can better engage in long-term planning and accumulation of assets, because now you know where things could go wrong in your plan. Examples of financial-planning weak links include unexpected expenses that cause inconsistent saving, increases in debt financing rates, illness, physical injuries for yourself and/or your family members, stock market crashes, housing market downturns, inflation, decreases in income, pregnancy, large home repairs, cars breaking down, etc. As a business owner, they may also include things like poor sales, poor products, or downturns in the business cycle.

There are many ways we can better plan for dealing with these challenges, including emergency accounts, cash savings that provide you with six to twelve months of living expenses, living well beneath your income, having health insurance, and long-term care insurance for elderly parents.

Avoid the Optimism Trap

Far too often, financial planners get swept away by their numbers without considering weak links. Financial planners' models and spreadsheets are so alluring and exciting that we become awed by their projections without stepping back to think about the reality and complete unpredictability of life. Many people are not going to be prepared for the future in the same way that the models indicate. This has a lot to do with the fact that weak links are likely to occur throughout our earning years, combined with the fact that many issues arise that drain our resources unexpectedly, both today and into the future. Personally, I've been able to avoid the optimism trap by making choices to live more frugally regardless of our income. Others will make the choice to increase their income while keeping a watchful eye on expenses. The point is that for many of us, we want to be conservative in the face of the fact that life happens and it is always going to be an adventure.

Avoid the Debt Trap

A lot could be said about the negative consequences of debt and how important it is to be planning to be debt-free at some point in the future. Granted, this won't be possible for everyone, but setting an intention to pay off debt is one of the most powerful things you can take away from this process. Debt is not something we ever want to get comfortable about; if you use it wisely it can help your life immensely, but at the same time, the goal is not to keep debt but to pay it off. Living a debt-free life is incredible because of the limitless number of choices that appear as a result. There is no reason to not want to be debt-free. Give yourself permission to live this way even if you don't know how to get there just yet.

Cash (Flow) Is King

You've heard it before, and it is a good time to remind you that cash flow is incredibly important whether you are managing your household or a business. Knowing how much cash you have available at any moment in time is a helpful skill to develop—at least so that you know you have what you need when you need it. Having a strong cash-management policy for yourself is what helps you avoid late fees, bank charges, unnecessary last-minute runs to the bank, and, ultimately, problems with your credit score, which drives up your cost of debt and financing.

By establishing a predictable and recurring revenue stream of income you become better able to mitigate risk in your finances. Plus nothing compares to the freedom that comes by knowing you've created an evergreen flow of cash into your accounts every month.

Finding ways to create cash flow without being dependent upon traditional forms of work was one of my goals when we sold everything and traveled for a year. While it was great to not have to worry about our finances and how we were making money, in the back of my mind I knew that without a stready stream of cash flow we weren't as free as we wanted to be. It also meant that we were living on our savings, which wasn't going to last forever. This inspired me to begin thinking creatively of how we could use our savings to create new streams of income that allowed our money to work harder for us.

Prior to moving to Sedona we bought our first commercial building with four rental spaces and spent the next few years learning how to become commercial real estate landlords. Once that was mastered we then built a guest home on the property we were living on in Sedona and began learning how to rent it out as a short term vacation rental. The combination of the two properties brought in enough income to pay all of our household expenses, which inspired us to purchase and rent out another property which created enough income that allowed us to start saving money again.

The point in sharing all of this is to inspire you to think of ways you can create predictable revenue streams beyond your job or business income—this ability becomes all the more important when you no longer wish to work primarily for the money. I've met many people over the years who've focused on buying real estate for this exact reason, which has led them to building wealth way beyond their wildest dreams as well as bring in cash flow that gives them the privilege of not having to work more than a few hours a week.

DAILY PRACTICES FOR P IS FOR PERMISSION

1. Engage in process of preparatory practices
2. Breath-work practice—5 minutes
3. Meditation practice—5 minutes

4. Journaling practice—20–40 minutes
5. Dedication and gratitude

MINDFUL MOMENTS OF REFLECTION

Developing Your Holistic Financial Plan

1. *Determine key decision makers in your life.* List the people who are closest to you. List key decision makers when it comes to important decisions for you and your family. List mentors you have to help with you financial matters. List other important figures when it comes to life planning.

2. *Define your resource base and financial resources; this is what you have to work with.* You'll want to start by completing your personal net-worth statement (see the facing page).

   If you discover that your net worth is a negative amount, please know this isn't all that uncommon. A Federal Reserve Bank of New York study[3] found that over 15 percent of U.S. households, or about nineteen million families have a less than or equal to zero net worth, often with the single largest culprit being student debt. Things like student loans, mortgages, the cost of health expenses, and upside-down car loans (where the car loses value faster than your loan is being paid off) can all contribute to having a negative net worth. The goal is to have this situation be a temporary one, and so by knowing where you are, it becomes more likely that you'll focus on ways to pay down debt faster while keeping track of your progress.

3. *Create quality-of-life goals (the Wealth Flower exercise).* Next you'll want to focus on creating quality-of-life goals; these are goals that reflect your more important and meaningful dreams and wishes. Begin by reviewing the following categories:

- Health
- Finance/money
- Business/career
- Relationships
- Spiritual and emotional health
- Environment

YOUR PERSONAL NET-WORTH STATEMENT

ASSETS

Liquid Assets $_____
(Cash, checking, savings, treasury bills,
   no penalty CDs)

Investments $_____
(IRAs, 401Ks, Other Stock, Bond and
   Investment Accounts)

Value of real estate $_____

Total assets $_____

LIABILITIES

Current Debt $_____
(Credit cards, student loans,
car loans, personal loans)

Long-term Debt $_____
(Mortgages)
Home Equity Lines of Credit
Total Liabilities $_____

TOTAL NET WORTH

(Total Assets minus Total Liabilities) $_____

Then take a moment to write down where you want to be in each of these areas of your life one year, five years, and ten years from now. Depending upon your age, you may wish to plan for longer time horizons to include college savings and retirement planning.

- Who and what do you love?
- How do you like to spend your time?
- What do you love to do?
- What do you most value?
- What do you enjoy spending money on?
- What are you doing in your career/business that you *love* doing?
- What do you wish you were doing more of when it comes to your career/business?
- If you were to have more free time, how would you spend it?

Fast-forward to the end of your lifetime. What did your life look like when you lived according to your own terms and fulfilled your dreams?

4. *Use your quality-of-life goals to help you establish financial goals.* As you establish and write down what you want to focus on, it is a best practice to make sure you are setting SMART goals. SMART stands for "specific, measurable, attainable, relevant, and timely." By paying attention to each of these factors as you put them down on paper, it becomes easier and more likely that you'll be able to bring your goals into reality.

Reevaluate this list after you've gone through "Step 7—E Is for Evidence," which is featured in chapter 16 and add anything additional that comes up. As you move through each of the seven phases of building your financial house, you will want to extract any financial tasks you have not completed and add them to your goals. Note: It is a good idea to limit the number of financial goals you are working toward to five, maybe ten if you are feeling particularly ambitious. This allows you to make sure these goals are completed before you add additional goals—which can help you avoid feeling overwhelmed and disappointed with your progress.

5. *Document your financial goals while breaking them into money actions that you take on a daily basis.* For each of the goals you have set for yourself in step 4, take time to break each of the goals into the smallest tasks necessary to complete them.

To give you an example, let's say you want to begin tracking your money so you know how much you are spending on a monthly basis. Your detailed task list could look something like this:

- Week 1—Research what software options are available for tracking money by asking friends and family (or post in the Mindful Millionaire Community) what applications people are using for tracking their money.
- Week 1—Determine features of what you most want to track.
- Week 2—Create a spreadsheet of the various apps and tools available, with the features most important to you highlighted.
- Week 2—Complete a comparison of the options and use this to decide which application to set up.
- Week 3—Purchase app and set up tracking system by linking it to banking, loans, and credit card data.
- Week 4—Begin process of using system, watching videos and other training tools to take advantage of features and benefits of the app.
- Week 5—Money tracking system is up and running. Time to set a new goal with detailed tasks broken out.

6. Put it all together. Share your financial goals with your financial partners (advisor, bankers, insurance agents, etc.) so they are familiar with the goals you've set for yourself.

At this stage you will want to continue to monitor and adjust your financial plan as you achieve your goals and set new goals for yourself. The idea is for your financial plan to be an ongoing tool you enjoy reviewing and adjusting according to its ability to help you create the life you really want to be living.

MINDFUL MOMENTS OF ACTION

1. How many days did you do your practices?
2. What was the experience like for you?
3. What did you struggle with completing?
4. Is there anything else you would like to note for this step—things to revisit in the future, areas of focus, questions you'd like to have answered?

SUMMARY OF STEP 6—P IS FOR PERMISSION

Now that you've explored your financial realities in greater specificity, you are ready to give yourself permission to create what you most want going forward. This permission stems from being conscious about who you really are, what you most want for yourself, and then bringing your finances into the equation to support the life you really want to be living. This process is drastically different from permission that centers around hopes, dreams, and prayers that things will someday turn around for the better. This process is here to help you take action and manifest from your highest sense of self so that you are motivated and inspired to do what it takes to get there. The life you've been wanting to create is awaiting your entry.

16

STEP 7—E IS FOR EVIDENCE

Life isn't about finding yourself.
Life is about creating yourself.
—GEORGE BERNARD SHAW

This step tackles the financial-planning process and details specific actions you'll want to put in place. You'll also be developing your practical financial knowledge based on what you've learned about your limiting beliefs and scarcity patterns of the past. You will identify immediate changes and strategies that will help you jump-start your future. The idea here is to ensure your financial life becomes a reflection of your True Self.

By now you've come a long way and you are ready to take all that you've learned about yourself and put it into practice with your money. *Woop!* This is the moment you've been waiting for (drum roll, please). It is *time* to take back control of your money and set yourself up for success. It's time to make some big changes that will last for the rest of your life. It's time to ensure that your finances are set up so they're reflecting your core values and supporting the wholeness of who you are becoming. It's time to use money to help you stretch yourself and expand into the life you really want to be living. After all, the meaning of life is to be found in the positive quest of achieving the goals you set for yourself while enjoying the process of getting there.

I am so excited for you. This has the potential to be magical in ways you might not be able to understand fully. I only know of its magic because I've been living this way for the past few years, and it is something I wish for you to experience from the bottom of my heart. So let's dive in!

BUILDING AND MAINTAINING YOUR FINANCIAL HOUSE

For nearly thirty years, my husband and I have been working together to build homes for our family: he does the design and building and I help in the planning, design, financing, and decorating. We make a great team, as we both know our strengths and we complement each other nicely. We've gone through this process more than eight times, and I feel like we're experts when it comes to building homes. After doing it so many times I've come to see that building your financial house is not all that different from building a traditional house, and for that reason I decided to connect IPROSPER to the stages of building your financial house—so you can clearly see all stages of the process.

My sense is that you will review the stages, activities, and goals and then decide where you need to go back and fill in the holes and gaps in your own financial house. For everyone it will be different, and yet if you wish to create financial freedom for yourself—whether you earn it or are inheriting it—you will want to take the time to make sure your house is rock solid. Your family will appreciate it, and you will sleep better at night knowing you are doing what you need to do to take care of these important aspects of life and financial planning.

The following tips, tools, and suggestions are broken down into the respective chakras you've already identified and are working on. The goal of following these suggestions is to help ensure you feel capable of taking responsibility for your money management. Aristotle once said, "For the things we have to learn before we can do them, we learn by doing them."[1] This applies perfectly to what you'll be embarking upon next, as it is all about taking action and learning by doing.

You may want to start at the beginning to ensure you've covered all the steps. Please remember to maintain your mindfulness as you move through this process. When you hit resistance, just allow yourself to understand that you are doing the best you can and that it's okay to not feel good about something. Then take some time to get curious and allow yourself to witness your feelings and pay attention to what they are revealing to you. Again, I can't help but quote Aristotle, who, like me, is cheering you on as you move through this process: "Men acquire a particular quality by constantly acting a particular way. . . . You become just by performing just actions, temperate by performing temperate actions, brave by performing brave actions."[2] Your bravery is evident here, and you are becoming exactly who you most want to be through your actions. By doing this process more than once, it will get easier and you'll find yourself living more consciously and deliberately.

STAGE 1: PREPARING THE BUILDING SITE— ROOT CHAKRA

As you know by now, the root chakra is about making sure you feel safe and supported by the life you've created. It's about knowing you have sufficient income to take care of your own basic needs without having to live in debt.

If you're currently supported by others, there's nothing wrong with that as long as it feels good to you and makes sense for all concerned. However, if you are feeling the need and desire to earn more money, then I encourage you to also heed that call and try out the following income generating ideas and activities.

Money Activities

Money Tracking

- Complete all the stages provided as part of writing your holistic financial plan in chapter 15.
- Start a money-fears journal. Rather than worrying about money, create a journal where you write about what you are afraid of and walk yourself through the process of relaxing and letting go of the fear, reminding yourself it is just a thought and you are taking daily steps to feel better.
- Daily and weekly income and expense tracking:[3] consistently track your income and expenses to determine any shortfalls. Learn what your monthly disposable income is.

Credit Score

- In the United States, go to www.annualcreditreport.com to obtain a free copy of your credit report. Bad credit can affect your life in a lot of ways, limiting your options and driving up the rates you pay for accessing credit, including for credit cards, car loans, and mortgages.
  As you review your credit report, take time to fix any mistakes by contacting your creditors or the three major credit agencies: TransUnion, Equifax, and Experian.

Close unused credit accounts, and use your credit report to identify items that need to be disputed with the agencies.

- Know your debt-to-income ratio, which is your total monthly debt (as determined by totaling up your minimum monthly credit payments) divided by your monthly gross income. This is a number that lenders use to determine your creditworthiness, and your target is to have it be less than 40 percent, while 20 percent or less is ideal; over 40 percent is stressed.

Income Generation

- In cases where income shortfalls exist, create income generating ideas to increase income: ask for a raise, create a freelance job on the side, create a new revenue stream for your business, or increase your prices.
- Your top priority at this time is increasing your cash flow, *not* accumulating stuff or even experiences—that comes later after you figure out how to have a strong, steady flow of cash coming in every month!

Emergency Funds

- Build an emergency fund with four months' worth of nondiscretionary (mandatory expenses that must be paid each month) in a cash savings account.
- Have access to a home equity line of credit to use in cases of emergency.
- Keep one to two months' worth of cash for personal expenses at home in a safe or in a safety deposit box.

Savings

- 401K retirement saving at work: at the very least take advantage of contributing enough to receive employer match.
- For any saving beyond emergency and retirement funds, put your money in stress-free investments, like CDs and high-interest-rate savings accounts.

Insurance Planning

- Confirm you have proper insurance for disasters, unexpected losses, and catastrophes, including auto, home, renters', health, and business insurance.

Estate Planning

- Complete a financial inventory for loved ones should anything happen to you, to ensure that everyone knows where your bank accounts and other important documents can be found.
- Complete a living will, also called an advanced-care directive, that stipulates what should happen for your care should you become incapacitated. Also ask your adult children to do the same.
- Complete a basic will that stipulates what should happen to your belongings, your assets, and also for the care of any minor children.

Money "Feeling" Goals

- Consider what can be done to help you sleep better at night, with the goal of helping you feel good about where you are with your finances.

STAGE 2: POURING THE FOUNDATION—SACRAL CHAKRA

The sacral chakra, when it comes to money, is about feeling good about your finances, and unfortunately for those who have a lot of debt, feeling good is *not* an easy thing to do. Knowing you have a plan for paying down your debt and saving money is a crucial part of balancing and harmonizing your sacral chakra. To do this you must have a strong, consistent, and reliable stream of cash flowing into your life. This part of your journey is about learning how to save money consistently. One way to think about it is to start with your income and then focus on saving money *before* you think about spending money. How much are you going to save each week, month, year? Commit to that goal and set up an automatic process so your saving happens no matter what. Then you use what is left over to fund your expenses and consumables. By paying yourself first through your saving behavior, you can't help but adjust what you are spending while telling yourself that you are your most valuable asset.

During this phase, you'll also want to pay close attention to your numbers (income, expenses, monthly saving, monthly fees, and so on) on a daily, weekly, and monthly basis so that you can become mindful of how you are spending your money and ensuring it is allocated in a way that supports your short- and long-term goals.

Money Activities

Money Tracking

- Complete your net-worth statement in chapter 15, if you haven't already.[4]
- Your priority is to continue growing your cash flow, paying off debt, and increasing your saving, *not* accumulating stuff or even experiences.

- Set up a budgeting software tool. Many of my clients use www.youneedabudget.com and have been very happy with their results. You might also consider Microsoft Money, Quicken, or other software programs. The most important thing is that you make a commitment and stick with it for ninety days before giving up; by then you'll have made using such a tool into a habit and it won't be so hard to keep it going.
- Decide on your allocations for expense management: consider limiting your mandatory monthly ("needs") expenses to 50 percent max of your disposable income, your discretionary expenses (for fun and extras) to 25 percent, and budget 15 percent for debt payoff, and 10 percent for mandatory and automatic saving.
- To curb spending, consider implementing a cash envelope system, in which all of your spendable income is divided into categorical envelopes to be used to meet your needs and wants. This is a way of ensuring you only spend what you have budgeted to spend and nothing more.
- Another approach that requires more diligence is to cut up credit cards and cancel accounts to prevent you from spending more money than you have.

Spending and Saving

- Establish a value-based spending plan that stipulates your goals for saving and debt payoff based on the values that are most important to you, knowing that if something doesn't fit into your core values, then you will need to wait at least three days before you make the purchase. If after three days the need is still there, then you can decide what you wish to do, after the emotion of the purchase has receded.

- Consider reducing access to your savings account and only putting money into your checking account when you know it is accounted for in your spending plan. To make your savings account more difficult to access, you could keep it at a different bank or credit union from where your checking account is held and have your paychecks or business income go directly into your savings account rather than checking. Even though electronically your money is mostly at your fingertips these days, the process of having to move money from one bank to another is one more step to prevent you from spending money you would prefer to save.

- Take a brutally honest look at your life to see where you could be just as happy and at the same time be spending less to live.

- Get familiar with the process of daily trade-offs to achieve your saving goals. Think, "If I am going to buy this, then I can't have that."

- If possible, establish an automatic savings account where 5–10 percent of the money in your checking account regularly sweeps into a savings account, so you're thinking of yourself as a saver rather than a spender.

Debt Management

- Establish a debt-payoff plan. Review strategies online to determine which makes the most sense for you when considering credit cards, student loans, car loans, and so on. Pick a debt-payoff plan and, whatever you do, stick with it until your debt is paid off. Especially focus on paying off any double-digit interest loans first.

Money Visioning

- Start a gratitude journal or practice wherein you spend five minutes every day focused on what you are grateful for in your life.

For Those in a Partner Relationship

- Discuss what you've learned about yourself during the IPROSPER process and encourage your partner to also go through the process by reading this book when the time is right.
- Get financially "naked" and share your completed exercises in steps 1–7 with each other. Talk about what is coming up and how you can support one another in the process of becoming financially well. The more open you are, the greater the mutual understanding and support you can give to each other. Approaching this process from love rather than fear will help the conversations flow more smoothly.
- Notice that if sharing your exercises in steps 1–7 with your partner seems too vulnerable, then it is an area for greater attention when you feel ready. Do not push yourself to do things that you do not feel right about; instead, focus on your own journey while mindfully thinking about what is holding you back from expressing it with your partner.

For Parents

- Adding family members requires long-term shifts in your budget. Do your best to keep expenses to a minimum: borrow or buy used when possible, and do what you can to save for college or an education account that can be used by your child when that time comes, rather than spending on unnecessary items.

Money "Feeling" Goals

- Knowing that your goal is to be more aware of how you feel, notice the ways in which you can provide greater self-compassion to yourself beyond things that cost money. It can be as simple as rubbing your own neck or feet, asking your partner to exchange massages, talking to a friend on the phone, or going for a walk in nature.

STAGE 3: THE FRAMING AND ROOF OF THE HOME— SOLAR PLEXUS CHAKRA

The solar plexus chakra, when it comes to money, involves feeling powerful with how you're managing your finances. This is a big leap for anyone who has struggled with money management in the past, because when you start engaging in these practices, you will be feeling your personal power in a bigger way than ever before. For that reason it is an exciting transition for many people, and if you are new to feeling powerful with your money, take a deep breath and proceed with a big smile on your face, because this is a big, big deal for you.

You are building your financial advisory team and learning about how to take greater responsibility for your finances. You are also keeping an eye out for increasing your income and giving yourself the opportunity to pay down debt and/or increase your savings.

Money Activities

Collaboration with Financial Partners

- Develop a list of money mentors. These are people in your life you'd like to learn from and seek the counsel of when making big money decisions. Then reach out and ask them to be on your money mentor team and what areas of speciality they are comfortable helping you with.
- If you haven't already, consider asking friends for referrals to a few CPAs to interview and to help you with tax planning. Compare options, ask pricing, and decide on the best person to assist you going forward. Make sure the person is eager to assist you with learning how to lower taxes in the near and longer term.
- Ask friends for referrals to two or three financial advisors. Meet with all of them to see how they can help you achieve your financial goals. Ask about fees and approaches to managing money. Make your final decision and move forward in getting initial accounts set up.
- Consider setting up your own investment account at a low cost brokerage firm like Vanguard or Fidelity Investments.

Income Management

- You may want to complete an income review, check inside about how you feel with your current income and whether or not you feel the need to begin testing ways to increase your income. If so, then start developing ideas and strategies accordingly. Don't be afraid to fail with your trials; just be afraid of what might happen when you don't try.

Money Tracking

- Increase your income or decrease your expenses so that your savings rate grows to 45 percent of your disposable income, your discretionary expenses (for fun and extras) to 25 percent, and use 20 percent to expedite debt payoff and 10 percent for mandatory and automatic saving. You may need to move to a less-expensive area or take a new job to be in a position to save this much of your income.
- Create a journal to keep track of large purchases you know you will need to buy in the future, according to approximate date of purchase and cost of purchase, so that you can begin to save and pay cash for those purchases (cars, college, home, etc.).
- Update your net-worth statement (from chapter 15).
- Conduct an inventory of the fees you are paying for your credit cards, bank accounts, financial advising, taxes, and anything else that comes to mind. Reach out to the companies you do business with to see if fees can be lowered per your good behavior and customer relationship.
- When monitoring your budget, pay close attention to opportunities to lower monthly fees whenever possible— including phone and internet services, cable, wireless service, satellite radio, and other satellite services. Never assume that your fees cannot be lowered.
- Consider debt consolidation as an option if it can help you become more effective at paying off your debt.

Insurance Planning

- Meet with your insurance professional and review your insurance policies. Ask the person to help you understand the benefits of purchasing umbrella policies to cover you for additional loss exposure. Also ask for information about disability and life insurance as needed. Ask friends for referrals to insurance professionals they've used in the past, if you don't have one already.

- Conduct a review of all your insurance policies to confirm that you have sufficient coverage for your home, cars, business, family members, household employees, and other insurable assets.
- Comparison-shop your policies with at least one other insurance company.

Tax Planning

- Meet with your CPA or tax-planning professional to discuss tax strategies.
- Do research on your own about tax rules and tax planning so that you know the questions to ask of your tax planner. Be sure you are accurately paying taxes, including any payments that need to be made throughout the year. Lack of understanding of your taxes can lead to tens or even hundreds of thousands of dollars in taxes over your lifetime. Additionally, it is a good idea to print out your taxes and review them each year for errors and mistakes that are very common and would not be caught without your review or, in some cases, an IRS audit, which is always better to avoid.

Debt Management

- Review any credit cards you are paying off and other outstanding loans to see if rates can be lowered by moving debt to another company. Pay attention to fees and penalties when applicable.

Home Mortgage Management

- Conduct a mortgage review to ensure your rate is in alignment with the current mortgage rates. Check if there is a chance of lowering the time to pay off your loan by accepting a ten-, fifteen-, or twenty-year term mortgage with a lower rate than you are currently paying. Or consider changing the amortization schedule on your existing mortgage so that you can pay it off faster by making larger payments.

For Parents

- Set up tax-advantaged college savings or tuition savings accounts for children.

For Business Owners

- If you do not already have an attorney, consider asking friends for referrals and establishing relationships for future reference.
- Establish a business savings account and start saving toward having two months' worth of business expenses saved for emergencies.
- Hire a bookkeeper, perhaps one recommended by your CPA or other business colleagues.
- Evaluate your business structure—sole proprietorship, LLC, S Corp—and speak with an attorney about costs to establish it, and speak with your CPA about tax benefits.
- Set up a retirement account for your business—IRA, SEP, SIMPLE—and speak with bankers, your CPA, and your financial advisor about options.

Money "Feeling" Goals

- With the goal of feeling more powerful in all aspects of your life, consider what you can do to help gain a greater sense of your own financial power.
- Give yourself a great deal of praise around all that you've accomplished.

STAGE 4: WALLS, WINDOWS, AND INSULATION— HEART CHAKRA

As you may recall, the heart chakra is about feeling loved and appreciated. This means you're feeling stronger than ever before about your money management, and you're acknowledging that it's time for the value you are providing in the world to be showing up with your money. If you're giving more value than you are receiving back, after a while you're likely to feel drained. So there you go: now it is time to check in and make sure your money is in alignment with what you are bringing into the world through who you are and what you're doing with your actions.

Your income and net worth are growing, and you feel a sense of appreciation for what you've created for yourself and for all those you are in service to. You're taking greater responsibility by learning about your money and starting to ask yourself questions about creating streams of passive income through your assets.

Money Activities

Income Management

- Complete an income review by asking yourself how you feel about your compensation. Remember that income

growth is a reflection of your inner growth. On a scale
of 1 to 10, 10 being highest—how well do you feel you
are compensated for what you are doing currently? If you
rated yourself under 5, consider what you need to do to
uplevel your offerings (at work or in your business) so that
you can increase your income in the coming six to twelve
months. If you feel your level is above 5 but lower than 8,
then ask yourself why you feel the value you are providing
in the world is worth more than you are being paid. Is
there anything you can do to ensure that others know your
value is worth more than what they are paying you? If so,
proceed accordingly to do what you need to do to increase
your income. If your level is at 8 or above, you may be fine
where you are now or you may consider asking for a raise
or increasing your prices. Remember to always consider
the fact that if you are paying close attention to the value
you are creating in the world for your employer, clients,
and so on, then it is a lot easier to ask to be paid for your
contributions.

- Continue to increase your business revenue by leveraging
  your strengths and talents, working with business mentors
  and coaches who can push you outside of your comfort
  zone.

Investing

- Begin investing in a balanced portfolio of stocks and
  bonds—either working with your advisor to develop
  the best options for you and your preferred level of risk,
  or reading books and taking classes to increase your
  knowledge of investing best practices.
- Depending upon your saved assets and interest,
  you may begin to research non-primary-home real

estate ownership opportunities (as a full-time or vacation rental).

Giving

- Establish a charitable-giving plan that includes 5–10 percent of your income, ensuring you are regularly giving to causes you believe in.

Estate Planning

- For those with families, now is a great time to begin learning about estate planning and ways to ensure that your family is taken care of should anything happen to you. This may include meeting with an estate-planning attorney to understand your options.
- Establish a vision for your legacy and then execute a properly documented trust or will and power of attorney for your estate.

Mortgage Management

- For those with mortgages, now is a great time to take a deep-dive look at your mortgage, the rate you are paying, and the amortization schedule. If you have already paid off all other debt, then you may shift gears toward paying off your mortgage more quickly than it was originally set up for or to refinance to a shorter term, if rates are lower enough for that to make sense—while there is no rule of thumb to follow, the most important factor to take into consideration when refinancing is to compare the total cost of financing for the various scenarios you are considering. People who refinance to a lower rate can

easily end up spending more on the total cost of financing
due to lengthening rather than shortening the time it
takes to pay off the mortgage.

For Business Owners

- As your income increases and you have more to contribute
  to savings, this is a good time to meet with your financial
  advisor to discuss upleveling your retirement plan—
  moving from a SEP to a 401(k) or from a SIMPLE IRA to
  a SEP—with the goal of saving as much as you can while
  giving yourself a tax break for doing so.

Money "Feeling" Goals

- Creating the opportunity to receive appreciation in the
  form of money is a wonderful experience. Receiving more
  so that it comes into alignment with giving is a balanced
  and harmonious state of awareness that fuels your desire
  to give even more.

STAGE 5: EXTERIOR FEATURES OF HOME— THROAT CHAKRA

The throat chakra is about speaking your truth authentically and
stepping into a sense of your own significance. When it comes to
your money, you're likely to be living in flow with your saving and
investment practices and growing your net worth more quickly than
in the past. Your investments are starting to pay off and you feel
more comfortable managing your advisors to create a cohesive team
that supports your growth. The other big realization that is likely to
come into your mind and heart is that no one is ever going to care

about your money like you do. This means that now it is your job to become an exemplary steward of your money.

One way to think about the throat chakra and better managing your money is that this stage is about knowing the difference between delegating money management responsibility and abdicating it. When you delegate aspects of money management to others you are still the person overseeing it, which means you are in charge of making sure your investment and financial advisors are following your directions. Far too many times people have left themselves vulnerable to the behavior of unsavory advisors because instead of delegating they are abdicating their responsibilities for the care and growth of their money. This is exactly what happened in the many Ponzi schemes over the years including the one orchestrated by Bernie Madoff.[5] A Ponzi scheme is a form of fraud where early investors are paid out a high rate of return at the expense of new investors who were also promised high returns. Granted not all investment advisors are out to get you, but when you know it is your responsibility and not anyone else's to be the director of your money you become far less susceptible to others' mistakes. Learning how to delegate your money and investment management requires you to know enough that you can ask good questions of your advisors, which takes time and energy, and yet it is one of the best investments you can ever make.

Money Activities

Income Generation

- Now more than ever before, you are leveraging your expertise to create a strong cash flow from your work.
- If you have a business and you've focused on the growth of your business, then your income is exponentially increasing.

- If you are working for others, your income is escalating according to increases in your salary, bonuses, and stock options.
- Building wealth is likely to come from channeling the money left over after bills are paid into investments like a business venture or real estate.

Debt Payoff and Savings

- Develop an automated process for moving saved assets into cash-flow-creating investments.
- Don't do anything with money unless it allows you to sleep soundly at night. Question your decisions and sit with them for at least seventy-two hours before buying anything.
- Take steps every day to be more deliberate with your money.

Money Tracking

- Update your net-worth statement (from chapter 15), revisit your financial mission statement, and establish your personal investment philosophy with your financial advisor (if applicable).
- Now that your income has likely risen, or at the very least your monthly expenses have been reduced, you can work toward taking care of your nondiscretionary expenses with only 30–40 percent of your income; another 20 percent allows you to take vacations and engage in fun activities, 10 percent goes toward charitable causes, and the remaining money (30–40 percent) is saved and/or used to pay off any remaining debt.

Collaboration with Financial Partners

- Your team of advisors is rock solid and they are willing to communicate with one another to help you save on taxes, protect your assets, and continue to grow your holdings. You have regular meetings calendared at least quarterly with your CPA, financial advisor, and annually with your insurance advisor.
- You're actively paying attention to ways you can save time, which is a far more precious asset than money is at this stage. Finding a harmonious balance here is an art not a science and depends upon your income level. The more you earn, the more priceless time becomes in comparison to money.

Investing

- Discover new ways to accelerate your investment income.
- As your portfolio of investments broadens to include those that allow you to diversify into not only stocks, bonds, and other publicly traded securities, perhaps you buy additional real estate through direct ownership or partnerships or you invest in other businesses.
- You may also meet with your investment advisor and/ or attorney to analyze investments and assess the risks associated to ensure they fit with your goals and objectives.
- Depending upon your willingness to take risks when investing in the stock market, you may wish to speak with your financial advisor about stop-loss measures to ensure that you are not more exposed to market swings than absolutely necessary, or at least so you know what to

expect if and when the market drops significantly. It is far better to be prepared for how you will handle downturns when you are not faced with reactive decisions.

- Your focus now is shifting toward earning economic freedom, where your non-work-related income exceeds your expenses.
- Depending upon your core values and concerns about the environment, you may wish to learn more about investing in socially responsible and sustainable strategies for your investments.
- Depending upon your saved assets and interest level, you may want to invest in non-primary-home real estate ownership opportunities (as a full-time or vacation rental).
- Depending on your income and saved assets, you may wish to begin establishing charitable-giving plans or consider other areas where you can be of greater service to others and the causes you believe in.

Mortgage Management

- For those with a mortgage, your focus may shift toward learning the best options for paying off your mortgage, taking into consideration any guidance from your CPA for the tax benefits of having a mortgage.
- Create a payoff plan so you eliminate all debt within a specified time frame.

Estate Planning

- Establish a formal process, including trusts, wills, and other needed documents with an estate-planning attorney so that your financial affairs are in order for the benefit

of your family and dependents should anything happen
to you.

Estate Planning for Business Owners

- Continue to scale your business revenue by leveraging
  your strengths and talents.
- If you are in a partnership and depending upon income,
  you may wish to discuss buy/sell agreements with your
  insurance professional to learn options for protecting
  partners and their families should anything happen to one
  or more partners.
- Additional estate- and tax-planning discussions will likely
  arise through this research.
- You may wish to create or join a mastermind group of
  other similar investors or business owners to share key
  learning with one another.

Money "Feeling" Goals

- Feeling the experience of flow in your life and with
  your money, take time to notice how this affects your
  surroundings and how you feel about life.

STAGE 6: LANDSCAPING THE GROUNDS OF YOUR HOME—BROW CHAKRA

The brow chakra is about moving into flow with your money and
your life—entirely. You feel like your intuition is guiding you to act
in all areas of your life, while your mind is taking care of the business
of money management as needed. You have reached a stage of wisdom and financial freedom. Now it is about finding your bliss in life

(in whatever way that speaks to you) and how you can help others do the same. You are also aware that money no longer controls you in any way. You feel great satisfaction about your life and your money.

Money Activities

Collaboration with Financial Partners

- You meet with your advisors on a quarterly basis to ensure your financial plan is working and helping you achieve your goals.

Investing

- If you haven't already reached economic independence, you're likely to be focused on achieving this goal within the coming three to five years. This is when your investment income exceeds your expenses and you have enough income that you no longer need to work. The goal is to have a consistent income regardless of economic conditions and stock market fluctuations.
- In search of higher meaning for your life and your money, you may find yourself becoming very focused on various types of charitable, socially responsible, and sustainable investments.
- As previous investments are sold or liquidated, you will want to have a strategy for reinvesting that resonates with your deepest values and intuition.

Personal Growth and Quality of Life

- You are continuing to find ways to spend less time focused on money and more time living your life.

- You may feel drawn to teaching others, including your family, what you've learned through your own process of financial enlightenment.
- You may feel drawn to living more like a minimalist, with your expenses much lower so you can save even if or when your income is not growing.

Money "Feeling" Goals

- You are living in a flow state with your money and have become a steward of your wealth and of the planet around you. Notice all the ways love is flowing through you and everyone around you.

STAGE 7: FINAL WALK-THROUGH—CROWN CHAKRA

The crown chakra is about witnessing the life you've created, remembering what you've learned along the way, celebrating how far you've come, feeling deep gratitude, and sharing your knowledge and experience with others.

Money Activities

You are living in the moment and creating your path each and every day from a place of service, love, compassion, and support of others.

Money "Feeling" Goals

- Celebrate each moment, including the joy and bliss that comes when living in abundance.

NEXT STEPS

Once you review the chakras that apply to you, write a list of the activities you are not doing and yet want to start doing over the coming ninety days.

From there, I suggest you break each of the projects down into the smallest steps possible so that you can take daily actions to create long-term success for yourself and your money. This will help lessen any sense of being overwhelmed and will increase your likelihood of success.

For example, you might want to have four months' worth of nondiscretionary expenses (those expenses that must be paid and don't include extras) in a cash savings account that isn't easily accessible (meaning you cannot easily sweep the money from that account to your checking account).

To do this you determine that you might need $8,000 in your emergency account—so, you'd divide this amount by twelve, meaning you would have to save $666 per month, which equates to about $22 a day, to reach your goal by the end of the year. If seeing this number causes you to think it's not possible, you may decide to instead focus on saving only $4,000 this year. To reach this goal that means you'd be saving $333 per month or about $11 per day.

You may have to come up with new ways to increase your income that could include a part-time job, a side gig or renting out your home either when you travel or on highly desirable weeks in your area through services like Airbnb. My in-laws, who are in their seventies, did this by renting out their home while they were staying in the RV in their backyard. They were able to earn over $8,000 in the first year alone!

When you do more research, you may find out that you could earn $5,000–8,000 a year or $600 a month by renting out your home while you are out of town,[6] with all of the money going into your emergency savings account. You can even rent your primary home out for up to fourteen days a year and not pay income tax due to it being a nontaxable hobby.[7] Another idea would be to start a side hustle, turning something you enjoy doing into a side business.

Now you have a way to achieve your goal, and the next step is to break down the action tasks you need to get your home ready to rent it out or your side business off the ground. The point is to find ways right now you can commit to that will allow you to meet your financial goals, and don't stop until you find a viable solution that you are willing to bring into reality.

Summary of Next Steps

To recap, your next step is to jot down the activities you need to focus on. For each money activity that you've highlighted, you will want to write down how you'll do it, when you'll do it, why you'll do it, and how you will hold yourself accountable to your goal.

MINDFUL MOMENTS OF REFLECTION

Taking one or more of the goals you've created for yourself in step 6, you can use the following questions to help you stay on course and continue to make progress in bringing your goals into reality.

Money Activity Goals

For each goal you've set for yourself, complete the following questions:

Why is this goal important to you?
What are the exact steps you need to take to bring this goal into reality?

By what date will you complete this activity?

What obstacles, if any, are there in getting this task completed? Write them down here and come up with a plan for dealing with these obstacles.

How will you hold yourself accountable to complete this goal?

DAILY PRACTICES FOR E IS FOR EVIDENCE

1. Engage in process of preparatory practices
2. Breath-work practice—5 minutes
3. Meditation practice—5 minutes
4. Journaling practice—20–40 minutes
5. Dedication and gratitude

MINDFUL MOMENTS OF ACTION

1. How many days did you do your practices?
2. What was the experience like for you?
3. What did you struggle with completing?
4. Is there anything else you would like to note for this step—things to revisit in the future, areas of focus, questions you'd like to have answered?

SUMMARY FOR STEP 7—E IS FOR EVIDENCE

While it is not possible to cover all the scenarios to shore up your financial house and ensure it accomplishes all of your goals, my hope is for this to give you many ideas to focus your attention on over the coming years. The more you learn about how to take better care of your money, the more confidence you will feel. Everything in life can become an expression of your fullest potentiality and money does not need to be any different. This is your chance to create all that you want for yourself—even if the pathway is not totally clear yet. The most important things are to keep moving forward and never give up. Opportunity for magic to appear along the way comes as a result of the seeds you are planting on a daily basis. While this road will likely be filled with many twists and turns that aren't always controllable, your intention for prosperity can prevail. Stay the course, stay the course, stay the course!

17

STEP 8—R IS FOR REINVENT

Your power to choose your direction of your life
allows you to reinvent yourself, to change your future,
and to powerfully influence the rest of creation.
—STEPHEN COVEY

In this final step, everything comes together. You realize how far you've come and celebrate your ability to make choices and decisions from a greater understanding of yourself. Now you get to learn about ways to set goals so you can put all that you've learned into practice. We'll also explore the remaining steps you will want to commit to ensure your ultimate success and financial wellness.

Living a prosperous life requires having faith that you will always be in the flow of life. Knowing you have the means and clarity to create that which is most important is what it takes to re-create your life. It also requires your ability to know and trust that your needs will always be met. Not that you can sit on your duff and do nothing and expect great things, but as long as you continue forward, accessing your wisdom and allowing guidance to appear whenever you need it, you can and will thrive.

Although life may have left us with inner wounds of separation and habits of retraction, recoil, and isolation, we no longer have to live from this limited sense of self. Instead, reinvention is about creating anew the life you have always wanted without feelings of limitation. It is your birthright to live in this way and it is within your control to create it for yourself. Knowing the truth of who you really are, you intuitively and heartfully understand how to live in accordance with that truth.

Financial wellness, under the right conditions, is as natural as breathing. The process of figuring it out is perfect for helping you on the pathway to spiritual evolution. There is no choice about dealing with financial matters as part of life, and yet now there is a way to turn these otherwise-mundane actions into spiritual epiphanies and teachings. With each test and trial that comes, you're given the opportunity to release any sense of limitation, seeing it as unreal, and then using it to get yourself back on track. It is in these moments that you can open your awareness and feel a sense of relief from the distorted perceptions of contraction that have plagued your money in the past.

By reinventing how we go about life, allowing it to unfold, realizing we are always doing the best we can, we land in a place so perfect that we have no desire to be anywhere else. We feel at home in the most profound way imaginable. Even when these feelings fade, we know deep inside that we can always find our way back home to our True Self.

THE TREE OF LIFE

A tree is only as strong as it is rooted within the ground beneath it. The ecosystem buffets a tree, yet it can stand and survive only as long as its roots remain firm. Knowing how to remain rooted in your own self is what keeps you strong in the face of adversity and challenge. No matter what storms life may bring your way, you will always have the tools you've learned here beside you, helping you meet whatever challenging conditions appear with a resilient heart and mind.

The truest power we have in life comes from knowing we are the love we seek and that we are the person we have been looking for all our lives. Knowing that life is not meant to be filled with struggle and that you have the tools you need to change it gives you the key you need to open the door to the freedom you've always wanted.

SETTING GOALS

The freedom we seek comes as a result of living a prosperous and purpose-filled life. In order to be living on purpose and achieving what others may think of as impossible, the setting of goals orients you toward success. Goals help us focus our direction so that we achieve all that matters while breaking free of the resistance of the past. Goals help us learn what we haven't yet learned. Goals help us create our future in advance of it actually happening. Goals help us grow and expand, pushing us to transform in ways we likely never imagined.

Many times people think they understand how to set goals, but then they never quite achieve what they were after. One reason this can happen is that if their goals aren't compelling or inspiring, they don't truly get to the heart of why they were setting them in the first place, so their goals lack the depth of meaning that is critical for their ultimate completion.

This is where returning to the Prosperity Ladder™ (in chapter 6) can help us become more deliberate in our choices. When we select goals that support our own feelings of completeness and wholeness, we save ourselves a great deal of time. We cut to the chase and leave out all the meandering paths we may have taken when we did not understand ourselves well enough. Instead, the seven prosperities remind us of our truth and our ability to accept, allow, and embrace all parts of ourselves. By focusing on the achievement of our goals, we give ourselves the opportunity to return to our own True Self again and again. When you know you are living in truth, your money becomes an expression of this truth.

THE PROSPERITY LADDER™

As you review the statements below, be sure to take time to customize them to your own situation:

- **I am safe and secure.** I have a consistent stream of income that supports my needs and my savings, which helps me prepare for my goals, dreams, and needs.
- **I am worthy.** I feel worthy of my life and my comforts. I enjoy paying off debt and saving money because of the confidence it brings into my awareness.
- **I am powerful.** I feel powerful when it comes to my money. I enjoy managing my money and watching it grow so that I have freedom to live my best life possible.
- **I am loved.** I feel loved and appreciated by myself and the world around me. I enjoy being well paid for my efforts and having the resources to give to causes I believe in.
- **I am trusting of myself.** I trust myself. I trust my ability to discern and choose those partners who can best support my financial goals. I trust myself to learn what I need to learn to be a steward of my financial responsibilities.
- **I am enough.** I am enough. When I recognize my own enoughness, the world reflects this enoughness back to me in my health, my relationships, my environment, my spiritual connection, and my money.
- **I am prosperous, whole, and complete.** I am prosperous. The world is a reflection of this abundance, and I enjoy the fruits of life in whatever form they come in.

LIVING DELIBERATELY

Going with the flow without setting goals and taking action is something you want to be very careful with. You can sacrifice your purpose and passion if you are not careful. Taking no action and going with the flow when you know what you really want is absolutely unnecessary. It slows you down and sends out very mixed signals to the universe. What is not essential is the forcing of what you want into reality, or thinking that you are in control of everything, or that only your efforts are all that is needed. Of course, there will be times when it is best to not be too specific about what you want and how you are going to get it. The trick is being able to discern when you are meant to set a goal and *make* it happen and when, at other times, you are meant to set a goal and *let* it happen. This is something you will likely be working on for many years to come. The point is that the more you decide to live deliberately, the easier it becomes to be in agreement and alignment with yourself and your goals.

Setting clear goals that align and support each other allows you to be precise in your efforts. By knowing the target, you can now aim for it. If you miss the target, then you know you've missed it. In knowing that you didn't get where you wanted, then you are better able to adjust and continue. I am reminded of something Lily Tomlin said in character as "Chrissy": "I always wanted to be somebody, but I now realize I should have been more specific."[1] Setting clear goals reduces the amount of time it takes to figure out if something is working or not. It also reduces any potential drama that your unhealthy ego and self-doubt might bring into the equation. Setting goals and taking massive action toward achieving them is what helps bring other things into your awareness and allows you to grow. When you know where you are going, you know if you got there. When you know where you are going, you can let go of the other destinations you were considering, which frees you up to focus more on the actions at hand.

By now you've learned that when you don't know your next step, a great option is to write about it. Ask yourself questions about what you are trying to accomplish, and take the time to journal answers back to yourself. Test things and always be willing to fail if needed. Always keep track of what you are learning—what works and what doesn't. What did you learn? What needs to change to be in greater alignment with your intentions? What is your intuition telling you about your goals?

HIGH-OCTANE FINANCIAL GOAL SETTING

The best goals are the ones that get you excited when you think about them. They empower and fill you up with lots of creative energy. Setting an intuitive and energizing goal (IAE goal) is done by using your knowledge, reasoning, and intuition. Not only do you feel like you can achieve it, it feels right, which gives you courage and determination to see it through to the end. When you are working on IAE goals, you lose track of time because the work is fun and enjoyable.

Once you've decided on your IAE goals, consider the process from my friend Dr. Brad Klontz, who did a study[2] that showed how people increased their savings rate by 73 percent when they followed these seven steps:

1. Pick your top three financial goals, based on what you've learned through this process. Notice the feelings you want to create inside by achieving these goals.
2. Passion-test your goals by making sure they are things you are excited about completing, by asking yourself, "What excites me most about these goals?"
3. Name your financial goals according to what you want. For example, if one of your goals is to save enough money to take a tropical vacation, then name your financial goal the "Aruba

Vacation Savings Account" (or whatever place fits). By naming it, you remind yourself about why you are saving rather than spending, which is helpful to keep you on track.

4. Time-stamp your goals. In order to achieve goals, you need to set a timeline of when you will complete them by.

5. Picture your financial goals. Now that you know what you want and when you want it, create a visual image of the goal. You can do this by creating a vision board that includes pictures and words about your goals, and once it is done, be sure to keep it close so you are seeing it every day. Also notice again how you want to feel by achieving these goals.

6. Create subaccounts. This is a way to make your savings accounts high-octane ones, in that they can be helping you accomplish many goals at one time. For each of your financial goals, you can ask your bank to help you create subaccounts, for example, you might have your "Hawaii Vacation Account" and your "Financial Freedom Account" under one umbrella.

7. Automate your success. Once you get your accounts created, then you can set up automatic direct transfers to go from your checking account into your savings subaccounts.

Using these seven steps is a practical way to apply what you've learned about yourself right away when it comes to your finances. The steps will help you see how easy it is to bring your financial goals into reality when they become crystal clear to you.

ONE FINAL STEP

In conclusion, take a few minutes to think about where you've been and where you are headed next. Ponder these questions to help you integrate and align all you've done: What did you set out to do when you started this process? What did you actually do? What happened for you?

Use these questions to clarify your intentions, actions, and results and to summarize the final process of resurrection noted in the hero's journey (chapter 14).

THE JOURNEY HOME

As you probably know by now, the Mindful Millionaire is a financial wellness journey that brings you home to your True Self. It's been teaching you the art of releasing fear and scarcity so you can engage in self-mastery and self-love by way of your experiences with money. While this particular journey is nearing its end, in reality, you are just getting started. Each time you embark on a new financial journey, you can return to this process to help ensure it is as smooth and easy to travel on as possible. IPROSPER helps you play to win in the adventure called life, so you can thrive in joy, peace, and prosperity.

DAILY PRACTICES FOR R IS FOR REINVENT YOUR LIFE

1. Engage in process of preparatory practices
2. Breath-work practice—5 minutes
3. Meditation practice—5 minutes
4. Journaling practice—20–40 minutes
5. Dedication and gratitude

MINDFUL MOMENTS OF REFLECTION

Journal about the Prosperity Ladder™

Ask yourself, "Is this statement true for me now?" If yes, write about the ways it is true for you. If not, then ask, "What can I do to help myself feel safe and supported by life . . . , to feel more worthy . . . , to feel powerful . . . ," and so on? From what you write, then further explore how you can establish goals that help you know this truth for yourself.

> I am safe and supported.
> I am worthy.
> I am powerful.
> I am loved and appreciated.
> I am trusting.
> I am enough.
> I am prosperous, whole, and complete.

Financial Ecosystem Goal Setting

Make time now to begin the high-octane goal setting process featured on page 282. Take what you've discovered by journaling about the Prosperity Ladder and begin to turn your goals into reality by walking through each of the 7 steps and creating a plan for moving forward. Don't skip this important step.

MINDFUL MOMENTS OF ACTION

1. How many days did you do your practices?
2. What was the experience like for you?
3. What did you struggle with completing?
4. Is there anything else you would like to note for this step—things to revisit in the future, areas of focus, questions you'd like to have answered?

SUMMARY FOR STEP 8—R IS FOR REINVENT

You've completed the eight steps to prosperity that have been outlined for you. You will likely want to do this process several times before it becomes second nature to you. Dropping away the small self and the drama of living in your past reality becomes easier and easier as long as you commit yourself to the big picture. Living your best life ever is completely within your reach. The more open you are to the magic that your life brings forth with each breath, the more the magic will become apparent to you.

Setting goals and continuing to take daily action toward achieving them is what it takes to change your life for the better. Remember too Jim Rohn's quote that becoming a millionaire is not so much about the amount of money you earn but the kind of person you become on your way of achieving your goals. Even if you didn't realize it until now (or are starting to realize it), you have always been perfect as designed. Your life is ready to reflect this perfection in every way possible.

You are incredible for investing so much time and energy in yourself. Be proud of all that you are and all that you do in the world. You are worth every bit of prosperity and abundance you can ever dream up and create for yourself!

CONGRATULATIONS—YOU COMPLETED THE IPROSPER PROCESS!

You did it! You've gone through each of the eight steps, and I want to let you know how excited I am that you did it! Not only have you done your best to understand and clear away your scarcity patterns with money, but you've created a holistic financial plan for yourself that can help you create the life you really want to be living.

As I mentioned, you can return to this process again and again, especially when you feel like you're reaching a ceiling in your financial-wellness process. There are always new things to learn and walls to break through to new understandings. I am always amazed at how far I've come and also how it's an ongoing journey. I hope you're very proud of yourself. You deserve to celebrate!

To continue to grow and expand into your fullest potential, I've created a "Prosperity Contract" that you can make with yourself. Feel free to customize it for your own life and what you most need in the way of support. My hope is for this contract to help you stay on course by remembering the truth of who you are and what you most want.

PROSPERITY CONTRACT

(to be copied and completed or obtain a template of the contract in the resource center found at www.mindful millionairebook.com)

I, _____,
am prosperous. My experiences with money are teaching me every day how to live in prosperity, freedom, and joy. I will no longer be held hostage by limiting and confusing beliefs about money, scarcity, and abundance.

I now commit myself wholeheartedly to the following self-mastery practices:

Daily meditation, breath work, and journaling.

Money dates on a monthly basis at a minimum.

I now commit myself to growing my wealth and my well-being.

I commit to frequent review of my finances for the coming ninety days. This will help me stay on target with setting, maintaining, and achieving the goals I've set for myself. This will help me solidify the positive habits I will apply to my life and my finances from now on.

I will make time on a consistent basis for my personal self-development, which includes reading financial books that help me learn things that will aid in the achievement of my financial goals. I know there is much to learn, and I will take it one day at a time.

I commit to repeating IPROSPER one or two times within the next six months. To see what I've learned and how far I've come in the process, I will explore what new things appear that I can learn and grow from.

I will reach out to those who support me in pursuing my goals and dreams, including friends, family, and therapists as needed.

I commit myself to excellent self-care, sleep, diet, exercise/yoga, and things that make me feel really, really, really good for the duration of my life. It is my responsibility to take excellent care of myself and pay attention to my inner voice at all times.

Initials: _____

Date: _____

PART III

A GUIDE FOR THE MINDFUL MILLIONAIRE

18

PROSPERITY IN ACTION

Prosperity is only an instrument to be used,
not a deity to be worshipped.
—CALVIN COOLIDGE

When it comes to living fully and prosperously, the quality of your experiences are what matter more than anything. If you've got about thirty thousand days to experience the game called life, then my sense is you want to play it out fully. To do this, you will want to engage with money as a tool rather than as your master.

As you've gone through the IPROSPER process, you've been learning how to earn, save, manage and invest your money in a holistic way that takes into consideration your mind and your heart . . . breaking free of old patterns that were driven by survival emotions like fear, anger, suffering, pain, and loss while mindfully leaning in to your feelings. As you've witnessed, your feelings are one of the greatest healing tools you have available to you—as you tune in to them and no longer make them wrong, you gain the power to turn your ship toward finding wholeness and completeness within. Dropping away all that doesn't serve you so you can welcome in something far more beneficial in its place.

When making big financial decisions going forward, you can do a few things. First, you can move through your decision reasonably and intuitively by considering your short-term and long-term goals, evaluating your choices, and deciding how best to holistically design and create your life on your terms.

Or you can surrender the decision to a higher power and ask for the guidance to appear in whatever way is most beneficial—through your dreams, in your meditation and breath work, or during your walks in nature.

While it is not sufficient to just sit back and meditate your way to prosperity, you've witnessed firsthand the power of gaining control of your mind and bringing the unconscious into conscious awareness. Noticing the numerous benefits that come when we take time to understand our own money stories and give ourselves permission to create that which we really want. Now it is your job to demonstrate the many ways you can move between making things happen and allowing things to happen so as to embody true prosperity in all of your endeavors. This will not be easy and yet we know it is imperative to go against years of conditioning and unconscious habits in order to affect the kinds of changes we want in our lives.

The greatest challenge, the one that far too many people succumb to, is falling back into mediocrity because we don't see evidence of our progress fast enough. This will require you to become a leader in your own life—someone who acts like a CEO that sets a vision for themselves and then goes about steering your actions (and those of others) in a direction that supports the vision. Raising awareness and illuminating truth and integrity through actions of body, speech, and mind. Becoming a leader in your own life helps you embody what you have learned here in ways that go far beyond money and success. I know you have the power and potential to do this and the satisfaction that comes as a result will be breathtakingly satisfying.

WHAT DOES PROSPERITY LOOK LIKE FROM NOW ON?

Let's examine the seeds of possibility going forward and how this book can help you continue growing prosperity in your life and the lives of those around you.

- **Feeling less financial stress and anxiety.** As a result of becoming more mindful about our reactions in times when they can get triggered, we no longer feel as much financial stress and anxiety. Mastering this tool enables us to integrate any experience, no matter how challenging. This is because we've learned how to let go of our emotional reactions, which have a way of escalating the uncertainties in life. We know that we can process the uncertainty and gain insight and wisdom from whatever financial mishaps occur. With this process we can turn confusion and emotional disruption into acceptance and understanding.
- **No longer criticizing ourselves about money.** We become more compassionate and understanding about our past behaviors with money. This leads to feeling less judgmental and more accepting of ourselves. By realizing how our reactions to situations in the past were often merely a cry for help from our child selves, we recognize the importance of giving ourselves the benefit of the doubt and seeing how we're always doing the best we can. Feeling a sense of unconditional love toward our past behaviors means there is no longer a reason to criticize, ridicule, and belittle ourselves. Instead, we value the fact that whatever happened in the past is how we got to where we are today.
- **Spending less and saving more.** Much of the time our reason for spending more money than we have has to do

with an unconscious cry for attention. The moment we discover how to reparent ourselves by providing guidance, support, and wisdom, we are ready to let go of our unconscious spending behaviors. When we no longer have the unhealthy ego running the show, we naturally shift our behavior, from doing things to ourselves that cause problems, to awakening our desire for ultimate self-care. Being able to build up a savings account that provides more choices and greater freedom is an act of self-care.

- **Making money becomes more enjoyable and easier.** When we are unconsciously nursing our emotional charges from the past, we do so by finding endless ways to distract ourselves away from how we feel. Being busy is not the same as being effective with our actions, and when we release our emotional behaviors, we diminish the distracting behaviors that stand in our way of making money. We naturally become more focused, effective, and oriented to the things that are most important when it comes to earning money and we stop wasting our time and attention on unproductive activities. This results in becoming a better leader within organizations and a more effective business owner—all of which lead to more enjoyment in the world and an increase in the flow of money.

- **Responding more and reacting less.** Learning about our physiology and our reactions to stress that come as a result of financial challenges helps us understand our behavior in new ways. Awareness of the reasons behind why we've reacted certain ways in the past and then releasing those causalities helps us evolve so we can face and embrace whatever circumstances are arising. Learning how to respond in a new way by living more in the present moment allows us to no longer get carried away by fear, anger, and/ or resentment. Reactive behavior progressively decreases as our responsive approach to life becomes our normal way of being.

- **Being less judgmental toward other people.** As we consciously come to see how everyone is a reflection of our own emotional state of being, we choose to respond to this reflection rather than react to it. This means we take responsibility for how others make us feel rather than projecting what they've triggered inside of us back onto them. As our inner condition changes, we feel more understanding and compassion toward all of life. By cleaning up our own emotional state, we no longer have reason to judge others, because we do not see their actions as being separate and isolated from our own perceptions. Instead, we seek to understand what's taking place in a new way as a result of our own emotional integration while appreciating the interconnectness of everyone and everything. Others may still behave the same way as they have in the past, but we no longer desire to criticize them for being who they are and doing what they are doing. Now we're simply accepting what is with love, peace, and compassion.

- **No longer stifling your dreams and settling for less than you want.** By realizing that money is a reflection of how you feel about yourself, your emphasis shifts toward creating the life you really want to be living rather than waiting for money to solve all your problems. This allows you to pursue things that you would not give yourself permission to do in the past. When we are consumed by our emotions, we cannot help but block the flow of money into and out of our lives, which causes an unhealthy fixation on money. When we are living in the present moment, we have a lot less fear about the flow of money because we realize that how we feel matters more than anything. When we are feeling good about being enough and having enough, we naturally become drawn to serving others, which affects how we show up in the world. Feeling like you are enough leads to abundance in a myriad of ways.

- **Completing money-oriented tasks easily.** I am always amazed at the dramatic shift for people who have gone through this process when it comes to managing their money. In cases where they couldn't even create a budget, much less stick to one, graduates of the program find themselves feeling inspired to pay off debt and build up their savings. When we no longer are stuck in limiting and scarcity-based patterns and behaviors, we feel empowered to create lives in which stress is not necessary. Releasing the desire for drama means you want to do everything in your power to create a stress-free life, and you know it's far easier when your money situation is under control.

- **Being more resilient to the unpredictable things that come up with money.** The more we surrender to the natural flow of life, the more we realize life has its own current. How everything that has happened in the past has led to our own awakening, and we see how the current of life is going to serve up whatever we need in order to evolve and grow as human beings. Noticing how natural it is for money challenges to appear and realizing that you have the tools with which to respond wisely to all that occurs, you feel a sense of buoyancy about life. Nothing really drags you down anymore. When times are good and you feel happy, you celebrate and enjoy that experience. When times are bumpy and filled with disruption, you know it is only temporary and you're going to do the best you can to respond with love. Living in a state of joy and loving acceptance means that we accept all that is because we are accepting ourselves as enough.

- **Fighting less with your family about money.** One of the biggest realizations that comes as a result of doing this process is gratitude for everything happening in your life. When we spend a lot of time with people, we cannot help but project our unintegrated emotions onto them. This can easily spiral out of control because it doesn't take many trapped emotions to cause us to react with anger and resentment. However, now you know the innocence that comes with being alive. You also know that the more you release, the more those around you transform before your eyes—not because *they* changed but because *you* have.

- **Letting intimate relationships deepen.** Knowing that our partners are reflecting back to us all that we have not yet integrated in ourselves, our relationships improve substantially. Now we recognize how we were attracted to our partners because we thought they'd be able to make us feel better. Now, instead, you see how you've selected each other to either perpetuate the problems you feel inside or to instigate the healing and releasing of that which causes you suffering. When we emotionally integrate all parts of ourselves back into wholeness, our partners transform before us. We can finally see them for who they are rather than who we've been projecting them to be. It can be quite startling when you see your partner for the first time in this way, because they really do look different. The love you feel toward this person is limitless and creates deep intimacy that grows and continues to blossom with the passing of time.

- **Releasing the propensity to attract negative people.** As we feel more prosperous, we also feel more positive. Some people in our lives are excited for these changes, while others aren't. Positivity is infectious for those who are ready for it, but highly repellent to those who are deeply attached to their negativity. Because like attracts like, we see how the more positive we become, the less attractive we are to those who feed off the negative. As the negative energy dries up, we can't help but attract new people into our lives who share in our joy of being.

- **Minimizing and getting rid of stuff and clutter.** One of the biggest shifts I've encountered over the past four years is that the more I clear out the emotional baggage of the past, the more I want my life to be simple and free from materialism. I was never a hoarder, but I definitely enjoyed expensive things—watches, clothes, shoes, food, recreational supplies, and so on. I know it was all a reflection of the desire to feel like I was enough. As you feel the weight released from your mind and body, you start to notice all the clutter that you've accumulated over the years and how it can weigh you down when all you want to do is soar. To be free means living more simply with less stuff, and so you may find yourself spontaneously giving things away to friends, family, and thrift stores. The more you get rid of, the more space you create in your life to simply be you, and that is more than enough.

- **Improving your health.** Just like everything else, health and well-being are two things that improve when you shine the spotlight of attention toward them. By becoming more conscious to the choices you are making about the care of your body, mind, and emotions, you find yourself feeling better about yourself. You also gain a greater appreciation for your body and how important it is to just about everything. The more I've awakened through this process, the less I've found myself getting sick (even when everyone else in the house has caught the latest bug). Taking responsibility for my body helps me make better choices about the care I receive, the types of doctors and healers I work with, and how I embody myself. Without your body being in its optimal state, *you* are not living optimally. To live fully you realize the importance of your body temple and do whatever you can to love it up.

- **Experiencing spontaneous feelings of grace.** Suddenly, without knowing where it comes from, you will likely start to feel moments of thankfulness. These may even be highly charged emotionally, to the point where it makes you cry because of how much gratitude you feel radiating within your being. Living gratefully with the fullness of life causes us to deliberately direct our attention toward all that is present and abundant, which causes us to feel incredible. This happens because when we are no longer taking life for granted, we automatically feel the conscious presence of the love and light that is within every person and every situation.

- **Letting synchronicity become commonplace.** The more we become our truest selves and recognize the wholeness that prevails in all aspects of life, the more we notice the synchronicity of events that are occurring around us. Simply by the act of being authentically you, the world responds accordingly and brings you all that you need and want. People appear with messages from out of the blue—people you haven't spoken to in years, as well as people you meet at the grocery store. All of life becomes in sync, so that you can gently flow down the river without needing to grasp on to the things that attract you and repel the things that don't. Instead, you feel confidence in whatever appears, as being perfect and divine for what you are ready to learn and integrate. No longer fearing what might happen or go wrong, now you are accepting all that is, which further expands your openness to synchronicity leading the way.

- **Experiencing prosperity and abundance 24-7.** You've awakened deep understanding about what it means to be living fully, freely, and joyfully. You feel blessed with gratitude and why you are here. You trust that the universe has your back at all times and that there is no way you can be left out of the love that is circulating constantly throughout the world. You no longer seek to fill the void within, because it is no longer there. Instead, you have accessed your true state of love, compassion, empowerment, and abundance. By realizing you are enough, you see the world as enough. By getting your financial house in order, you see how good it feels to take care of yourself so that you don't have to worry about the basics. You also see how money is a terrible master and a great tool to help you become the person you've always wanted to be.

19

A BROADER VIEW FOR YOUR FINANCIAL REALITY

You are the light of the world.
—MATTHEW 5:14.

No matter what financial questions you were trying to answer when you came across this book, I'm guessing you didn't realize it could help you improve your life way beyond money. Yet that's exactly what happens by diving into this complicated relationship. Only when we calm ourselves enough to sense and feel the truths hidden deep inside can we truly begin to understand what's taking place. While it's impossible to completely remove all of our biases and conditioning, in developing alternative ways of seeing, we're able to look beyond the dollars, emotions and behaviors to notice the qualities that give rise to them. From this new lens it becomes apparent that by continuing to see money as anything other than a tool, we miss out on our own true brilliance.

Having spent what seems like a lifetime exploring my own and thousands of others' experiences with money, I've concluded that the key to mastering your money comes down to believing in yourself as a whole and complete being. For many this requires becoming more mindful of lack and limitation-oriented thoughts while no longer allowing fear and resistance to dictate your actions. This new way of being serves as a form of protection over your mind, body and spirit reminding you of your ability to make choices and decisions that help you live your best life possible. The power that comes upon realizing that money is not your enemy, nor a scorecard of self-value, and not even something that will solve all your problems, is incredibly redeeming. Reaching this level, the level embodied by those who are truly prosperous, requires that you return to yourself and become comfortable in your own skin. Facing your inner critic, as well as your doubts and fears without letting them pull you astray means you have gained the reigns to reinvent and redesign your life on your terms. There are no magic pills for achieving this kind of inner mastery. It is only in this final phase when you take full ownership of your destiny that you tap into the flow of life.

My greatest hope is that you can apply what you've learned here to your life and to your money. It's the reason I've written this book, and I can't wait for you to accomplish your goals in the days, months, and years to come. Learning without execution is worthless.

Now is the time to decide exactly how you're going to put what you've learned into practice. It is only through planning, taking action, and then learning from your actions that you can make the biggest shifts and improvements with money. Becoming a Mindful Millionaire isn't about instant success as much as it is about the power of applying yourself, letting go of what's not serving you, and then changing your financial habits so they are in alignment with the True You. It isn't likely to happen overnight, but it can and will happen when you're focused on creating it. It is completely within your power.

To sing the song that you are here in life to sing, you must have a certain degree of financial stability. This is why applying what you have been learning is so critical. Do not let this go to waste, even if it takes years to master. It's okay to be patient and persevere over time. It's okay if things feel like they are a mess right now. This book, my courses, the books mentioned in the bibliography, the Mindful Millionaire Community, and so much more are available to help you make this transition. No matter what, be sure to find a group of people who help you feel inspired and encouraged along the way. Everyone needs support—me, you, and all those who want a better life for themselves. None of us are meant to be islands; we're so much more powerful when we band together and remind one another of our truth and of our potential.

YOU ARE NOT BROKEN

As I said early on, just because you had situations of brokenness in your past does not mean you are broken. You cannot be broken. It's simply impossible. For many of us, we thought this was the case for years; now we know it is not true and can never be true. Instead, we see how all of those challenging situations were just bringing us home to our True Selves.

This journey has cultivated your awareness of everything from grounded strength to your connection with the Divine, balancing the polarities of life so that you can dance and surrender into wholeness, releasing patterns of fear and scarcity so you can find your own sense of prosperity. Everything that's happened has been a gift to help you fall deeper into self-understanding and self-love. It is only by understanding yourself that you can understand others and then be in a position of serving all of humanity. From this place of no longer needing to fix anyone or anything, including yourself, you know the truth of your nature, of the greater good, and of how you fit into the bigger picture of life.

YOU ARE THE HEROINE OR HERO

You are the hero or heroine of your own story. By going through the eight-step process you've learned what it means to be in the world but not of it. You're here in this world taking responsibility for your life while being guided by the truest parts of you. This is the ultimate experience of what it means to be a human being having a spiritual experience. This is what money is asking you to become with it, to do the dance of being here, now, in physical form, and at the same time to let go, because you know that the human mind is limited by its physical realities and is limitless when it comes to the seat of your soul. It is here that you realize that your money is one of the least interesting things about you or about anyone else, for that matter. It no longer defines who you are and merely supports the life you've come here to live.

Honoring and cultivating your own strength, courage, tenacity, and compassion allows you to balance the polarities and escape duality so that you become more open to the constant flow of love, support, and bliss that life brings. You know that all you need to do is put your hand out anytime you start to waver and feel a sense of isolation, separation, or despair. Support is waiting for you in all directions, and it is during these times you can ask yourself, "What's really going on here? How am I in my own way? What greater message can I take from this experience? What is my True Self calling me to become in the face of this adversity?"

THE LIGHTNESS OF BEING

It is from this higher perspective that you are capable of cultivating the light wherever you are and showering yourself with unconditional love to help you find your way back home. Know that you have all the faith, humility, and kindness you need to take wonderful care of yourself. Living in a state of integrated consciousness, awakened to the truth of yourself, encourages you to fully experience all that you are here to be, without needing to suffer. No one deserves to suffer for any reason, including you. You are not to blame for any of the experiences you've had, and now that you've witnessed your own innocence, you no longer need to project pain and problems out into the world and onto others.

Being true to your own feelings means you no longer need to fill the role of victim in your life. Instead, the victim has transformed into the heroine in your story. By becoming grounded and rooted in your body, in your heart, and in your divine connection, you realize that everything is a choice that is within your power to make and create. You attracted all the adversity you needed to learn how to disprove your own limiting beliefs. You now realize your own power to not only survive but to thrive.

We've come a long way together, and I'm excited to see what comes next in your journey. This is only the beginning, and you have the tools that will help you enormously. Anything you don't have now is within your reach when you surrender to asking for it. My hope is that you feel better prepared than when you picked up this guide. I also hope you can see your own light better than before, and that you are ready to shine it brightly into the world. The world needs more of your light. Let it shine.

See yourself going through your daily activities, now that your life is heading the way it is intended to be. See yourself getting up in the morning, meditating, dressing, eating, doing your work, meeting with friends and family, and taking a walk in nature. See yourself and how beautiful you are. See how others are picking up from your energy. Savor how good it feels to be here now. Focus on your own life as a creation that you decide, and at the same time surrendering all final outcomes. Take the best possible care of yourself at all times, and discover the light that you truly are.

YOU ARE THE GIFT

There's no part of your life that you can't put up against what you've learned. Every story is here for the sake of your own freedom and liberation. When you experience anything as separate or intolerable, the Mindful Millionaire process can bring you back into the peace and understanding you are feeling right now. Whenever you feel cut off from your wholeness, return to the story that you are telling yourself, question it fiercely, and walk through the hero's journey to see what is ready to be healed, released, and what the new story is that you're ready to create.

Always remember that everything is a reflection of your own thinking, your own beliefs, and your own storytelling. Investigate what's going on under the surface so you can feel what you need to feel and heal what you are ready to heal. Forgiveness is the greatest gift you can offer to all of life. Take advantage of it whenever possible, and also know that sometimes you're just not going to be ready yet. Never push yourself beyond what feels right, because as we know, you only trigger resistance, and we know how that goes.

Until you can see the world and everyone in it, including yourself, as a dear, loving friend, you will know that there is still work to be done. Your life is a gift, and it's a seed of potentiality that you are here to take to its fullest expression. Your potentiality emerges as a consequence of your evolution. Trust that you are always on this path, even when you don't see it.

A MEANINGFUL LIFE

It is a relief to know that you no longer need to be anyone other than who you are. While aspects of your past with money may have seemed like a nightmare at the time, now you can see how pivotal they were for bringing you to this moment—where you're learning ways to no longer see the world through the lens of limiting and confusing belief systems. Instead, you're empowered to investigate and question the assumptions so you can consciously break free from patterns of illusion. From that place of power, you can create greater wealth for yourself and your family.

Now you are free to live a life of great meaning and purpose, without confusion. You are so much more than your money. You are the True Self that lives within, and you are the source of your own happiness. In the same way, you are the creator of your prosperity, wealth, abundance, and financial well-being. You are the light. You are the path. You are everything you have ever hoped for. You are beautiful and perfect just the way you are. You are the unwithholding lover of life. You are whole, complete, and awake to your own essence. You are a Mindful Millionaire. Embracing all that you are allows you to live in full expression and to light the pathway for yourself, your family, friends, and the world around you.

I wish you well.

XOXO, Leisa

ACKNOWLEDGMENTS

I've been blessed to be surrounded by incredibly loving human beings throughout my life and the process of bringing this book to life was no exception.

To my soulmate, Tim, whose infinite patience and support helped make this possible, I am beyond grateful for your unconditional love and unwavering commitment to our family.

To Zoe and Aidan, you've helped me learn the essence of truth, abundance, and prosperity.

To my brother Aaron, thank you for being you and for unconditionally accepting me. I hope this book brings you as much healing as it has me.

To my parents-in-law, Paul and Helen, thank you for your love, support and excitement over the past few extremely adventurous years.

To the heroes and heroines who bravely engaged with this work, you've helped bring this book into reality, and you inspire me every day! I am especially grateful to those whose personal stories are featured in these pages. You are extraordinary examples of what it means to uncover and let go of the patterns that no longer serve you, and the resulting transformation! Your strength, determination, and resilience have earned my highest and utmost admiration, appreciation, and respect.

To the Atlas Collective community, your love and support these past few years has meant everything to me. Thank you for being a part of breaking new ground—trying the meditations, reading the many drafts and providing feedback too many times to count. None of this would be possible without your contributions.

To my incredible agent, Jessica Faust, you encouraged me to write this book and helped bring it to life. Thank you for your coaching along the way and your encouragement when I didn't think I had it in me. And for that small detail of coming up with the most brilliant title I could have imagined, thank you!

To my writing coaches, Celeste White and Tom Bird, thank you for your wisdom and compassion—you helped me learn the craft of writing, storytelling, and communicating in new ways that opened my heart and soul to the depths of my being. You helped me see beyond my limiting beliefs about writing and for that I am forever grateful.

Many thanks to the mentors who have helped me along the way: George Kinder, Jonathan and Stephanie Fields, Henry Cuenca, Barbara Kramer-Kahn, Ellen Stein, Todd Herman, Alexia Vernon, Vicki Howe, Jennie Joy, Grant Sabatier, and Dana Wilde to name a few. It has been an honor to learn from you—your wisdom energy travels far and wide in touching people's lives and I'm blessed to have benefited from your work and your kindness.

I am so very grateful to Daniela Rapp and the entire team for giving *The Mindful Millionaire* a home at St. Martin's Press. It is a dream come true for any writer to work with such a brilliant editor and a visionary publisher. The fact that you believed in and supported this work is invaluable to me.

To Holly Riley, our work together transformed my life during this journey. Thank you for always being there. Your knowingness of what I needed to explore and release kept me moving forward. Thank you for your encouragement to share that wisdom with the world. I pray that these discoveries help countless living beings move beyond their suffering.

To my parents, I miss you both and love you from the bottom of my heart. Thank you for giving me the absolutely perfect life.

And finally, to my readers, I hope this book helps you create the life you most desire to be living. It is waiting for you!

NOTES

AUTHOR'S NOTE
1. Gabrielle Oettingen, *Rethinking Positive Thinking: Inside the New Science of Motivation* (London: Current Publishing, 2014).

1. A TALE OF TWO (MONEY) PATHS
1. Senhil Mullainathan and Eldar Shafir, *Scarcity: The New Science of Having Less and How It Defines Our Lives* (New York: Picador, 2014), 7.
2. Bruce Greyson, "Near-Death Experiences in a Psychiatric Outpatient Clinic Population," *Psychiatric Services* 54, no. 12 (December 2003): 1649–51, doi:10.1176/appi.ps.54.12.1649, PMID 14645808.
3. Jonathan E. Sherin and Charles B. Nemeroff, "Post-Traumatic Stress Disorder: The Neurobiological Impact of Psychological Trauma," *Dialogues in Clinical Neuroscience* 13, no. 3 (September 2011): 263–78.

2. THE POWER OF YOUR MONEY STORY
1. C. G. Jung, *Psychology and Religion* (New Haven, CT: Yale University Press, 1938), 131.
2. Joseph Murphy, "The Treasure House Within You," *The Power of Your Subconscious Mind* (Eastford, CT: Martino Publishing, 2011), 11–26.
3. David Whitebread and Sue Bingham, *Habit Formation and Learning in Young Children*, Money Advice Service, 2013, https://www.moneyadviceservice.org.uk/en/corporate/habit-formation-and-learning-in-young-children
4. Elisabeth Kübler-Ross, *On Death and Dying*, repr. ed. (Scribner: 1997).
5. Brené Brown, "The Power of Vulnerability," Tedx Houston video, June 2010, https://www.ted.com/talks/brene_brown_on_vulnerability?language=en.
6. "Suicide Rising Across the US," Centers for Disease Control and Prevention, last reviewed June 7, 2018, https://www.cdc.gov/vitalsigns/suicide/infographic.html#graphic2.

7. Paul Yakobowski, "Financial Literacy Linked to Financial Wellness," Teachers Insurance and Annuity Association of America (TIAA), April 2, 2019, https://www.tiaa.org/public/about- tiaa/news-press/press-releases/pressrelease748.html.

8. Holly Riley, *Allowing Handbook: Simple Strategies for Manifesting Dreams . . . They Work on Everything, All the Time, No Matter What*, vol. 1 (Reno, NV: Peace in Peace out Productions, 2012).

9. Byron Katie and Stephen Mitchell, *Loving What Is: Four Questions That Can Change Your Life* (New York: Three Rivers Press, 2002).

10. Vincent J. Felitti, MD, FACPA, et al., "Relationship of Childhood Abuse and Household Dysfunction to Many of the Leading Causes of Death in Adults," *American Journal of Preventive Medicine* 14, no. 4 (May 1998): 245–58.

3. STOPPING THE WAR WITHIN

1. Stuart Wilde, *Sixth Sense: Including the Secrets of the Etheric Subtle Body* (Carlsbad, Hay House, 2000), 7–8.

2. Robert B. Cialdini and George Newbern, et al., *Influence: The Psychology of Persuasion* (New York, HarperCollins Publishers, 2009), 237–71.

3. *The Allianz Women, Money, and Power Study: Empowered and Underserved*, Allianz Life Insurance Company of North America, 2016, www.allianzlife.com/-/media/files/allianz/documents/ent_1462_n.pdf?la=en&hash=2955C0DCE4 F0BCC290A41345D 5C0FBF36D87F976.

4. Steven C. Hayes and Elizabeth V. Gifford, "The Trouble with Language: Experiential Avoidance, Rules, and the Nature of Verbal Events," *Psychological Science* 8, no. 3 (May 1997).

5. T. Richardson, P. Elliott, and R. Roberts, "The Relationship Between Personal Unsecured Debt and Mental and Physical Health: A Systematic Review and Meta-Analysis," *Clinical Psychology Review* 33, no. 8 (December 2013): 1148–62.

6. Wenqi Yang et al., "The Impact of Power on Humanity: Self-Dehumanization in Powerlessness," *PLoS One* 10, no. 5 (May 2015).

4. OVERCOMING RESISTANCE TO CHANGE

1. Steven Pressfield, *The War of Art: Break Through the Blocks and Win Your Inner Creative Battles* (New York: Black Irish Entertainment, 2002).

2. Armstrong, John, How to Worry Less About Money (New York: MacMillan, 2012).

3. Thich Nhat Hanh. *Fear: Essential Wisdom for Getting Through The Storm* (New York: HarperCollins, 2012), 1.

4. Brad Klontz, PsyD, and Ted Klontz, PhD, *Mind over Money* (New York: Broadway Books, 2009), 129–33.

5. "PTSD: National Center for PTSD," U.S. Department of Veterans Affairs, accessed September 2, 2019, https://www.ptsd.va.gov/understand/common/common_adults.asp.

6. Sara Blakely. "Spanx Founder: My dad encouraged me to fail." CNN Business video, March 30, 2018. https://www.youtube.com/watch?v=_TeV9op6Mp8

7. Watty Piper. *The Little Engine That Could: An Abridged Version* (New York: Grosset and Dunlap, March 15, 2012).

6. CLAIMING YOUR PROSPERITY

1. A. Shorrocks, J. Davies, R. Lluberas, "Global Wealth Report 2019," https://www.credit-suisse.com/about-us/en/reports-research/global-wealth-report.html.

2. A. Shorrocks, J. Davies, R. Lluberas, "Global Wealth Report 2018," https://www.credit-suisse.com/about-us/en/reports-research/global-wealth-report.html

3. Jodi Thornton-O'Connell, "What Percent of Americans Think They Will Be a Millionaire?" GOBankingRates, June 8, 2018, www.gobankingrates.com/making-money/wealth/percent- americans-think-millionaire/.

4. Jim Rohn, "The Real Value in Setting Goals." *Success*, article republished from past interview on August 30, 2019, https://www.jimrohn.com/get-inspired-by-your-goals/.

5. Simon Sinek. Quote published on @Simon Sinek Facebook page. February 28, 2012. https://www.facebook.com/simonsinek/posts/10150702227276499

6. Thomas Corley, *Change Your Habits, Change Your Life: Strategies that Transformed 177 Average People into Self-Made Millionaires* (Minneapolis, MN: North Loop Books, 2016), 60.

7. Thomas C. Corley and Michael Yardney, *Rich Habits Poor Habits: Discover Why the Rich Keep Getting Richer and How You Can Join Their Ranks* (Melbourne: Wilkinson Publishing, 2016), 223.

8. "Wells Fargo Survey: Affluent Investors Feeling Good on Financial Health; Yet More than Half Worry about Losing Money in the Market," *Business Wire*, July 15 2015, www.businesswire.com/news/home/20150715005418/en/Wells-Fargo-Survey-Affluent- Investors-Feeling-Good.

9. Thomas J. Stanley and William D. Danko, *The Millionaire Next Door: The Surprising Secrets of America's Wealthy* (Lanham, MD: Taylor Trade Publishing, 2010), 9.

10. "42 Best Millionaire Statistics, Facts & Resources 2019," Millionaire Foundry, accessed May 1, 2019, https://millionairefoundry.com/millionaire-statistics/.

11. Dave Ramsey, "The National Study of Millionaires," Dave Ramsey, January 7, 2019, www.daveramsey.com/research/the-national-study-of-millionaires.

12. Thomas C. Corley, *Rich Habits: The Daily Success Habits of Wealthy Individuals* (Minneapolis, MN: Langdon Street Press, 2009).

13. *Financial Literacy: Do the Rich Know Something We Don't?* Spectrem Group, 2015. https://spectrem.com/Content_Whitepaper/financial-literacy-white-paper.aspx

14. "42 Best Millionaire Statistics, Facts & Resources 2019." Millionaire Foundry, accessed May 1, 2019. https://millionairefoundry.com/millionaire-statistics/.

15. Matt Wells. "Illusionist plans 44 days in suspension." *The Guardian*, August 19, 2003. https://www.theguardian.com/media/2003/aug/20/broadcasting.uknews

7. YOUR MIND AND YOUR MONEY

1. Shana Lebowitz, "A Psychologist Says Feeling Stressed Is a Sign Your Life Is Meaningful," *Business Insider*, May 1, 2015, https://www.businessinsider.com /stress-means-your-life-is-meaningful-2015-5.

2. Mara Mather and Nichole R. Lighthall, "Both Risk and Reward Are Processed Differently in Decisions Made under Stress," *Current Directions in Psychological Science* 21, no. 2 (February 2012): 36–41, doi:10.1177/0963721411429452.

3. E. Luders et al., "Bridging the Hemispheres in Meditation: Thicker Callosal Regions and Enhanced Fractional Anisotropy (FA) in Long-Term Practitioners," *NeuroImage* 61, no. 1 (May 2012): 181–87, doi:10.1016/j.neuroimage.2012.02.026.

4. Alice G. Walton, "7 Ways Meditation Can Actually Change The Brain," *Forbes*, February 9, 2015, www.forbes.com/sites/alicegwalton/2015/02/09/7-ways-meditation -can-actually-change-the-brain/#16506d2e1465.

5. Joseph Wielgosz et al., "Long-Term Mindfulness Training Is Associated with Reliable Differences in Resting Respiration Rate," *Scientific Reports* 6, no. 1 (June 2016), doi:10.1038/srep27533.

6. Clifford Nass, in an NPR interview, as quoted in *Fast Company*, February 2, 2014.

7. Amishi P. Jha et al., "Mindfulness Training Modifies Subsystems of Attention," *Cognitive, Affective, & Behavioral Neuroscience* 7, no. 2 (June 2007): 109–19, doi:10.3758/CABN.7.2.109.

8. Emma Seppala, "The Scientific Benefits of Self-Compassion," The Center for Compassion and Altruism Research and Education, May 8, 2014, ccare.stanford .edu/uncategorized/the- scientific-benefits-of-self-compassion-infographic/.

9. "John Bradshaw (Author)," Wikipedia, April 19, 2019, en.wikipedia.org/wiki /John_Bradshaw_(author).

8. KNOWING YOU'RE ON THE RIGHT PATH

1. St. John of the Cross, "Dark Night of the Soul" (poem), Christian Classics Ethereal Library, July 13, 2005, http://www.ccel.org/ccel/john_cross/dark_night.toc .html.

10. STEP 1—I IS FOR INTENTION

1. You can access these meditations at www.mindfulmillionairebook.com.

2. Julia Cameron, *Artist's Way* (New York: TarcherPerigee, Anniversary edition, 2016).

3. Carol S. Dweck, *Mindset: The New Psychology of Success* (New York: Ballantine Books, 2007).

11. STEP 2—P IS FOR PATTERN

1. Abraham H. Maslow, *Motivation and Personality* (New York: Harper & Row, 1954).

2. Joseph Campbell, *The Hero with a Thousand Faces* (Novato, CA: New World Library, 1949).

3. To access these guided meditations, go to www.mindfulmillionairebook.com.

4. To access all seven of the complete money stories, go to www.mindfulmillionaire book.com.

5. Gary Keller, *The One Thing: The Surprising Simple Truth Behind Extraordinary Results* (Austin, TX: Bard Press, 2013).

14. STEP 5—S IS FOR STORY

1. Christopher Vogler, *The Writer's Journey: Mythic Structure for Writers*, 3rd ed. (San Francisco, CA: Michael Wiese Productions, 2007).

15. STEP 6—P IS FOR PERMISSION

1. "About Holistic Management," Savory Global, accessed September 2, 2019, https://www.savory.global/holistic-management/.

2. A. Savory and J. Butterfield, *Holistic Management: A New Framework for Decision Making* (Washington, D.C: Island Press, 1999) 17.

3. O. Armatier, G. Topa, W. Van der Klaauw, and B. Zafar *"Which Households Have Negative Wealth?"* Liberty Street Economics, August 1, 2016. https://libertystreeteconomics.newyorkfed.org/2016/08/which-households-have-negative-wealth.html

16. STEP 7—E IS FOR EVIDENCE

1. Aristotle, Nicomachean Ethics, Book II, as translated by W. D. Ross. Written 350 B.C. http://classics.mit.edu/Aristotle/nicomachaen.2.ii.html

2. Ibid.

3. To access the tracking forms, go to www.mindfulmillionairebook.com.

4. To access additional resources including a net worth template, go to www.mindfulmillionairebook.com.

5. Stephanie Yang, "5 Years Ago Bernie Madoff Was Sentenced to 150 Years in Prison—Here's How His Scheme Worked" *Business Insider*, July 1, 2014. https://www.businessinsider.com/how-bernie-madoffs-ponzi-scheme-worked-2014-7

6. Dan Caplinger, "Renting Out Your Home? 3 Tax Rules You Need to Know" *The Motley Fool*, May 26, 2017. https://www.fool.com/taxes/2017/05/26/renting-out-your-home-3-tax-rules-you-need-to-know.aspx

17. STEP 8—R IS FOR REINVENT YOUR LIFE

1. Lily Tomlin, "Chrissy", http://www.lilytomlin.com/wordpress2/team_item/chrissy-2/

2. B. Klontz, F. Zabek, C. Taylor, A. Bivens, E. Horwitz, P. Klontz, "The Sentimental Savings Study: Using Financial Psychology to Increase Personal Savings," *Journal of Financial Planning* 43, no.10 (October 2019), 44–55.

FOR FURTHER READING

BROW CHAKRA

Clauson, George S. *The Richest Man in Babylon*. Shippensburg, PA: Sound Wisdom, 2019.

Kinder, George. *The Seven Stages of Money Maturity: Understanding the Spirit and Value of Money in Your Life*, repr. ed. New York: Dell, 2000.

Kramer, Michael, Hal Brill, and Christopher Peck. *The Resilient Investor: A Plan for Your Life, Not Just Your Money*. Oakland, CA: Berrett-Koehler Publishers, 2015.

Little, Kenneth E. *Complete Idiot's Guide to Socially Responsible Investing: Put Your Money Where Your Values Are*. New York: Penguin Group, 2008.

CHAKRAS

Dale, Cyndi. *The Complete Book of Chakra Healing: Activate the Transformative Power of Your Energy Centers*. Woodbury, MN: Llewellyn Publications, 1996.

———. *The Subtle Body: An Encyclopedia of Your Energetic Anatomy*. Louisville, CO: Sounds True, 2009.

Judith, Anodea. *Eastern Body, Western Mind: Psychology and the Chakra System as a Path to the Self*. New York: Celestial Arts, 1996.

Myss, Caroline, PhD. *Anatomy of the Spirit*. New York: Three Rivers Press, 1996.

CROWN CHAKRA

Dispenza, Joe. *Becoming Supernatural: How Common People are Doing the Uncommon*, 2nd ed. Carlsbad, CA: Hay House, 2019.

Foundation for Inner Peace, *A Course in Miracles*, combined ed. Temecula, CA: Foundation for Inner Peace, 1975.

Hawkins, Dr. David. *Letting Go: The Pathway of Surrender*, repr. ed. Carlsbad, CA: Hay House, 2014.

Maharshi, Sri Ramana. *Be As You Are*, reissued. London: Penguin UK, 1988.

Selig, Paul. *I Am the Word*. New York, Gildan Media, 2014.

Wilde, Stuart. *Infinite Self*. Carlsbad, CA: Hay House, 1994.

Yogananda, Paramahansa. *Autobiography of a Yogi*. Los Angeles, CA: Self-Realization Fellowship, 2014.

HEART CHAKRA

Bach, David. *The Latte Factor: Why You Don't Have to Be Rich to Live Rich*. New York: Atria Books, 2019.

Brach, Tara. *Radical Acceptance: Embracing Your Life with the Heart of a Buddha*, repr. ed. New York: Bantam, 2004.

DeYoe, Jonathan K. *Mindful Money: Simple Practices for Reaching Your Financial Goals and Increasing Your Happiness Dividend*. Novato, CA: New World Library, 2017.

Hill, Napoleon. *Think and Grow Rich*. New York: Chartwell Books, 2015.

Mellan, Olivia. *Money Harmony: A Guide for Individuals and Couples*. London: Walker, 1994.

Richards, Carl. *The Behavior Gap: Simple Ways to Stop Doing Dumb Things with Money*. New York: Portfolio, 2012.

Stanny, Barbara. *Overcoming Underearning: A Five-Step Plan to a Richer Life*, repr. ed. New York: HarperBusiness, 2007.

Twist, Lynne. *The Soul of Money: Transforming Your Relationship with Money and Life*. New York: W. W. Norton, 2017.

Wattles, Wallace D. *The Science of Getting Rich*. Scotts Valley, CA: CreateSpace Independent Publishing Platform, 2013.

MEDITATION

Easwaran, Eknath. *How to Meditate*. Tomales, CA: Nilgiri Press, 2011.

Goleman, Daniel, and Richard J. Davidson. *Altered Traits: Science Reveals How Meditation Changes Your Mind, Brain, and Body*. New York: Penguin Random House, 2017.

Salberg, Sharon. *Real Happiness: The Power of Meditation: A 28-Day Program*. New York: Workman Publishing, 2010.

ROOT CHAKRA

Birken, Emily Guy. *End Financial Stress NOW*. Avon, MA: Adams Media, 2017.

Cagan, Michele, CPA, and Elizabeth Lariveire. *The Infographic Guide to Personal Finance*. Avon, MA: Adams Media, 2017.

Mullainathan, Sendhil, and Eldar Shafir. *Scarcity: The New Science of Having Less and How It Defines Our Lives*. New York: Picador/Henry Holt, 2014.

Ramsey, Dave. *The Total Money Makeover: A Proven Plan for Financial Fitness*, 3rd ed. Nashville, TN: Thomas Nelson, 2009.

Robin, Vicki, and Joe Dominguez. *Your Money or Your Life: 9 Steps to Transforming Your Relationship with Money and Achieving Financial Independence*, rev. ed. New York: Penguin Books, 2008.

Stanley, Thomas J., and William D. Danko. *The Millionaire Next Door: The Surprising Secrets of America's Wealthy*. New York: Pocket Books, 1996.

SACRAL CHAKRA

Ariely, Dan. *Dollars and Sense: How We Misthink Money and How to Spend Smarter*, repr. ed. New York: Harper Paperbacks, 2018.

Benson, April Lane. *To Buy or Not to Buy: Why We Overshop and How to Stop*. Boulder, CO: Trumpeter, 2008.

Chatzky, Jean. *Women with Money: The Judgment-Free Guide to Creating the Joyful, Less Stressed, Purposeful (and, Yes, Rich) Life You Deserve*. New York: Grand Central Publishing, 2019.

Mundis, Jerrold. *How to Get Out of Debt, Stay Out of Debt, and Live Prosperously*, rev. ed. New York: Bantam, 2012.

Rind, Valerie. *Gold Diggers and Deadbeat Dads: True Stories of Friends, Family, and Financial Ruin*. Washington, DC: VSJ Enterprises, 2014.

Stanny (Huson), Barbara. *Sacred Success: A Course in Financial Miracles*. Dallas, TX: BenBella Books, 2014.

Steinberg, Amanda. *Worth It: Your Life, Your Money, Your Terms*. New York: Gallery Books, 2017.

Tessler, Bari. *The Art of Money*, repr. ed. New York: Parallax Press, 2018.

For spending and debt problems, also consider Overspenders Anonymous and/or Debtors Anonymous for local support and guidance.

SOLAR PLEXUS CHAKRA

Bach, David. *The Automatic Millionaire: A Powerful One-Step Plan to Live and Finish Rich*, expanded, updated ed. New York: Currency, 2016.

Corley, Thomas. *Rich Habits: The Daily Success Habits of Wealthy Individuals*. Minneapolis, MN: Langdon Street Press, 2009.

Hawkins, David R. *Power vs. Force*. Carlsbad, CA: Hay House, 2014.

Kiyosaki, Robert. *Rich Dad Poor Dad: What the Rich Teach Their Kids about Money That the Poor and Middle Class Do Not!*, 2nd ed. Scottsdale, AZ: Plata Publishing, 2017.

Sabatier, Grant. *Financial Freedom: A Proven Path to All the Money You Will Ever Need*. New York: Avery, 2019.

Warren, Elizabeth. *All Your Worth: The Ultimate Lifetime Money Plan*, repr. ed. New York: Free Press, 2006.

THROAT CHAKRA

Graham, Benjamin. *The Intelligent Investor: The Definitive Book on Value Investing*, rev. ed. New York: Collins Business, 2006.

Lowry, Erin. *Broke Millennial Takes on Investing: A Beginners Guide to Leveling Up Your Money*. New York: TarcherPerigree, 2019.

Mackey, John. *Conscious Capitalism: Liberating the Heroic Spirit of Business*. Brighton, MA: Harvard Business Review Press, 2014.

Murray, Gordon, and Daniel C. Goldie. *The Investment Answer: Learn to Manage Your Money and Protect Your Financial Future.* New York: Business Plus, 2011.

Robbins, Tony. *Money, Master the Game: 7 Steps to Financial Freedom,* updated ed. New York: Simon & Schuster, 2016.

———. *Unshakeable: Your Financial Freedom Playbook,* repr. ed. New York: Simon & Schuster, 2018.

Town, Phil. *Rule #1: The Simple Strategy for Successful Investing in Only 15 Minutes a Week!* New York: Currency, 2007.

INDEX

ABOUT THE AUTHOR

Kristie Pellegrino

Leisa Peterson, CFP® is on a mission to help one million people elevate their financial consciousness. As a money coach, business consultant, and spiritual teacher, Leisa hosts the *Mindful Millionaire* podcast as well as virtual workshops and deep-dive retreats. Her masterful blend of sound financial strategy and mindfulness training helps people break free of patterns of lack, scarcity, and money fears, allowing them to finally lead the rewarding, fulfilling, and abundant lives they most desire.

Leisa has appeared in *The Wall Street Journal*, *FastCompany*, *Forbes*, *The Week*, *Huffington Post* and has been featured on many podcasts and radio shows. Prior to starting WealthClinic®, LLC, Leisa worked with some of the largest financial and business services companies in the world including Wells Fargo, State Farm Insurance, UNUM Life Insurance, New York Life, Federal Express, Pitney Bowes, Ford Motor Company, and General Motors.